"Cedar Koons has written a t[...]
people with intense emotions[...]
mysterious, and explaining them to another person is like trying
to help someone understand what chocolate tastes like when
they have never tasted it before. Koons bridges the gap between
Eastern/Buddhist practice and a way to know and regulate
intense emotions by providing the reader with concrete examples, case stories, and practices. I will recommend this book to all
of my emotionally intense clients."

> —**Shari Manning, PhD**, founding partner of the
> Treatment Implementation Collaborative, LLC, a
> group that provides dialectical behavior therapy (DBT)
> training, consultation, and supervision worldwide; and
> practicing DBT therapist of over twenty years who was
> trained by Marsha Linehan, PhD

"A seasoned expert in both dialectical behavior therapy (DBT)
and mindfulness, Cedar Koons has packed a ton of wisdom into
this book. She brings the material alive with vivid writing and
her use of illustrative case examples and practical mindfulness
exercises. Even more impressively, she unpacks concepts such as
'wise mind' in a way that is both true to DBT, and practical for
readers who are first learning about DBT mindfulness skills. I
would highly recommend this book for anyone struggling with
intense, hard-to-tolerate emotions. Clinicians helping people
with intense emotions will also benefit greatly from Cedar's practical guidance on how to understand and use mindfulness skills."

> —**Alexander L. Chapman, PhD, RPsych**, professor
> of psychology at Simon Fraser University, president
> of the DBT Centre of Vancouver, and coauthor of
> *The Dialectical Behavior Therapy Skills Workbook for
> Anger*, *The Borderline Personality Disorder Survival
> Guide*, and *The Dialectical Behavior Therapy Skills
> Workbook for Anxiety*

"Reading Cedar's wonderful book was an exercise in beginner's mind. It is a reminder that there are infinite ways to practice mindfulness, and so the book will resonate with the person new to mindfulness as well as with the expert who is open to the richness of new teachings. By practicing the skills in this book, the result for the person struggling with intense emotions will be greater mastery and control of their experience; and the expert, too, if open to new learning, will continue to strengthen and broaden the delivery of skilled and compassionate care."

—**Blaise Aguirre, MD**, medical director at McLean 3East Continuum of Care, assistant professor of psychiatry at Harvard Medical School, author of *Borderline Personality Disorder in Adolescents*, and coauthor of *Mindfulness for Borderline Personality Disorder* and *Coping with BPD*

"I highly recommend *The Mindfulness Solution for Intense Emotions* to anyone—Koons's teaching, examples, and stories are so clear, engaging, and inspiring. If you are wondering which self-help book to buy, this is the one. It gets right to the heart of the matter!"

—**Mitch Ditkoff**, cofounder and president of Idea Champions, and author of *Storytelling at Work*

"Two things are certain: the path through suffering involves an active practice of mindfulness, and the way is much smoother and direct when guided by a skilled, compassionate, and astute teacher. Cedar Koons, a gifted writer, inspiring mindfulness practitioner, and dialectical behavior therapy (DBT) master, is just that person, and her book, *The Mindfulness Solution for Intense Emotions*, is just the road map many of us need to begin or strengthen our own mindfulness practice. Cedar's deep wisdom about mindfulness and DBT resonates throughout each page—through story, vignette, explanation, and practical exercises. Her style is personal, accessible, and direct. For those of us who seek solace from suffering, to live freely with our eyes and hearts wide open, this book is for you!"

—**Linda A. Dimeff, PhD**, president and chief scientific officer at Evidence-Based Practice Institute in Seattle, WA; institute director at Portland DBT Institute in Portland, OR; and coeditor of *Dialectical Behavior Therapy in Clinical Practice*

The
MINDFULNESS SOLUTION FOR INTENSE EMOTIONS

Take Control of Borderline Personality Disorder with DBT

Cedar R. Koons, MSW, LCSW

New Harbinger Publications, Inc.

Publisher's Note

Distributed in Canada by Raincoast Books

Copyright © 2016 by Cedar Koons
        New Harbinger Publications, Inc.
        5674 Shattuck Avenue
        Oakland, CA 94609
        www.newharbinger.com

Cover design by Amy Shoup

Acquired by Catharine Meyers

Edited by Susan LaCroix

Library of Congress Cataloging-in-Publication Data on file

Printed in the United States of America

18   17   16

10   9   8   7   6   5   4   3   2   1   First printing

For Prem Rawat
and for Eddie

CONTENTS

FOREWORD

Practically everyone has struggled with strong emotions at some time during their lives. Emotional turmoil often accompanies life events like divorce, serious illness, or long-term unemployment. For some people, however, emotional suffering can feel constant and overwhelming, because their emotions are particularly intense and difficult to manage. Attempts to escape such emotional pain can lead to failed relationships, addictions, even suicide.

Learning to tolerate emotional pain until it passes is very difficult and requires tremendous courage and will. But courage and will alone cannot take one from emotional turmoil to emotional acceptance, or from chaotic behavior to effective behavior. Such change requires complex skills. Luckily, such skills can be learned!

The mindfulness skills described in this book are at the core of a treatment I have spent my entire career developing and researching: dialectical behavior therapy (DBT). DBT helps people achieve an improved quality of life by replacing harmful behaviors with more effective ones, even when intense emotions are present. When I was first developing DBT at the University of Washington I was also a new student of Zen. I wanted to find a way to share what I was learning from Zen with the people I was treating in order to help them reduce their emotional suffering.

I knew most of my clients would not be able to sit in meditation, at least not at first. They needed simple, concrete tools that could help them take control of their attention enough to learn other skills they desperately needed to master. With the help of my teacher, Willigis Jager, Roshi, I attempted to distill the essence of Zen into tools for highly emotional people. The result was the seven mindfulness skills of DBT. The mindfulness skills allow us to focus attention in the moment in order to recognize that we have a choice about how to proceed. Taking control of attention with the mindfulness skills is a prerequisite to mastering the other DBT skills, including distress tolerance, emotion regulation, and interpersonal effectiveness.

Since I developed DBT, mindfulness has become a valued part of many other psychotherapies. As Cedar Koons mentions in this book, studies have been published that demonstrate the value of mindfulness practice in the treatment of chronic pain, depression, substance abuse, post-traumatic stress disorder, couples therapy, and more. Neurobiologists have found lasting changes in the structure of the brain related to mindfulness practice. While the research to determine what part mindfulness plays in DBT's overall effectiveness has not yet been done, I continue to suspect that it plays a significant role.

I am very pleased that a book has been written on mindfulness especially for people who experience difficulty managing intense emotions—the people for whom DBT was developed. This book covers not only the seven mindfulness skills but also several key distress tolerance skills from DBT, including Radical Acceptance. The book brings fresh insights to all of these skills, including stories, practices, and scientific research. It also addresses the spiritual side of mindfulness, something I have also chosen to emphasize in the recent revision to my skills training manual. But most of all, the book emphasizes the role of mindfulness in emotion regulation.

I am also very pleased that it is Cedar Koons who has written this book. I have known Cedar for more than twenty years and have always noted her passion for mindfulness. Before I met her, Cedar started the first DBT program in a Veterans Administration

(VA) Medical Center in the early 1990s and conducted important research on DBT for female veterans. In 1995 I invited her to join my training company, where she continues to teach and consult on DBT. In 2000, Cedar became the first president of Marie Institute, now Linehan Institute, and suggested to me that we develop retreats for DBT therapists. Over the years Cedar has closely assisted me at numerous retreats, and also at mindfulness trainings.

Cedar's writing is informed by her own mindfulness practice that she has maintained for more than forty years. She explains each skill in clear and readable prose with numerous examples and metaphors so that you can really grasp the essence of the skill, and she offers simple exercises to help you begin to master them. Her engaging stories illustrating how people have used these skills provide inspiration and hope. This book is a valuable resource for anyone who wants to take control of intense emotions and end emotional suffering.

—Marsha M. Linehan

INTRODUCTION

Have you ever been swept up in powerful emotions that prompted you to do things that damaged your relationships or caused you to feel overwhelmed and lost? Have you often regretted emotional behavior or felt that it cost you your self-respect? Have you thrown away your dreams and acted against your deeply held beliefs because of being emotionally out of control?

Most people, at one time or another, have done things they regret under the influence of emotion. But if you feel that you constantly go from one crisis to another because of your emotions, *and you want to change*, this book is written for you. The mindfulness skills taught here can help you find shelter from the devastation caused by powerful, out-of-control emotions so you can ride out the storm without being harmed. Instead of being swept away, you can take shelter in your own strength and intention through mindfulness.

We all experience pain in life, and most of us, at one time or another, go through periods of suffering. I am no exception. I grew up a highly emotional child in a home where the expression of emotions, especially anger, was very much discouraged. Though my parents were loving, caring people, the solution they proposed for handling emotions could be summed up as "Don't show or talk about your feelings and they will go away." When this strategy didn't work for me, which was often, I didn't know what to do.

Although I excelled in school and in sports, and had a few close friends, I was often embarrassed because emotions seemed to rule my life. I coped with them in adolescence and early adulthood by suppressing them during the week with my studies and acting them out on weekends with various risky behaviors. This pattern made my emotions even more difficult to manage. At this time, when I was trying to establish my identity and values, my emotional behavior made life more turbulent and confusing for me. Nothing brought me the sense of self-control and of feeling grounded that I was seeking. I was searching for something, looking everywhere but where it actually resided, fully operational—inside of me.

In my twenties, some friends who were learning to meditate invited me to join them at various workshops and ashrams. I was curious but skeptical. Methods abounded, from those you could purchase to those for which you had to change your name, shave your head, and renounce the outside world. The challenge was to find a path that felt right *to me*. I wanted my path to be straightforward, nonreligious, and free or low-cost. After an extensive search, I found a path that drew me, one that included formal meditation and mindfulness practice throughout the day.

For the first few years I struggled with the contrast between how calm I could feel during meditation with how caught up in emotions I felt in my day-to-day life. Formal meditation was easier than mindfulness! Whether I was working at my job, interacting with friends, or taking care of my family, I found it easy to lose focus under stress. Some days I felt pretty discouraged. Because of my teacher's inspiration I stuck with my meditation practice, and over time I started to experience the integration I sought. Through mindfulness, I not only learned how to handle stress better, but also felt a higher level of joy and contentment. My relationships improved and so did my self-respect.

In the early 1990s I took a job as a clinical social worker on an inpatient psychiatric unit at Duke University Medical Center. My new colleagues had just returned from training with Dr. Marsha Linehan, the developer of dialectical behavior therapy

(DBT). DBT was developed as a treatment for borderline personality disorder (BPD), a disorder that is characterized by pervasive problems with emotion regulation (Linehan 1993). People with BPD often suffer intense emotional pain and are at increased risk for suicide. I had worked with many BPD patients, but much of the treatment available at the time wasn't very effective. The diagnosis itself carried the stigma of being untreatable. But DBT had scientific evidence behind it, indicating that it might actually help patients with BPD find a reason to live (Linehan et al. 1991).

In DBT, mindfulness is broken down into specific skills that can be learned, even by people in emotional turmoil. These concrete skills can help highly emotional people take control of their attention so they can focus on making better choices (Linehan 1993a). I saw that I could use these skills to teach others some of what I had gained from years of meditation and mindfulness practice.

At first I was doubtful about how people who experienced intense, difficult-to-manage emotions—a problem called *pervasive emotion dysregulation*—would be able to focus long enough to use the skills. I knew how difficult it was to take control of my attention even when I wasn't emotional. But I also knew that learning to take control of one's attention in the moment was a ticket to real and positive change. So even though I questioned whether my clients with pervasive emotion dysregulation would be able to learn the mindfulness skills, I was excited to try and hoped they would benefit.

I learned not only that people with emotion dysregulation can learn these skills, but that they can use them to transform their lives. Over the past twenty years I have applied DBT as an individual therapist, skills trainer, and team leader, and have been the principal investigator on research studies of DBT. I have also trained and consulted with numerous teams providing DBT treatment to adults and adolescents in outpatient, inpatient, and

3

residential treatment, and in forensic and juvenile justice settings. These experiences have confirmed my belief that mindfulness skills are crucial to recovery from emotion dysregulation and BPD.

My main goal in writing this book is to provide a resource for people with emotion dysregulation problems, from the most severe BPD to emotional suffering not related to a psychiatric diagnosis. The book presents the seven mindfulness skills of DBT and focuses on the connection between mindfulness and emotion regulation. Mindfulness skills help you to focus in the present moment and therefore reduce impulsive behavior and increase a sense of connection to yourself, even during times of stress. I discuss how mindfulness addresses some of the most troubling mental health problems people experience, such as depression, anxiety, post-traumatic stress disorder (PTSD), substance use, and eating disorders.

While the mindfulness skills of DBT sound deceptively simple, they are challenging to apply. First you have to understand them, and then you have to practice, practice, practice. I hope the structure of the book will help you meet these challenges. Chapter 1 explains key concepts about mindfulness and how it can be used to manage your emotions; chapter 2 describes states of mind and how they influence our behavior; and chapter 3 describes the benefits of *wise mind*, or inner wisdom. Chapters 4 through 9 teach each of six mindfulness skills individually, and include stories to illustrate their application as well as exercises to practice and strengthen them. Chapter 10 teaches three acceptance skills to increase your ability to tolerate emotional distress while remaining mindful. Chapter 11 offers guidance on developing a formal mindfulness practice. There is also a resources section with a list of suggested books, links to audio files, and websites for further learning. And audio versions of a number of the practices in this book are available for download at http://www.newharbinger.com/33001. (See the very back of this book for more information.)

If you are participating in DBT treatment, this book can bolster the skills you acquire in class and with your therapist. If you are a graduate of DBT, the book can serve as a helpful refresher and companion for deeper understanding and sustained practice. For those of you who have never been exposed to DBT, this book offers an opportunity to learn and practice the core skills of a highly popular and effective psychotherapy treatment on your own. It may serve as an adjunct to other kinds of psycho-therapy or spur you to seek full DBT for more severe problems. Even if you are a seasoned practitioner of mindfulness or medita-tion you may find these skills valuable, especially if emotions get in the way of your practice.

It has been my experience that the dedicated practice of these skills can promote recovery from emotional suffering, even suffering that has persisted for years. I hope that this book will make the DBT mindfulness skills accessible to you so that you too can find the here-and-now solution for intense emotions.

Chapter 1

USING MINDFULNESS TO MANAGE YOUR EMOTIONS

On New Year's Day a few years ago, my husband and I had a terrible argument about my shopping. He grabbed my purse and snatched the credit cards out of my wallet. It made me so angry that I ran out of the house with just my car keys. I didn't even put on my winter coat. I drove for an hour in rain and sleet, crying and screaming in anger. It was so unfair, how he disrespected me! I was never going back. Never! But once I got to the next town it was getting dark and I realized I had no money, no phone, no credit card, no ID. I didn't even have enough gas to get home. I finally scrounged some coins out of the glove compartment to make a call at a pay phone, but he didn't answer. I had to beg a woman pumping gas next to me for a few dollars' worth of gas. When I got back to the house, my husband was gone. There was a note on the kitchen table that read: I am done. Don't contact me. It's over. —Chloe, 29

Pervasive Emotion Dysregulation

Do you find that your emotions often cause problems for you, especially in your relationships? Have people consistently told you that you are too sensitive? Do emotions interfere with your thinking? Because of your emotions and emotional behavior do you ever wonder who you really are? When you feel negative emotions, are the sensations in your body so strong and unpleasant that sometimes you feel you would do anything to make the sensations go away—even hurt yourself? Do strong emotions hang around for days, even weeks, making you feel bad? Have emotional situations made you wish you were dead?

If you answered yes to many of these questions, chances are you experience pervasive emotion dysregulation. This means your sensitive nature is difficult to manage, and this difficulty negatively affects the overall quality of your life.

For nearly a hundred years mental health professionals have recognized a pattern of emotional dysregulation that showed up in a variety of problems, some of which are very severe (Gunderson 2009). Psychiatrists described the disorder as "on the border" between psychosis and neurosis (Stern 1938). Some dedicated psychiatrists, such as Otto Kernberg (1967), devoted their lives to trying to help people with these problems, but their treatments reached only a few. Many mental health professionals refused to treat people with pervasive emotion dysregulation (Paris 1993).

In 1980, as part of the development of the *DSM-III*, the third *Diagnostic and Statistical Manual of Mental Disorders*, a committee of psychiatrists constructed borderline personality disorder (BPD) to describe their understanding about this group of problems (Gunderson 2009). The committee agreed upon the following nine criteria and determined that the disorder could be composed of any five or more of these criteria that were firmly established by age eighteen and persisted throughout life. These nine criteria continue to describe BPD today (American Psychiatric Association 2013).

Criteria for Diagnosing Borderline Personality Disorder

1. Frantic efforts to avoid being or feeling abandoned by loved ones.

2. Instability in relationships, including a tendency to idealize and then become disillusioned with relationships.

3. Problems with an unstable sense of self, self-image, or identity.

4. Impulsivity in at least two areas (other than suicidal behavior) that are potentially damaging, such as excessive spending, risky sex, substance abuse, or binge eating.

5. Recurrent suicidal behavior, including thoughts, attempts, or threats of suicide, as well as intentional self-harm that may or may not be life-threatening.

6. Mood swings, including intense negative mood, irritability, and anxiety. Moods usually last a few hours and rarely more than a few days.

7. Chronic feelings of emptiness.

8. Problems controlling intense anger and angry behavior.

9. Transient, stress-related paranoid thoughts or severe dissociation.

Source: American Psychiatric Association 2013

To understand BPD better, it is helpful to know a few demographic facts. For example, 75 percent of people diagnosed with BPD are female, and up to 75 percent of people with BPD intentionally harm themselves at least once during their lifetime. About 10 percent of people with BPD actually kill themselves. Because of their suicidal tendencies, people with BPD make up about 20 percent of patients in psychiatric hospitals, even though they account for only about 2 percent of the national population (Gunderson 2009).

Also, people with BPD are statistically very likely to have additional accompanying problems, called *comorbidities*. The most common accompanying problems are major depression, panic disorder, PTSD, and substance use disorders (Biskin and Paris 2013). The accompanying problems can complicate treatment, as the problems tend to be interrelated and to interact with each other in ways that can make treatment more difficult (Eaton et al. 2010). For example, if you have depression in addition to BPD, the depression may make the BPD problems more prominent and the BPD may make the depression harder to resolve. What statistics cannot show is that regardless of stereotypes, people with BPD look very different from one another (Paris 1993). What they all have in common is the experience of severe emotional distress and difficulty managing emotions.

Mindfulness for Severe Distress

In the 1980s, Jon Kabat-Zinn (1990), a mindfulness practitioner who worked as a microbiologist at the University of Massachusetts, decided to teach mindfulness techniques to people with chronic pain. His students were people suffering intense physical distress who had not been helped by other treatments. Over the next few years he developed an eight-week class, mindfulness-based stress reduction (MBSR). MBSR is now backed by abundant data showing its effectiveness at reducing suffering and improving quality of life for its participants (Godfrin and Van Heeringen 2010).

Around the same time as Kabat-Zinn was developing MBSR, Marsha Linehan, a psychologist at the University of Washington, became interested in whether mindfulness could help suicidal people suffering from intense emotional distress, especially people not helped by standard behavioral therapy. Linehan believed that these clients, all with severe BPD, would benefit from learning basic mindfulness skills to take control of their attention and tolerate painful emotions. Like MBSR, DBT is now backed by a lot of data that prove its effectiveness (Linehan et al. 2014). Thus we now know that mindfulness practice really helps people in severe distress, whether that distress is physical or emotional.

Linehan originally tried standard behavioral methods with her clients but found that these methods did not work because intense and painful emotions got in the way. The very behaviors that wrecked her clients' lives—such as self-harm—actually brought them relief from painful emotions in the moment. The more desperate they felt to escape their emotions, the more they sought relief with problematic behavior. The emotional pain was so intense that it was impossible to imagine giving up the behavior, even though they knew they were destroying their chances at a decent quality of life. If her clients were going to survive, they needed to learn skills, some of which were pretty complicated and hard to learn. But first they needed a simple way to stay present in, and tolerate, the present moment (1993, 1993a).

Mindfulness Becomes a Skill

How can people in intense pain manage to stay in the present moment long enough to learn complicated skills? Linehan, a mindfulness student, decided to try to translate what she had learned of Zen principles into simple skills to teach her clients (Van Nuys 2004).

Zen is a school of Buddhism now practiced all over the world. Buddhism originated in northern India, from where it spread south and east. In China, Buddhism took on elements of Taoism and became a school called Chan. After thriving for many centuries in China, Chan took root in Japan, where it was called Zen. In the last century, Zen traveled to western countries, including the United States. Zen teaches that the path to enlightenment is through meditation, self-contemplation, and intuition, rather than through faith and devotion (Suzuki 1964).

Linehan's translation of Zen principles into mindfulness skills resulted in the three *what* skills and the three *how* skills of DBT (Van Nuys 2004). Linehan also described the wisdom inside all people that could be accessed through mindfulness practice. She used the name *wise mind* to describe this inner knowing and explained how the *what* and *how* skills could connect people to their inner wisdom (Van Nuys 2004). Wise mind together with the three what skills and the three how skills make up the seven mindfulness skills I will present in detail in chapters 3 through 10.

The Seven DBT Mindfulness Skills

Wise Mind

What Skills	**How Skills**
Observing	Nonjudgmentally
Describing	One-Mindfully
Participating	Effectively

Source: Linehan 1993a

Kabat-Zinn's mindfulness-based stress reduction teaches formal meditation as a way to become more mindful. In DBT, Linehan wanted to help people take control of their attention without needing to learn formal meditation. The seven mindfulness skills developed by Linehan and described in this book can be used in a variety of ways and in all kinds of settings to operationalize the benefits of mindfulness for people who struggle with intense emotions, without the requirement to sit for formal meditation. Each skill isolates a step in the process of becoming more aware. When used correctly, the mindfulness skills can make the difference between a chaotic, emotion-driven life and a focused, intentional one by increasing our distress tolerance, emotion regulation, and interpersonal capabilities (Linehan 1993a).

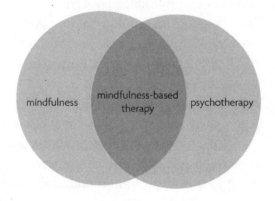

Figure 1

What Is Mindfulness?

Mindfulness is intentionally focusing in the present moment and accepting what is in that moment without evaluating it as good or bad (Germer 2004). We can be in a mindful state for a few moments, for most of a day, or for days, weeks, or years at a time. We can be mindful while undertaking all kinds of activities, from putting out a forest fire to eating a popsicle, from carrying on a conversation to having sex.

How Mindfulness Helps People with Emotion Dysregulation

Researchers have studied how mindfulness can lead to a reduction in people's experience of pain and improve their ability to cope with a variety of problems, including depression, chronic pain, and addiction (Godfrin and Van Heeringen 2010). Evidence shows that mindfulness reduces emotional pain by bringing our attention into the present moment and helping us focus on what is real in the moment (Grossman et al. 2004). As we will see in chapter 2, strong emotions produce powerful urges to act before we think. When we focus mindfully, we are building in a brief pause before we act. Within that pause we can actually recognize that we have a choice about how to act, rather than being slaves to our emotions and their urges.

Mindfulness practices also can help a person become calmer and feel more grounded—the exact opposite of how we feel when we are in the grip of emotions. Even when we are going through a prolonged crisis, such as coping with cancer treatment or recovering from an episode of depression, mindfulness practices can increase our experiences of connection to ourselves and enhance our spirituality (Greeson et al. 2015).

Is Mindfulness a Religion?

Because mindfulness is from the Buddhist tradition, some people fear that if they practice mindfulness they will be asked to give up their own spiritual or religious beliefs and adopt new ones. These worries affect both religious and nonreligious people.

Although some religions make use of it, mindfulness is not a religion. The practice of mindfulness, however, can open one to certain experiences that could be called spiritual, mystical, or flow-type experiences (Kristeller 2010). The present moment, it turns out, is a pretty exciting place to hang out. When contact with the present moment increases, we notice things in a new way. It is easy to interpret what happens in a spiritual dimension, but it is not necessary to do so.

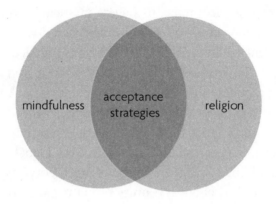

Figure 2

Mindfulness requires no beliefs and neither prescribes nor disagrees with the beliefs of any religion (Batchelor 1998). Religions might offer specific belief systems about God and correct behavior, morality, and the afterlife. Religions also usually offer specific scriptures to inform nearly every aspect of life. Mindfulness practice does not include or exclude any of these things.

What religion and mindfulness have in common are strategies to help with acceptance of reality. In religion, activities such as prayer, turning things over to God, reading scriptures, and participating in liturgy can help us accept painful realities, such as death, and appreciate joyful interpretations of reality, such as feeling loved by God (Diamond 2012). In mindfulness, we accept what is in the moment without interpretations of good or bad or assigning any particular meaning to reality.

Mindfulness and Mysticism— What's the Connection?

All mystics are in some way mindfulness practitioners, but not all mindfulness practitioners are mystics. Mystics may be secular or associated with a religion. Mystics use mindfulness, contemplation, and meditation to enter into communion with ultimate reality. Most religions have a mystical component that cultivates some kind of mindfulness activity. Hindus and Buddhists engage in meditation, Christians practice contemplative or centering prayer, Judaism has the Kabala, and Islam contains the practices of Sufism. Mystics encourage us to be awake to reality in the present moment (Borchert 1994).

Atheists and other nonreligious people also have described mystical experiences. Scientists such as Max Planck (1949) and Erwin Schrödinger, pioneers in quantum theory and quantum mechanics, talked about the unity of matter and consciousness almost like mystics, though neither was religious. Schrödinger, reputedly an atheist, connected his theory of wave mechanics with Hinduism's belief in the unity of all things, mind and matter (Moore 1992).

Many poets and naturalists have described mystical experiences. William Blake, in "Auguries of Innocence" (1789), describes seeing infinity in a flower and eternity in an hour (Harmon 1990). Many of Blake's poems, like those of Emily Dickinson, Robert Frost, and Walt Whitman and contemporary poets such as Mary Oliver and Gary Snyder, describe insights attained, often in nature, that sound like mystical experiences (Lehman 2006).

We don't have to be mystics to practice mindfulness. We can draw our own conclusions about our experiences. A feeling of joy arises in me: is it because God loves me, or is joy simply a sensation passing through me, not unlike sadness but more pleasurable? Mindfulness skills allow us to notice feelings as they come and go. What we say to ourselves about our inner experience is up to us.

Do I Have to Learn to Meditate?

Mindfulness skills allow us to be in the present moment while carrying on with the business of life. In meditation we set aside time from daily activities to focus exclusively on a particular practice. To meditate you must be mindful, but being mindful does not require that you meditate. (Note the way the meditation circle is contained inside the mindfulness one in figure 3.) The practice of meditation may improve your mindful awareness throughout the day.

Figure 3

Many meditation practices emphasize concentrating on something, such as a mantra, a prayer, or the sensation of the breath while sitting still and silent. In other meditations it is as if the lens of the mind is wide open but no images are captured. The meditator attempts to observe the mind's activity without becoming lost in it, remaining alert to *all that is*, not attending to breath, mantra, or any focusing technique nor following any thoughts. This challenging practice teaches you to step back from your thoughts and observe them as thoughts only (Mipham 2004).

Meditation has been described as sitting under a waterfall and mindfulness as walking through a redwood forest on a rainy day—both activities result in getting thoroughly "wet."

Mindfulness, with practice, can also increase our experience of "flow" (Csikszentmihalyi 1997).

Mindfulness and Flow

When you feel an energized focus, full involvement, and immersion in whatever you are doing, you can be said to be in a state of flow. Mihaly Csikszentmihalyi (1997), a developer of the concept, describes flow as the experience people associate with the best moments of their lives, those that give their lives meaning. Athletes refer to it as being "in the zone," religious mystics as being in "ecstasy," artists and musicians as "aesthetic rapture." The practice of mindfulness can lead to highly pleasurable experiences, whether you are making dinner, playing in the waves of the ocean, or teaching third graders how to sing in rounds. Being mindful also can enhance the possibility of remaining more present to flow experiences that arise spontaneously, sometimes when you least expect them. Since those of us with pervasive emotion regulation often have difficulty experiencing spontaneity and joy, mindfulness techniques are useful not only to regulate painful emotions but also to increase awareness of positive emotions and to increase the possibility of experiencing flow.

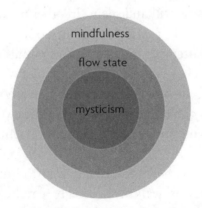

Figure 4

Twin Obstacles: Emotional Intensity and Emotional Avoidance

If mindfulness is so simple and great, why is it so hard for people with emotion regulation problems to learn and use these skills? The first step of mindfulness is to take control of your attention. This is especially difficult for people who experience emotional intensity and often practice emotional avoidance (Chapman, Gratz, and Brown 2006).

Emotional intensity refers to the experience of excruciating bodily sensations associated with emotions and the sense that it is impossible to resist the "action urge" of that emotion. (For a list of emotions and their hardwired action urges, see the box titled "How to Recognize Emotion Mind," in chapter 2.) Even when we know better, following an action urge can feel like *what we must do*. Once we act on an urge, we start down a slippery slope that can lead to more emotion and more urges, and eventually to confusion and misery. Giving in to emotion-based action urges can seem so right in the moment but often leads to long-term suffering (Linehan 1993).

Though seemingly the opposite of emotional intensity, emotional avoidance can lead us to the same impasse (Chapman, Gratz, and Brown 2006). When we feel we cannot tolerate emotional pain, we want desperately to escape. Our attention wanders to all the distractions available to us, such as food, alcohol, drugs, sleeping, eating, having suicidal thoughts, lashing out in anger, isolating—anything to avoid feeling the emotion. These temporary escapes are easy to access. We forget about the promises we've made to others or ourselves, we forget the long-term consequences of these "solutions," and we fall victim to old patterns.

By design and linked to our survival mechanisms, emotions function to get our attention and organize us to act in accordance (Ratey 2001). The very nature of emotion makes it difficult to focus the mind on anything else. The following stories illustrate how two people used mindfulness skills. Colleen struggled with emotional intensity; Christina, with emotional avoidance.

• Colleen's Story

Colleen had worked for the state department of revenue for nearly eight years, sitting in a cubicle answering taxpayers' questions over the phone. Forty-two and divorced, Colleen worked almost fifty hours a week but was paid for only forty. Her boss could be verbally demeaning to her. Although Colleen hated her job she could not afford to leave it, with its benefits and promise of a pension. Taxpayers were often rude—cursing, calling her names, and sometimes even hanging up in the middle of her explanations. She was expected to always act in a professional manner.

Colleen often came home at the end of a workday with a pounding headache. She had dreams about trying to kill people. Colleen knew her anger was a problem, but she didn't know what to do about it.

One day, Colleen's boss told Colleen that her caller-disapproval rate was above 30 percent. "This is unacceptable," the boss said, "and you know it!" She then smiled in a way that Colleen interpreted as condescending. Colleen stood up, feeling anger like a white-hot ingot in her chest. She had the urge to slap the smile off her boss's face. Colleen managed to run from the cubicle instead, but she accidentally bumped into her boss's shoulder as she escaped. Colleen was written up for this incident, and the human resources manager required her to take a class in anger management.

Colleen needed to regulate her anger urges and get her anger to diminish. In DBT she learned to notice the signs that anger was building and how to step back and mindfully observe it without suppressing or acting on it. When Colleen felt her tension building, she tried to take breaks to breathe, stretch, and relax. During her lunch break she often took walks, counting her footsteps instead of ruminating about rude taxpayers. On the weekends Colleen increased her exercise. Her blood pressure came down and she began to sleep better. She also made a promise to herself to find another job just as soon as she could get her performance ratings to improve.

"The most powerful skill for me," she said after completing the skills class, "was learning that I could simply observe my emotion. I do not have to stuff it down or act when the emotion is strong. It is a miserable feeling to be that angry, but I have learned to focus and endure it until the intensity passes. After just a few moments it does, then I make a choice about what to do. When I remain calm, people usually calm down too, and we can work together on solving the problem." With her new skills, Colleen was eventually able to land a better, less stressful job.

• *Christina's Story*

Christina, a college student majoring in theater, planned to pursue an acting career after graduation. Christina was talented, but she struggled with intense self-doubt and a tendency toward perfectionism. Since her freshman year, Christina had been binge eating at night and then exercising to burn the extra calories she'd consumed. The problem had grown worse as she progressed in her acting program, until Christina felt completely out of control. "I don't know how to stop it," she said. "I don't even know why I do it." Christina's eating disorder was so effective at helping her avoid her emotions that she didn't know what she felt.

Christina ate small, light meals during the day and binged at night after everyone in her dorm had gone to sleep. In the space of about forty minutes she might consume as many as 1,500 calories, mostly carbohydrates. Then she ran on the treadmill in the basement, often for two hours or more, and finally fell into bed in the middle of the night. The next day she would be exhausted and feel even more vulnerable. She avoided friends and activities and hid out in her room when she wasn't in class.

Christina started therapy in the fall of her junior year. She learned mindfulness skills and used them to help recognize her bodily sensations and emotions, especially before, during, and after the bingeing and exercising. This took a number of weeks, since Christina had been avoiding feeling bodily sensations for years. She first identified the bodily sensations she felt before bingeing as "wanting to hide," which was actually an urge associated with an emotion, rather than a sensation. After the binge she felt "sedated," followed by the desire to hide again. After running on the treadmill she felt both physical and emotional relief.

Christina recognized that "wanting to hide" was actually the emotion of shame. Her experience of shame was so powerful that she ate to make it go away. Eating did make it stop for a short time, but then it returned stronger than ever, accompanied by fear, which caused her to run off the calories she had consumed.

Christina's shame most often arose around her performance in class and any critical feedback she got from peers or professors. She interpreted criticism as evidence of rejection and failure. She would later realize that her interpretations were probably exaggerated, but in the moment she couldn't reassure herself and she felt too ashamed to ask for anyone's support. Instead, she went numb and acted as if everything were fine, although her thoughts turned to self-loathing. She didn't eat regular meals, so by evening she was hungry and vulnerable.

In therapy Christina came to understand more about how over-exercising was connected to the whole pattern. Exercising gave her a sense of empowerment and distracted her from the further shame she felt about having just binged. After she had exercised she was able to sleep soundly and her shame was forgotten. These strategies for managing shame—going numb, avoiding, bingeing and exercising—worked in the short run, but they were ruining Christina's life.

Mindfulness skills gave Christina the power to recognize when shame was arising, putting her at risk for a binge/exercise cycle. She was also able to improve her eating habits during the day and to tolerate the emotion of shame at night, without bingeing, until it passed. Mindfulness also helped Christina notice and reduce perfectionist thinking and critical self-talk. She got better at asking for feedback and clarifying any communications she might interpret as rejecting.

As she began to regulate shame, Christina was able to decrease and finally eliminate bingeing and over-exercising. By recognizing her emotions and experiencing rather than avoiding them, she developed new ways to cope with the stress of acting. Mindfulness skills enhanced her sense of self-control and freedom. "I use the mindfulness skills every day," she said. "I know when I am vulnerable and I take steps to protect myself. I still have urges to escape uncomfortable feelings, but I have learned to accept them. I feel like I have some control over the bingeing and that feels really good. I say to myself, 'You can deal with this.' And then I do."

Reduce Emotional Intensity and Emotional Avoidance with Mindfulness

Mindfulness helps by waking us up in the middle of an emotional storm. It helps us see what is going on (bodily sensations and urges) and what choices we have (to act on urges or not) by bringing our attention into the moment. First we notice the sensations we are feeling. Even if the sensations are intensely unpleasant, we recognize they are only sensations and they will pass in a short while. When we can tolerate the sensations of emotions and not feel compelled either to act on or to avoid them, we begin to notice something important: urges are only urges, not imperatives. We can simply notice the emotion and ride it like a wave, knowing that eventually it will pass, even if only to come again. The more we can stay present and accept the moment, the less we feel the need to either act on how we feel, like Colleen, or escape from how we feel, like Christina. When the intensity and urgency pass, the way forward becomes easier to see. Over time, we begin to hear the quiet voice of our true selves gently advising us.

When we stay in the present we find that the moment is, in fact, tolerable. We are not ruminating about our intractable problems or agonizing over the loneliness and shame we feel. We give up trying to fix everything and stop blaming ourselves for what we imagine to be the gigantic mess we have made of our lives. Instead, our own inner voice might say, *Okay, maybe I am not happy with what is going on, but I can accept this moment.*

Our first experiences of practicing mindfulness skills may be painful. We have to get over the initial barrier of intense emotions or emotional avoidance to experience what the skills can offer us. We have to *experience* our emotions, thoughts, and bodily sensations, rather than avoid them. At first this can feel overwhelming, even wrong. We may become more aware of negative thoughts or feelings of grief, anger, fear, and unpleasant

24

bodily sensations we have been suppressing. They don't feel good! It is easy to want to give up at this point and return to the more familiar strategies of acting on urges or avoiding feelings.

The changes we experience at first may be so subtle that we might not notice much difference right away. Our thoughts will still wander; our attention will drift to the negative; we frequently will return to old behaviors. After all, reining in the mind after years of letting it run wild is going to be slow. But over time our practice will pay off.

Mind Wandering Versus Present-Moment Awareness

When the mind wanders, it often ends up in unpleasant territory and can lead to a downturn in mood, even when we aren't depressed, according to a mindfulness study conducted at Harvard University. Letting your mind wander is associated with worsening mood even when you are on vacation or engaging in your favorite activities. Focusing in the present moment, on the other hand, leads to improved mood even when you are doing things you typically do not enjoy, such as being stuck in traffic or attending a work-related meeting. The study showed that the relationship between present-moment focus and overall happiness affected people who were already happy as well as those who described themselves as unhappy—that is, otherwise happy people became unhappy when they lost focus in the moment and unhappy people improved their mood by focusing in the moment, *independent of what they were doing in the moment* (Killingsworth and Gilbert 2010)!

Present-moment awareness could be as important to our feeling better, and is arguably much easier to accomplish, than other changes we might need to make, such as moving, taking a vacation, changing jobs, or meeting new friends. Present-moment focus alone might help us improve our mood enough to give us the energy and focus to approach other, more complicated changes.

In summary, mindfulness is useful for anyone who wants to be able to cope with distress and make better decisions. For people with emotion regulation problems, the main obstacles to learning and using mindfulness skills are emotional intensity and emotional avoidance. The specific mindfulness skills of DBT teach us how to notice when our intense emotions are in control, as well as how to focus and what to focus on. The very act of choosing to focus mindfully builds in a pause that allows us to remember we have choices about how to respond to our emotions. Using mindfulness skills on a daily basis can help anyone leave behind chaotic, emotion-driven behavior and enter into the present moment where it is possible to feel more acceptance, peace, and contentment.

Now that you have been introduced to the overarching concepts of this book, we are ready to drill down into each of the skills in detail. In the chapters to come, you will learn first to identify your state of mind and then how and when to use each of the seven mindfulness and three acceptance skills of DBT to gain more control of your mind, even in times of emotional distress.

Chapter 2

WHAT IS YOUR
STATE OF MIND?

I always feel at war with myself. Last year a part of me desperately wanted to drop out of graduate school and use the money I had saved to focus on my writing. The other part of me wanted to finish my degree and get a teaching job. I couldn't make up my mind! I went back and forth, but eventually I dropped out of school. Then I got really depressed. I haven't written a single story in six months. Now I'd kill to be back in school! I wish I knew whether or not to trust my feelings. The problem is my feelings flip-flop all the time. It makes me feel crazy not to know my own mind. —Rudi, 26

Reasonable Mind and Emotion Mind

Why do we sometimes have problems trusting our perceptions and knowing what is real? Why do we think or feel one way one minute and completely differently an hour later?

Having a history of making bad decisions based on emotions contributes to believing you cannot trust yourself. Emotions and their urges get in the way of brain processes that help us figure out whether a particular thought or emotion should be considered valid, justified, or appropriate to the current situation (Ratey 2001). When we learn to recognize our state of mind and how it influences our perceptions, we can make smarter choices. Recognizing our state of mind can help us determine how much to trust what we are feeling and thinking in the moment (Linehan 1993a).

This chapter introduces two important states of mind: *reasonable mind* and *emotion mind*. Understanding reasonable mind and emotion mind will prepare us to learn *wise mind*, the first of the seven mindfulness skills and the topic of the next chapter (Linehan 1993a). But first, what do I mean by "mind"?

Think of mind as pure awareness, like an empty sky. Through the mind travel our thoughts, images, body awareness, memories, urges, dreams, and more—always moving and transforming, like weather in the atmosphere. This "weather" is our state of mind at any given time. When we are in reasonable mind it is just another day, and we don't even notice the weather. The mind is hyper-rational, focused on the facts and tasks at hand. When we are in emotion mind, emotions are in control and storms blow in. Rationality flies away like leaves in an autumn gale. Under the influence of very strong emotions, thoughts jump from the past to the future and back to the present, and emotions and urges feel as unstable as tornados. The weather of wise mind is peaceful, even if a storm has recently passed by. Emotions may be present, like clouds in a blue sky, but the weather is calm. We are aware both of the facts of a situation and of our feelings about it. The mind is quiet and the attention is focused in the moment.

Most of the time a part of your attention is quietly observing everything you are doing, even your own state of mind. To identify your state of mind, tune in to yourself from that observing part of you. How do you feel in your body? What are your thoughts like? Is emotion present? Can you name it? Do you feel any urges? Do you feel a loud intensity; a cool, logical focus; or a quiet inner knowing? Being able to look at your mind this way will help you identify your state of mind (Linehan 1993a).

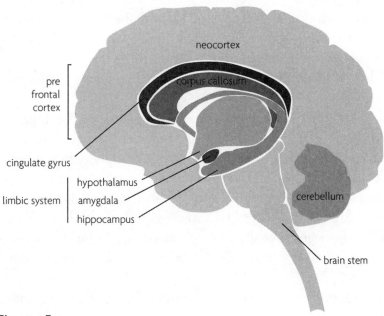

Figure 5

The Brain and States of Mind

Looking at how our brains are structured (see figure 5) can help us understand the importance of physiology on states of mind. Reasonable mind—the state of mind concerned with facts, tasks, and concrete problem solving—resides in a part of the neocortex called the prefrontal cortex, or PFC. The PFC takes information from other parts of the brain and determines what is and is not useful. The PFC controls starting and stopping actions, prioritizing and sequencing steps toward a goal, and using information to adapt to novel situations. The PFC allows us to think abstractly, stay focused on what is relevant to any situation, predict outcomes, and manage time (Fuster 2008). A well-functioning PFC contributes to the ability to suppress behavior that others might find offensive or inappropriate, such as telling a sexually explicit joke to a new supervisor at work. Many of the tasks of reasonable mind require a working PFC. Collectively, these tasks are called "executive functioning." (For a list of these tasks, see the box titled "Abilities Associated with Effective Executive Functioning," in chapter 8.)

Unfortunately, the PFC, like other parts of the brain, is subject to malfunction. Problems such as obsessive-compulsive disorder, attention deficit/hyperactivity disorder, schizophrenia, depression, autism, and traumatic brain injuries can reduce executive functioning, as can chronic alcohol abuse and drug addiction. A malfunctioning PFC interferes with the ability to focus, follow through on goals, delay gratification, and inhibit urges. A compromised PFC can make it harder to access reasonable mind (Ratey 2001).

Emotion mind resides in structures deep in the brain called the limbic system, which includes the amygdala, the hypothalamus, the hippocampus, and other structures. These structures make up the "threat alert" part of our brains. The limbic system is a "first responder" to information in the environment that pertains to our survival. When a threat is perceived, the limbic system responds immediately, communicating through its dedicated neural pathways to our brain stem. Certain kinds of stimuli—such as loud sounds, the sight of an attacking animal, or the feeling of falling—cause us to react immediately and involuntarily without interpretation. Such reactions are "hardwired." That is why you will jump back if a snake lunges toward you, even if it is in a glass box. Your hardwired response does not require input from other parts of the brain, such as the PFC (Ratey 2001).

When something triggers the limbic system it immediately activates the brain stem, which regulates the sympathetic and parasympathetic nervous system, affecting breathing, temperature, and alertness. Also activated is the cerebellum, an adjacent structure controlling movement, muscle tension, and balance. Instantly your heart starts pounding, your muscles tense, and you feel the sensation of fear—flight, fight, or freeze. You've made no conscious assessment. Emotion mind is in full control, pressing you to act (Whalen and Phelps 2009).

Our brains, always prioritizing threat avoidance, also store our emotional memories through the hippocampus, which enables us to recall these memories quickly. Whenever a set of stimuli has produced strong, unpleasant reactions in the past, the hippocampus stores a special kind of memory of those stimuli. When we encounter them again, our reaction is immediate (Ratey 2001).

Let's say a man on a motorbike came up behind you, grabbed your purse, and knocked you down. Every time a motorbike passes you thereafter, you are likely to be braced for an attack.

Even hearing a motorbike might cause you distress. In fact, the fear associated with the motorbike might be activated when any vehicle, even a bicycle, passes you. You don't have to remember the reaction you paired to that stimulus. Your limbic system does that for you, activating your autonomic nervous system to prepare for the threat.

Like the PFC, the limbic system is vulnerable to malfunction. Long exposure to traumatic stress or severe depression can weaken the hippocampus (Fuster 2008). Depression distorts thinking in a variety of ways. It decreases concentration, increases rumination and hopeless thoughts, and reduces our ability to experience pleasure (American Psychiatric Association 2013). Bipolar disorder and schizophrenia are thought to impair the functioning of the cingulate cortex, a structure that connects the limbic system to the PFC, to communicate about emotions, pain, and aggression (Fuster 2008). All of these brain impairments make us more vulnerable to emotion mind.

By activating the entire brain, wise mind functions as a clearinghouse where the information coming in—facts, emotions, learning from the past—can be processed more effectively. When we are in wise mind we have access to the executive functions of the PFC as well as information from the limbic system, including the old, perhaps distorted, interpretations from the hippocampus (Paulson et al. 2013). No one area exerts complete control. Wise mind allows these centers, with their differing perspectives, to communicate rather than dominate.

Identifying Reasonable Mind

Now that we've looked at the brain to understand more about states of mind, let's look at how to identify them in ourselves. How does it feel to be in reasonable mind?

Reasonable mind feels cool and nonurgent. When we are in reasonable mind we are not paying much attention to the emotional content of a situation. Sometimes we can operate in reasonable mind without much awareness of what else is happening, including the emotions we are feeling (Linehan 1993a).

Reasonable mind focuses on tasks. We want to get to the destination by the most direct route, make the soufflé according to the recipe, or reconcile the checking account according to the bank statement, without any drama. Reasonable mind helps us notice what belongs in a sequence and what does not. It helps us categorize and label things to solve concrete problems (Linehan 1993a). See the following box, titled "How to Recognize Reasonable Mind," for a checklist that can help you identify when you're in reasonable mind.

We also need reasonable mind to function in relationships. We use it to agree on a set of facts and make logical decisions with another person. Reasonable mind is necessary when we work on a team, such as a task force or jury or with relatives planning a family event. Reasonable mind allows us to collaborate more effectively with people who may not share our emotional reactions. Having a working reasonable mind is necessary to function in almost all work environments and is key to balanced friendships.

Reasonable mind can even save our lives by helping us to stay calm and focused on facts under pressure. Captain Chesley Sullenberger, who landed his jet on the Hudson River in January of 2009 with 150 passengers and five crew members aboard, used his reasonable mind to avert a crisis. There was no room for emotion during that landing. If Sullenberger and his crew hadn't been able to make quick logical decisions that day, many lives would have been lost (Batty and Weaver 2009). Functioning in a crisis may require that emotions be suppressed and reasonable mind be in charge. This may be why people sometimes collapse in tears after coolly dealing with a crisis.

How to Recognize Reasonable Mind

☐   I am focused on the task at hand.

☐   I am concerned with facts.

☐   I have considered pros and cons.

☐   I am not that influenced by emotions, my own or those of other people.

☐   I feel cool and nonurgent.

☐   I don't get what all the fuss is about.

☐   I am not able to understand why someone is upset with me.

☐   I can't say exactly how I feel other than "fine."

Check all that apply. If you checked one to three statements, you may or may not be in reasonable mind; four to six, you probably are in reasonable mind; seven to eight, you are certainly in reasonable mind, but you are potentially clueless about your emotions!

When Reasonable Mind Is Out of Balance

Reasonable mind is necessary in making good decisions. When reasonable mind is offline we can't listen to what is sensible. We can't even agree on the facts. This prevents us from being able to solve problems that arise with other people. But as we will see, reasonable mind must be balanced with awareness of emotion. We will look at three stories that illustrate how a person's decision-making process can be out of balance: too little reasonable mind, ignoring feelings in reasonable mind, and being stuck in reasonable mind. At the end of this chapter is a list of practices that can help you strengthen your reasonable mind.

• *Vince's Story*

Vince, a talented designer, had lost a well-paying job and was having a hard time finding another when he first came to see me. He had expressed anger toward the man who had fired him and was considering suing the firm for breach of contract. Vince acknowledged that he was frequently absent from work due to his mood and that he almost never met his deadlines, but he refused to consider that these might be the reasons why he was terminated. Instead, Vince stuck to believing that his employer had fired him because he was envious of Vince's talent and some clients liked Vince's work better than his. Vince further believed, without evidence, that the firm was giving him bad references because they did not want him to compete with them.

Vince had spent so much effort being angry at and blaming others for his problems that the facts of his own behavior were hard for him to face. After much discussion, he was able to recognize and admit that his problems began with anxiety around his job performance. Even though he knew he had good skills, he lacked confidence and feared rejection.

Vince's fears led to procrastinating on important projects. The more he procrastinated, the more his boss demanded that Vince meet client deadlines. His boss was getting negative feedback from clients about the delays, and without Vince's product he could not collect the money he needed to operate. As a result, he was very caustic toward Vince.

Privately, Vince felt guilt and shame about his procrastination. Publicly, Vince vilified the boss for not understanding the creative process, and blamed his procrastination on a toxic work environment. Vince began not showing up for important meetings with clients, and sometimes put the blame on coworkers who hadn't followed through on their parts of a project. Blaming his boss and coworkers for his problems allowed Vince to avoid his part in the situation, providing temporary relief from his pain. But blaming others meant denying the facts, further damaging relationships, and losing access to his reasonable mind. If he couldn't accurately describe the facts to himself and to me, how could he ever solve his problems?

Eventually, by repeatedly accessing reasonable mind, Vince was able to look at the facts without emotion overwhelming him and admit that he had played a role in his termination. When he finally got a job in another firm, he worked hard to access reasonable mind and not overlook the facts whenever his anxiety spiked. With awareness of his state of mind, Vince was able to reduce avoidance on the job, which improved his work, his relationships, and his mood. By accessing reasonable mind, he was better equipped to solve the real problems before him, rather than the ones he had created by refusing to face facts.

Because reasonable mind doesn't access information that comes mainly from emotions, it doesn't grasp how we feel about a situation. In reasonable mind we can be clueless and cut off from our feelings. Some people hide in reasonable mind to avoid their own and other people's emotions, especially when those emotions are uncomfortable or have unwelcome consequences. When we ignore our feelings because they don't line up with the facts we can end up making unwise choices, especially in matters of the heart.

• *Denise's Story*

Denise, a thirty-five-year-old emergency-room physician, was worried that she would never get married. She had dated many men but never found Mr. Right. At services over Jewish New Year, she met Jeff, an accountant, the kind of "nice Jewish boy" her mother had always wanted her to marry. Jeff was immediately attracted to Denise and shared her interest in settling down. Denise was flattered by Jeff's attention and grew fond of him.

Denise and Jeff dated for a year. When he proposed marriage, she couldn't decide what to do. On the one hand, Jeff made an excellent salary and had no real vices; in addition, her mother loved him. And Denise's biological clock was ticking. If she wanted to have a family it was time to act! On the other hand, Jeff's conversations about investing, his politics, and his passion for remote-controlled airplanes bored her. Most of all, she wasn't physically attracted to him. Denise felt betrayed by her emotions because they didn't line up with the facts— Jeff was a good catch! Denise married Jeff. Within five years they were divorced. Denise promised herself she would never overlook her emotions about a relationship again.

• *Sarah's Story*

Sarah was a thirty-seven-year-old former soldier with two young sons. Her husband was deployed overseas. She worked as a licensed practical nurse at a home for developmentally disabled adults and lived in a house next door to her mother, who lived on disability.

Sarah's employer felt she was not handling the stress of her circumstances well enough to do her job effectively. She had been falling asleep on the job. He suggested she contact the employee assistance program to set up an appointment. At the appointment Sarah told the counselor she simply did not have the time to come to therapy. "I'm just stressed out. It's no big deal. Lots of people have problems like mine and they get through them."

Sarah was "reasonable" about everything. She was focusing on facts without considering the emotional factors. She had no time for herself; her mother was not much help; her husband was away; she was not sleeping; she had headaches; she was in trouble at work. Sarah chose to ignore her needs. *Everybody has stress*, she reasoned.

Sarah told herself she didn't have a choice. If she had been able to acknowledge the problem, she might have found ways to get support. Instead, she pushed her feelings aside to get on with the business of surviving. Sarah was stuck in reasonable mind. It didn't make sense to her to take care of herself, but she was facing long-term problems with her physical and mental health.

Sarah's story is a familiar one. The demands of family and work can be so overwhelming that pushing aside emotions becomes a way of life, especially when facing unusual demands such as being a single parent, having a disabled child, or being married to someone with a chronic illness. Unfortunately, being stuck in reasonable mind over time, living a highly stressful life, and suppressing emotions can lead to long-term problems such as chronic pain, illness, and depression. The checklist in the following box can help you determine whether you are stuck in reasonable mind.

Am I Stuck in Reasonable Mind?

☐ I keep pushing aside my own feelings, thinking they are unimportant.

☐ I try to ignore body complaints such a headaches, backaches, and stomachaches.

☐ I consistently ignore my intuition.

☐ People I love frequently tell me I "just don't get it."

☐ I coolly and rationally keep making the same mistake over and over, especially in relationships.

☐ I often feel clueless when someone I care about is really emotional.

☐ It is sometimes hard for me to understand why other people are so worked up about an issue that also affects me.

☐ I rarely experience strong emotions of any kind other than frustration.

☐ I am lacking in experiences of joy or love, and instead feel flat and dry.

☐ I am often in a caregiving role for others while I ignore my own needs.

Check all that apply. If you checked one to three statements, you may not be stuck in reasonable mind. If you checked four to six statements, get in touch with your emotions now. If you checked seven to ten, call the tow truck; you are stuck in reasonable mind!

Reasonable mind is only part of our awareness. Emotions are central to who we are and are necessary for effective communication, both verbal and nonverbal. Sometimes, however, reasonable mind is the only way we can ground ourselves during storms of emotion. Here are some practices you can undertake to strengthen your reasonable mind.

Practices to Strengthen Reasonable Mind

1. Check the facts of an emotional situation. List every relevant fact you can think of. Do not discount *any* relevant facts.

2. If you are struggling with an urge to act or avoid, write a list of pros and cons.

3. Study logic and learn to identify logical errors.

4. Play games that require sequential thinking, such as chess, bridge, or Scrabble.

5. Ask yourself, *What would Data or Spock (from* Star Trek*) say about this?*

6. Ask someone who is objective and whom you trust to tell you whether you are being reasonable, and listen to the answer.

Why We Need Emotions

All social animals—whether gorillas, elephants, dogs, or humans—are emotional creatures by design (Goleman 2011). Emotions help social animals to function in herds, packs, or bands to hunt, escape enemies, and raise their young by motivating action, amplifying communication, and providing quick information about their environment. Because of our social nature, emotions are a necessary part of what it means to be human. Emotions make us feel connected to others, help us communicate, motivate us to act, and literally help us survive.

We use emotions as a first line of communication because the body language and facial expressions associated with them communicate more quickly and powerfully than words. Emotions also give us important information about other people and ourselves; we are influenced by how something makes us feel, even when feelings conflict with facts (Ekman and Friesen 2003). It is through our emotions, at least in part, that we understand who we are, what we value, and what makes us feel safe and secure (Goleman 2011). Our emotions give us gut feelings in which we tend to place a lot of trust.

Emotions also motivate us to act in ways that are crucial to our survival. Emotions inspire us to protect those we love and to seek out and rescue people who are lost, even strangers. Emotions inspire acts of heroism and sacrifice for the greater good, such as fighting forest fires or disarming bombs. Emotions inspire artistic expression and performances that unite us, from singing our national anthem at a sporting event to reading a literary classic aloud. We seek experiences of affiliation, love, and joy to enrich our lives, thereby coming into closer contact with others (Goleman 2011). The experience of positive emotions increases our ability to tolerate adversity. Positive emotions even strengthen our immune systems (Davidson et al. 2003).

Painful emotions are also necessary for our survival and functioning. If we had no fear, we would take unwise risks. Without anger we would not be able to defend our rights. Without shame and guilt we would act in ways that would make it impossible for us to live in community. Every emotion plays an important role in our quality of life and relationships.

Of course, powerful emotions must be regulated. When we let our emotions run unfettered, we are apt to make serious mistakes, possibly harming others and ourselves. When emotions are in full control, whether they are positive or negative, we enter the state of mind called emotion mind (Linehan 1993a).

Identifying Emotion Mind

Emotion mind can be useful for short, extreme episodes, such as when you are escaping from an angry bear or fighting off an intruder in your home. In dire circumstances like these you don't need to stop and consider the consequences. Your survival is threatened and you have to act. But for most of us and in most situations, emotion mind can be a dangerous country to visit. That is why it is especially important to know when you've crossed the border.

As with reasonable mind, identifying emotion mind is a crucial first step in becoming mindful. Recognizing when you are in emotion mind allows you to pause, step back, and resist following your urges. The following four steps will help you to identify the presence of emotion mind.

Step 1. Notice your body sensations. Emotion mind causes you to feel intense sensations, such as a churning in your gut, a pounding in your chest, a lump in your throat, or a tightening or loosening of your muscles. (Positive emotions also cause sensations, which are pleasant but may be harder to notice.) Each emotion has its own distinct sensations, and sometimes you can recognize and even name the emotion based on the sensation.

Step 2. Notice any action urge. Depending on how strong the emotion is, the action urge can feel almost irresistible. As you'll see in the following box, each emotion has its own distinct action urge. If you realize you are in emotion mind, you can learn to name the emotion you are feeling.

Emotions and Their Corresponding Action Urges

Emotion	Action Urge
Anger	Attack
Fear	Escape
Sadness	Isolate
Shame	Hide
Guilt	Make amends
Love	Approach
Joy	Go for the gusto

Source: Linehan 1993a

Step 3. Pay attention to the thoughts that accompany the action urge. Emotion mind narrows our attention so that we can focus only on what is relevant to that emotion (Ratey 2001). Thoughts influenced by that emotion crowd out reasonable thoughts. The more we think about what caused the emotion, the more we dwell on the emotion. It can be hard to observe emotions without acting on them. But observing thoughts can help us recognize that we are in emotion mind and step back from acting. We will discuss this further in chapter 3.

Step 4. Pay attention to your own body posture and facial expression (Linehan 1993a). Are you scowling? Is your jaw set? Are your arms crossed? The face and body language associated with an emotion are hardwired and help us communicate to others what we are feeling (Ekman 2003). Even if we try to hide how we feel, sometimes others will recognize our emotions (Linehan 1993a). Someone might say, "You look sad," or "You look angry," before we recognize our own feelings. Being mindful of your face and body language can help you recognize when you are in emotion mind. The following list will help.

How to Recognize Emotion Mind

☐ I am very focused on the emotion I feel.

☐ I can't take my mind off what I want to do.

☐ The outcome I am seeking feels very urgent.

☐ My body is full of strong sensations (either pleasant or unpleasant).

☐ It is hard to consider alternative behavior.

☐ I notice I am pushing aside misgivings about acting on my emotion.

☐ Some facts seem more relevant than others.

☐ I am thinking of immediate rewards only.

☐ I don't want to talk it over with anyone who might disagree.

☐ My body temperature is up.

Check all that apply. If you checked one to three statements, go slow—emotion mind is engaged; four to six, build in a pause before taking any action; seven to ten, caution! Emotion mind is fully in charge!

Situations That Make Us More Likely to Enter Emotion Mind

Certain emotional or physical conditions make us more likely to have a strong emotional response in any situation. These include having had a recent loss, being sleep-deprived, or having physical pain or discomfort. We are also more vulnerable to emotion mind when we don't have enough pleasant activities in our lives (Linehan 1993a). Being under the influence of alcohol or drugs generates a self-inflicted vulnerability to emotions, as these influences depress the executive functioning of the brain, impair judgment, and increase the likelihood that emotion mind will take charge (Whalen and Phelps 2009). Even pleasant events, such as having a new baby or getting promoted at work, can make us feel vulnerable.

Interactions with others can also make us more vulnerable to emotion mind. As social animals we are influenced, for better or worse, by how comfortable we feel with others. In some environments we might feel supported and acknowledged, while in others we might feel out of place, even disregarded. Being isolated from others, with few friends or social contacts, makes us more vulnerable to emotion mind. On the other hand, having supportive relationships increases our ability to cope with adversity, including painful emotions (Goleman 2011).

The physical environment can affect our vulnerability to emotion mind. The jury is still out on how significantly weather affects mood, but most of us experience a lift on the first sunny day after a cloudy period. We might habitually react negatively to crowds or loud sounds, such as those at a carnival midway or in a nightclub with strobe lights and loud music. Research has shown that residents in public housing showed improved physical and mental health when they moved to places with access to more attractive and well-maintained surroundings (Evans 2003).

Thinking patterns we develop in our families of origin or through our struggles with anxiety or depression can also make us more vulnerable to emotion mind. The following box contains key thinking errors identified by cognitive psychologists; some may sound familiar to you.

Common Thinking Errors

1. Overgeneralization. Drawing broad conclusions from one situation: "German Shepherds aren't likely to bite. Bear never did."

2. Filtering. Paying attention only to the details instead of the big picture: "So what if he deals drugs? He is so nice to his mother!"

3. Imperatives. Believing there is only one correct way to behave, for both you and others: "She should have come to my party no matter how tired she was. That's what friends do."

4. Fortune-telling. Believing your own predictions about the future as if they were bound to be true: "I know I'll get stuck with the blame for this even though it isn't my fault. It always happens."

5. Mind reading. Telling yourself you know what someone else is thinking and refusing to consider other possibilities: "She thinks I am a loser. I can tell, even though she is nice to me."

6. Catastrophizing. Telling yourself that the worst is going to happen without considering other possibilities: "Lisa is moving. I'll never find another friend in all of New York."

7. Emotional thinking. Believing that if you feel it, it must be true: "I feel that if I take this (more expensive) apartment (that I can't afford) I will be happier."

8. Discounting. Acting as if positive information doesn't count: "I got one bad evaluation, so I failed. Who cares about the nine positive ones? They were just blowing smoke!"

9. Black-and-white thinking. Seeing things as polarized, without shades of gray: "She was the best friend I ever had. Now she is my worst enemy."

10. Control fallacy. Believing you are responsible for how someone else feels or behaves, in the absence of evidence: "I can't stand it when Mom is depressed because I feel it is all my fault."

Source: Beck 2011

The following box contains a summary of conditions that increase our vulnerability to emotion mind.

What Makes Us Vulnerable to Emotion Mind?

Physical vulnerabilities

Being hungry

Being sick

Being sleep-deprived

Being in chronic pain

Not exercising

Using drugs or alcohol

Overeating, undereating, eating the wrong foods

Being jet-lagged

Needing to go to the bathroom

Being constipated

Starting, changing, or being off a medication

Emotional and cognitive vulnerabilities

Being emotional about something else

Having untreated depression or anxiety

Having a sick family member, friend, or pet

Being lonely

Making faulty interpretations

Making persistent thinking errors

Feeling unprepared

Environmental and Social Vulnerabilities

Not having enough money to pay bills

Being unemployed

Moving

Coming back from vacation

Being exposed to loud sounds

Being exposed to bad smells

Being lost

Being alone in unfamiliar circumstances

Having a very messy house

Pleasant Event Vulnerabilities

Going on vacation

Getting a financial windfall

Planning a wedding

Having a new baby

Buying a new house

Retiring

Falling in love

Getting a new puppy

• *Heidi's Story*

Let's see how emotion mind can operate in a decision-making process. Heidi, recently divorced and feeling lonely, volunteers at the local animal shelter. A particularly cute Schnauzer there looks just like the dog she grew up with, activating many associations in her hippocampus. The dog looks at her with his soulful black eyes and she wants to adopt him immediately. The primary emotion she feels is love, and the universal urge of love is to go toward and embrace the beloved.

When Heidi looks at the little dog, her heart rate ramps up. She feels excitement and desire and can think of nothing except how to take him home. She has already named him Salty, after her childhood pet. Unfortunately, some facts get in the way: Heidi lives in a townhouse that doesn't allow pets, and she has no money to pay for the neutering required to adopt him. She argues with herself about the dog, but she is unable to focus on the facts.

Heidi calls her sister and talks her into coming to see Salty and loaning her the neutering fee. The shelter staff allows her to pay for the neutering, but she has to wait a week to take him home. As she pays she has her first misgivings. Now she will owe yet more money to her sister. Another fact intrudes: what will she do if the landlord finds out? Will he tear up the lease and give her a thirty-day notice? What if he won't give back the security deposit? Still, she signs the paperwork for Salty. How can she abandon this dog that has become the love of her life?

All week long Heidi agonizes over her decision. She doesn't want to leave her cozy home, which is affordable and close to work. But she also can't stand the thought of giving up Salty; she is certain he is already counting on her. *Maybe I can keep Salty a secret,* she thinks. *I can walk him early in the morning and late in the evening when no one is around. I can take him to doggie day care near work, but I'd better find out what they charge.*

A week later, Heidi brings Salty home, delighted to have his warm body in her arms. She shows him his new bowl and bed. He runs around the town house, sniffing everything and wagging his stub of a tail. Then he stops, sits down, cocks his head, and begins to bark. It is the loudest, most piercing bark Heidi has ever heard. He barks off and on for the next hour. She had forgotten that her childhood dog also barked this way and how much it bothered the neighbors. Now someone is knocking at her door!

Can you see how this story typifies emotion mind? Heidi couldn't resist her attraction to Salty, so she ignored the facts presented by reasonable mind. She plotted about how to over-come the facts and avoid the outcome that part of her knew could happen. Impulsively, she gave in to the action urge, paying for the dog to be neutered and signing the necessary papers. Suddenly she felt buyer's remorse and started to worry. The facts were penetrating her emotional dream. Finally, when she took Salty home and he began barking, Heidi experienced one of those "oh, no!" moments for which emotion mind is famous. Already the secondary emotions of fear and sadness were waiting in the wings to take over from the first rush of love.

Why Some People Are More Vulnerable to Emotion Mind: The Biosocial Theory

Although almost everyone has a hard time resisting the action urge of a powerful emotion, some people have a harder time reg-ulating their emotions due to their temperament and learning history. As a result, they have more problems with impulsivity, relationships, and a sense of self. When people with this kind of temperament grow up in environments that don't teach them the skills they need to manage their moods and emotions, the result is pervasive emotion dysregulation. This theory, the Biosocial Theory of borderline personality disorder, is one of the foundations of DBT (Linehan 1993).

Parents know that each baby is born with a unique temperament. Temperament is more stable than personality and has a powerful influence upon it. The New York Longitudinal Study (Chess, Thomas, and Birch 1970) followed a group of children and observed their development as they grew. The researchers identified nine different temperament factors or traits that appear to be inborn: activity level, rhythmicity (how regular a baby is with eating, sleeping, and so on), approach/withdrawal (shyness), adaptability, intensity, mood, persistence and attention span, distractibility, and sensory threshold.

Developmental researchers combined these traits to come up with three basic temperaments for babies: (1) easy and flexible, (2) active and feisty, and (3) slow to warm up. These temperaments have nothing to do with good or bad parenting, although obviously some temperaments are easier for parents to manage (Chess, Thomas, and Birch 1970).

Many of us began life as infants whose temperaments were more emotional—either feisty or slow to warm up, or a combination of the two. If we did and if our families and communities understood and were supportive, we may have struggled at times, but without developing pervasive emotion regulation problems. However, if we grew up in a family in which our emotional needs were disregarded, or one that was abusive or neglectful, our childhoods were fraught with intense stress and risk. Even in supportive families, emotional children may have more problems and place more demands on their families as they grow up (Morris et al. 2002). Children with special emotional needs make a lot of demands on their parents and are at risk for being blamed for how their needs affect the family (Linehan 1993).

Emotional Vulnerability

Being highly emotional is not a problem per se. Many artists, teachers, health care providers, community activists, politicians, ministers, and other "people people" are highly emotional. Highly emotional people can lead passionate, intense lives full of meaning and purpose—as long as they learn how to regulate their emotions. But, according to Linehan (1993), when you have a highly emotional temperament and you also lack the skills to regulate your emotions, you are at risk for developing BPD.

The temperament of emotionally vulnerable people includes three important factors: (1) a low threshold of emotional reaction, (2) emotions that are strong and long-lasting, and (3) a slow return to baseline (Linehan 1993). Let's look at each of these characteristics.

A low threshold of emotional reaction. Having a low threshold of emotional reaction means that it doesn't take much to upset you. Whether you have a higher baseline of emotion present all the time or are more sensitive and reactive than the average person, you are more likely to register a higher-than-average emotional response to something that happens in your environment (Jacob et al. 2009; Linehan 1993).

If you have a low threshold of reaction, something that prompts mild apprehension or even goes unnoticed by someone else could be intensely anxiety-provoking to you. Similarly, a behavior that others might find only annoying might enrage you. News that provokes mild sadness in your friend might leave you feeling grief-stricken. This phenomenon can be true with "positive" emotions, too. The ability to feel love and joy easily can strengthen your ability to cope with negative emotions. Often, however, people with a low threshold for negative emotions also have trouble feeling positive emotions (Linehan 1993). It may be that frequently being flooded with powerful negative emotions makes it hard to feel the subtler sensations of love and joy.

Strong, long-lasting emotions. Emotionally vulnerable people have more intense and persistent emotions. The sensations accompanying emotions are strong and often profoundly unpleasant, and therefore are difficult to distract from or ignore. Action urges and urges to avoid are extremely powerful and last a long time.

Slow return to baseline. Your reactions can move from "easily upset" and "intensely upset" into "upset for a long time." It may take you much longer to recover from a sense of being mistreated than your less emotionally vulnerable friend or family member. Long-lasting reactions make you more vulnerable in terms of reacting to the next stressor that comes your way (Linehan 1993).

When the social environment, especially the one in which we grow up, doesn't teach us skills for managing our emotions, but instead regularly criticizes us for how we react, the result is pervasive emotion dysregulation. Pervasive emotion dysregulation is created by repeated transactions *over time* between emotional vulnerability and something called the "invalidating environment "(Linehan 1993).

The Invalidating Environment

The invalidating environment can include family, institutions (such as schools, the foster care system, the church), and even the prevailing culture. Environments become invalidating when they fail to protect you or neglect your basic needs. Environments for children invalidate when they regularly communicate that their needs, feelings, and preferences are bad, or wrong, or otherwise lack validity (Linehan 1993).

We all have our own private inner experiences, experiences that no one else can really know unless we talk about them. We are the only ones who truly know what we feel we need; what we like and dislike; what scares, delights, or saddens us; what our pain threshold is; and what we find intolerable. Such experiences develop early in life and are held in our limbic system, becoming part of our personality. Sometimes our families or communities react negatively and judgmentally to our expressions of these deeply personal experiences, independent of any consideration of whether or not they are actually valid.

Here is a story that illustrates how a parent can fail to understand the private experiences of a child: A father cut a watermelon slice for his five-year-old daughter with a knife that, unknown to him, had just been used by his wife to cut a cayenne pepper. The girl tasted the ripe red melon and screamed that her mouth was burning. Her father laughed, joking about what a "drama queen" she was and how she was always trying to get attention. "Watermelon may be red," he said, "but it isn't hot!" The child, now sobbing, rubbed her eyes with her hands, which were smeared with stinging pepper oils. She was so hysterical that her father became alarmed. Her mother came in from the garden and soon deduced what had happened. She validated the girl's experience; washed her hands and face with warm, soapy water; and soothed her. After an hour of being soothed, the girl finally calmed down.

The father's reaction to his daughter was extremely invalidating in the moment. He failed to understand what caused her reaction and instead blamed her anguish on a defect in her character—being a "drama queen." Luckily, the mother was able to explain to them both that the child's reaction was valid, and she also soothed her daughter for as long as she needed. The father explained to his daughter that he hadn't known the knife had pepper oils on it and apologized. This event in isolation caused no lasting harm to the girl, although it took a long time for her to like watermelon after that! If, however, the father had frequently dismissed or minimized his daughter's emotional reactions, the long-term results might have been much more damaging.

Effects of the invalidating environment. When a child, especially a highly emotional child, is repeatedly told that what she feels is wrong; that she should not feel the way she does; that she is stupid, selfish, sinful, or just plain wrong, the child gets confused about what to believe about herself and the world. When people we are supposed to trust, people who have authority over us, tell us it is wrong to be the way we are or to feel the way we do, we have limited ability to contradict them. Should we believe our own feelings, or what others are telling us to feel? Chances are, especially as children, we will believe what others tell us and reject our own feelings as bad or wrong. Invalidation like this can lead to problems understanding, and therefore regulating, our emotions (Linehan 1993).

Environments in which children are not taught how to manage their emotions but instead are blamed and punished for not knowing are also highly invalidating. Parents who do not take the time to teach their highly sensitive children how to manage their temperaments may fail to do so for many reasons. They may lack emotion regulation know-how themselves, may be depressed or addicted, or may be too overwhelmed with the struggle to survive to take the time to teach their children. Sometimes these parents then blame the child for needing help to manage. The child may criticize herself for not knowing how to do things "right." The child might believe that others know instinctively how to behave and conclude that she is at fault for not knowing. As a result, the child might set perfectionist standards and then give up when they are not attained (Linehan 1993). The child could even feel that it is better not to try at all since success is so far out of reach.

In addition, invalidating environments often ignore children's appropriate requests for attention and only notice a child's needs when the child is desperate and demands attention

(Linehan 1993). When families or institutions ignore moderate requests for attention, some children will then suffer in silence for a long time before they make demands. Others resort to extreme, demanding behavior right away, since it obviously works. In any case, whenever extreme demands get the attention denied to moderate asking, a child learns to be more intensely demanding. Linehan (1993) identified going from not asking at all to demanding intensely as a direct result of the invalidating environment.

Invalidating environments in adulthood. We can find ourselves in invalidating environments in adulthood also. Living or working in an invalidating environment can make anyone more vulnerable to his or her emotions. Whether in prison, in medical school, at boot camp, in a low-paying job with a micromanaging boss, or even when dealing with an airline over lost luggage, invalidating environments can put anyone in emotion mind.

For people who developed pervasive emotion dysregulation in childhood and still lack skills to manage their emotions, the invalidating environments of adulthood—including, unfortunately, many institutions created to help us, such as hospitals—become almost intolerable. Learning to identify invalidating environments in adulthood can help us transform our reactions to them, rather than falling into old, ineffective patterns dictated by emotion mind. The following box lists some characteristics of invalidating environments.

Five Characteristics of Invalidating Environments

1. The environment does not consider your individual needs, special circumstances, or other unique situations. Its rules apply to all situations.

2. The environment assumes you will figure out on your own how to interact with it when you have a problem.

3. The environment offers little or no substantive assistance when you report a problem, even when it acknowledges that your problem is real.

4. The environment assumes it is right and you are wrong. Your negative reactions to interactions with it are evidence of a defect in you.

5. The environment ignores most of your requests at first. It responds to your requests only when you become intensely demanding, and then only intermittently.

In summary, this chapter taught us about two states of mind: reasonable mind and emotion mind. Reasonable mind sticks with the facts but can be clueless about emotions, and emotion mind often plays fast and loose with the facts in service of emotional action urges. Some people are more susceptible to emotion mind because of temperament and upbringing. Having an emotionally vulnerable temperament and growing up in an invalidating environment put people at risk for developing BPD (Linehan 1993).

Neither reasonable mind nor emotion mind gives us all the information we need to make wise choices. However, *recognizing* the state of mind we are in allows us to consider that we may not be attending to all the data—facts and feelings—required to make a wise choice.

How do we balance the facts of a situation with how we feel about it and move toward a solution that takes both into consideration? To find out, let's turn to the third state of mind and our first mindfulness skill: wise mind.

Chapter 3

FIND YOUR TRUE SELF: WISE MIND

I grew up never knowing who I was. I was doing my best just to survive, going from one foster home to another. Most of the time I felt empty and confused. I had no idea what my values were, what I really believed, even whether I was a good person. I couldn't have given you a long-term goal if my life depended on it! The problem was I couldn't count on myself—Who was this person called "me"? That all started to change when I learned about wise mind. Wise mind introduced me to myself. —Tracey, 49

The Problem: "Who Am I?"

A life spent in emotion mind is not conducive to developing a stable relationship with yourself. Emotionally vulnerable children who grow up in invalidating environments do not learn to trust their own perceptions, because they have been taught to view them as inaccurate; and as we learned in the discussion of Biosocial Theory, when you are repeatedly told that your feelings, preferences, and perceptions are wrong, you tend to turn to others to tell you the right way to feel and think (Linehan 1993). Unfortunately, no one can really tell us how to feel and think, at least not if we are to have our own identity. If we are going to develop and maintain a sense of who we are, we have to learn to recognize our true feelings and perceptions for ourselves. We have to find our inner wisdom.

The third criterion in the diagnosis of BPD is "Identity disturbance: markedly and persistently unstable self-image or sense of self" (American Psychiatric Association 2013). To understand the problem outlined by this criterion, let's look separately at each of these factors—identity, self-image, and sense of self.

Identity is related to factors such as age, class, gender, race, ethnicity, sexual preference, work or school performance, marital status, and whether one has children. And it is affected by both predictable and unpredictable events in life. An example of a predictable change is aging, which alters our functioning and employment identity in ways we can anticipate. Examples of unpredictable changes include getting a serious illness, going through divorce, losing a job, failing a class, inheriting a lot of money, or finding your sexual or gender identity changing. Identity disturbances are hard for anyone, even people with stable self-images and a strong sense of self (Jorgensen 2006).

Self-image is constructed from our thoughts about ourselves through time. Self-image can be affected by many of the same factors that affect identity. Our stability of self-image is related to the narratives we tell ourselves and others about who we are

(Adler 2012). These narratives can either have or lack the characteristics of consistency and agency. When consistency is lacking, for example, our stories do not help us decide whether we are a good and worthy person. When agency is lacking, we tend to believe we have no control over what happens to us, perhaps even over our own behavior. A consistent, positive self-image is correlated with good mental health. The sense of agency has been correlated with improved mental health among people with BPD (Adler 2012).

Then there is the elusive term *sense of self*. What is a sense of self and where does it come from? Linehan (1993) hypothesizes that the sense of self arises out of observing oneself over time, especially in a calm and secure environment. Thus people who grow up with an emotionally vulnerable temperament in invalidating environments are definitely at risk for lacking a strong sense of self. Instead of knowing that you can trust your perceptions about your experience, you might feel confused about what you feel and whether it is what you *should* feel. You might find that you are too easily influenced by others, or that your feelings and beliefs swing between polar opposites. When you try to go inside and figure out who you are, you might feel profoundly empty and confused.

When your identity is disrupted, your self-image is unstable, and a sense of self is lacking, it becomes impossible to know who you are and what you value in life. This can feel like being in a boat without a rudder, adrift on a turbulent sea. How can this problem be corrected? Must we stabilize our identities and self-image with more achievements, a better resume, a higher paying job, or a more ideal living situation? How about a romantic relationship, more friends, or becoming a parent? What if these changes are out of reach for us? Or what if we attain some of these goals and a sense of self remains elusive?

In Buddhist philosophy no emphasis is placed on the separate ego (Nhat Hanh 2002). This is quite different from Western psychology, which focuses on the ego as necessary to survival. Egos want all sorts of things, many of which are unattainable, and some of which are destructive. But egos also want love and fulfill-ment, which are certainly worthy goals. How do we separate the goals of our egos from our sense of self? Buddhist philosophy directs us to moment-by-moment experiencing to help us connect with a sense of self, apart from our turbulent, fickle egos.

Mindfulness teaches us to cultivate present-moment aware-ness first and to experience reality without judging it. Thus we develop a sense of self by noticing again and again how we feel in the moment and accepting it. The more we practice this simple awareness, the more we come to know and accept ourselves as unique feeling, and perceiving individuals. Present-moment experiencing acts as a portal through which we access our true selves. It is from this portal we can then pursue worthy goals such as love and fulfillment.

Okay, so am I saying that if you don't have a sense of self that says, "I am an achiever," or "I am a loner," don't worry about it, you don't need it? Not exactly. Each of us needs enough of an ego-self to take care of our basic needs and responsibilities. I am saying that there is a surefire way to grow into a sense of self without having to get your dream job or relationship, losing fifty pounds, or winning the lottery. That way is to get in touch with your wise mind.

The Solution: Wise Mind

Wise people have been talking about something like wise mind for millennia. Some of its aliases are the soul, the in-dwelling of the holy spirit, the conscience, Buddha nature, gnosis, the atman, the heart of hearts, the true self. According to countless sources, it lives inside of everyone. And just as inner wisdom is called by many names, it also can be reached by many different methods.

The genius of the DBT skill of wise mind is that it demysti-fies the process into a discrete skill to be practiced and, eventually, mastered. The skill of wise mind can be used for decisions as elementary as "Should I have a glass of wine?" to those as complex as "How can I live serenely in a world where there is so much suffering?" To use this skill, ask your wise mind a question and listen carefully for the answer. Asking is the easy part. The hard part is heeding the answer when it comes.

Recognizing Wise Mind

Unlike emotion mind, which tends to raise its voice, or reasonable mind, which talks in a modulated tone, wise mind often speaks in a whisper. We have to cultivate the habit of listening for wise mind, and asking for its input, which doesn't usually come in the form of an opinion. It comes as a sense, awareness, or noticing—states which can be quiet, even wordless.

Wise mind, with its soft voice, can feel at first like uncertainty. Reasonable mind can be smugly sure of itself when we are armed with the facts. In impulsive people, emotion mind can also feel certain of itself, even aggressively so. In fearful and avoidant people, emotion mind may be reticent or confused, but still feel certain that this anxious response is the right stance. But wise mind usually doesn't come on at first as such a strong opinion. It is subtler, less cocksure.

Here's an example of how wise mind feels: Let's imagine you are backpacking in the wilderness and at the end of a long day you come to a fork in the trail about an hour from base camp. Reasonable mind pulls out the map and points out that the uphill fork is a shortcut. Emotion mind, exhausted and demoralized, wants to take any shortcut. Wise mind looks at the map and notices that the shortcut is very steep and ungraded. It might be a little shorter but it looks very difficult. "Wait a minute," wise mind says. "I'm not sure we should take this trail." It can be easy to pass right by this whisper of uncertainty when other states of mind are signaling loudly. Reasonable and emotion mind might get us back in camp more quickly, but we will be worn out and overextended. Wise mind will get us back to camp safe and sound.

We are approaching wise mind when we begin to feel compassion and concern for ourselves. We become willing to take our time and consider our options. We start to think of long-term consequences of our actions, and the short-term relief we crave feels less compelling. A wider perspective opens and our intuition gets engaged. We begin to consider our values as we get closer to a decision. We may even feel less fearful of not getting immediate relief from emotional pain and more able to tolerate not getting the outcome we want.

As we step back from urges and emotions, we can access the treasure that is our own inner wisdom. But only rarely do we recognize wise mind right away. Usually recognizing wise mind is a process that unfolds through time.

Accessing Wise Mind: The Process

When we attempt to access wise mind, we become more calmly alert. We don't exactly know what to do and are aware that we could make a mistake, especially by acting on urges. I like to call this state "being in wise mind's waiting room." Here we consider our options. We may not be completely ready to give up engaging in impulsive behaviors that relieve us in the short run, but we are willing to consider options other than leaping headlong into action urges that have gotten us into trouble in the past. We don't yet have the clarity we need, but at least we have arrived in the right frame of mind. We are willing to take our time to consult wise mind. Eventually, if we sit tight, the answer about what to do will emerge from within us. Eventually, wise mind will show up. In the meantime we are calmer and wiser just sitting in wise mind's waiting room. The following checklist will help you recognize whether you are there.

Am I in Wise Mind's Waiting Room?

☐   I am aware I am vulnerable to emotion mind.

☐   I care about using a skillful approach, at least a little.

☐   Even though I am very emotional I am not acting on my urges.

☐   I can remember feeling this way and making big mistakes I don't want to repeat.

☐   I am asking for help.

Check all that apply. If you checked one or two, you are approaching the waiting room; three to five, your appointment time with wise mind has nearly arrived—be patient! After you have answered all these questions in the affirmative, write a paragraph about what you think wise mind might have to say and read it slowly, aloud to yourself. This process will bring you closer to wise mind.

Once we enter wise mind's waiting room it is only a matter of time before our wisdom shows up. Emotional arousal decreases, and when emotion is present, it feels quieter and gentler. Our heart rate starts to slow, breathing deepens, and urgency abates. The parts of our brain begin to communicate with each other. We can settle into the moment with a bit more ease and take stock of our situation. The facts, as presented by reasonable mind, take their proper place in our contemplation. The prefrontal cortex is engaged. Emotions are accepted and integrated, even if we are feeling a lot of pain.

Acting from Wise Mind

Sometimes a situation seems to demand that we act immediately and we can't access wise mind. When this appears to be the case, it is a good idea first to consider all the facts. Must we really act now? (Remember that urgency is a hallmark of emotion mind, and the urgency may be more emotional than actual.) If a situation seems urgent but we are not sure what our wise mind says, we next might seek advice from someone we know to be trustworthy. To arrive at what is wise, we can double-check our feelings against that advice, then proceed carefully and hope for the best. As we wait for wise mind, we can gather information about the situation and compare that information against our feelings and intuition. Wise mind will often show up while we are doing our due diligence.

To get closer to wise mind, ask yourself these five questions:

1. Have I looked at the pros and cons of following my action urges?

2. Have I considered how acting on my action urges will affect my long-term goals?

3. Have I slept on the decision to act for at least one night?

4. Have I consulted a trusted person for input on my urges?

5. Have I asked, *What do I feel in my heart of hearts?* and really listened for the answer?

Occasionally, especially in a dangerous situation, wise mind can come as a flash of insight, a powerful intuition. Such a flash can feel almost like divine intervention, especially when it results in our escaping a threat. Usually our encounters with wise mind are not so dramatic, however. As mentioned above, wise mind can be drowned out by the loud voice of emotion mind, which has the force of survival evolution behind it. Because wise mind sometimes just whispers or nudges us, we have to train ourselves to hear it, especially through the din of daily life. Highly emotional people have to learn to hear it through the strong static of pervasive emotion dysregulation.

The Obstacle: Intense Emotions Obscure Wise Mind

When we are in a lot of confusion, pain, or misery, emotion mind will masquerade as wise mind and try to tell us it is in our best interests to do something drastic. For example, emotion mind might say we should harm ourselves or that other people would be better off if we weren't around. In the middle of an uncomfortable conversation with a family member, emotion mind might scream, "This is your wise mind speaking: Get in the car and drive away right now!"

People I have worked with have told me that their wise mind tells them they are idiots or losers. This is not wise mind, but emotion mind. Wise mind is consistent with all the other mindfulness skills covered in this book and thus is nonjudgmental. It never calls anyone names. We have to become expert at recognizing the voice of emotion mind, which says one thing one moment and another the next, in a loud, urgent voice.

Sometimes we have to let time do its work before we become clear about how to proceed. We may need to build in a pause before we act, by sleeping on any decision. We need to practice tolerating uncertainty and refraining from action when we are still oscillating between anger (*I'm going to go right in and quit!*) and fear (*But then I won't have a job!*). Time is often wise mind's friend.

Going through a complex decision-making process sometimes requires a long journey following an obscure trail through the country of uncertainty. It is good to have wise mind as a guide. The following list of statements can help you determine whether you are following wise mind.

Am I in Wise Mind?

1. My wisest friend would understand and agree that my decision is wise.

2. I feel a sense of peace, even though emotions may also be present.

3. My feelings about my decision have remained stable over several days.

4. I do not feel intense urgency.

5. I am not judgmental of myself.

6. I don't necessarily need others to agree with me.

7. I feel a sense of "letting go" rather than clinging to the outcome.

8. I can accept what is happening.

9. I am neither denying facts nor suppressing emotions.

10. I am not giving up, resigning myself, or being willful.

11. My decision is in harmony with what I know are my values. (If confused about your true values, refer to number 1.)

Overcoming Obstacles to Wise Mind with Dialectics

In the last chapter I mentioned the common thinking errors that create vulnerabilities to emotion mind (see the box titled

"Common Thinking Errors," in chapter 2). In this section we will explore dialectical thinking, a way of thinking that helps us access wise mind. Let's start by contrasting dialectical thinking with two other types of thinking: absolutist and relativistic.

Absolutist Thinking

Absolutist thinking is grounded in opposites such as good and evil, right and wrong, true and untrue. Absolutist thinking is characterized by comparing *what is* to an ideal of *what should be* and explaining the difference based on a rigid belief system rather than looking at the situational context (Ostell and Oakland 1999). For example, an employer with absolutist thinking may think that attendance at work is so paramount that all employee absences show a lack of responsibility, even those associated with having to care for a sick child or parent. People with absolutist thinking experience stress when they encounter situations that don't correspond to their ideals, expectations, and frameworks of beliefs. Research has identified absolutist thinking as being associated with poor psychological health, anger problems, and diminished effectiveness in relationships (Ostell and Oakland 1999). Absolutist thinking has a lot in common with emotion mind.

Relativistic Thinking

Relativistic thinking, on the other hand, says that what is true, moral, or ethical depends in part or entirely on the situation—it's all relative (Swoyer 2014). Taken to extreme, relativistic thinking can lead to a person's holding no objective standards, relying entirely on subjective beliefs from situation to situation. Relativistic thinkers might be unwilling to condemn practices like torture or child marriage, for example, if they believe some good can come from them. "It depends on the

71

situation," they might say. Relativistic thinkers also might value anecdotal evidence as highly as evidence based on scientific research—for example, relying on the opinions of friends over abundant data collected by experts in rigorous studies. Relativistic thinkers may forego absolutist standards, such as "Thou shalt not kill," in favor of justifications that serve a particular worldview— for example, the killing of some people sometimes is justified in this or that situation, depending on some circumstances. By removing familiar standards of justification, including agreed-upon facts and standard codes of conduct, relativistic thinking can lead to confusion about what to believe, what to value, and how to make decisions (Swoyer 2014). Relativistic thinking can have a lot in common with reasonable mind out of balance.

Dialectical Thinking

Dialectical thinking is neither absolutist nor relativist; rather, it sees truth as unfolding through time due to the struggle of opposing arguments (Buckingham et al. 2011). "Truth" never stands still; rather it is always growing. Consider the argument that marriage should be a contract only between one man and one woman. There have been many arguments in opposition, including the idea that the institution of marriage can or should include relationships between two people of the same sex, and the idea that it can or should include relationships between one man and more than one woman. Over time, these different ideas about marriage have conflicted culturally, religiously, ideologically, legally, and at the ballot box. In the West, societies that once accepted polygamy have either given it up or mostly hidden the practice from view. Societies that once vilified homosexuality have reached toward marriage equality for all couples, thus changing the definition of marriage. This is how "truth" grows.

In dialectical thinking, a strong argument is not one that overwhelms a weaker argument—as in absolutist thinking—but one that absorbs and transforms a weaker argument, thereby becoming more whole, more total, and true (Gonzalez 1998). This process has been likened to a spiral, which appears to fold back on itself even as it expands into totally new territory. For example, the statement enshrined in the U.S. Declaration of Independence that "all men are created equal" once meant all white men who owned property were equal with each other before the law. This gradually evolved to include all white men, even those who didn't own land, even the poor. Through struggles like the Civil War and the Women's Suffrage Movement, the statement grew to include first men of color, then all women. This expansion has not cancelled out the original statement; rather it has expanded and strengthened it. The struggle for equal rights continues for many groups of people. Dialectics shape the course of these ongoing arguments.

Let's examine the structure of a dialectical argument. The *thesis* is the first and least adequate stage of the argument, a view advanced, often without proof. The *antithesis*, the second stage of dialectics, poses its opposite. Over time, these two arguments struggle until a synthesis emerges. A synthesis creates a new reality and sometimes a new problem to solve. Synthesis is not a compromise; rather it is a new entity, born of the opposing forces yet different and unique. This synthesis then starts the whole cycle over again. Once one issue is resolved, another is created (Gonzalez 1998).

For example, a person wrongfully convicted of a crime (thesis) struggles to get his case retried (antithesis) and to be released from jail (synthesis). Eventually, his efforts are successful. Hurrah! However, now he has a new set of problems and a new thesis: he needs a job, housing, health care, and friends—all things that the jail had more or less provided. These needs will not be met without considerable effort and struggle, and for a time he could be unemployed, even homeless. Each synthesis we experience becomes a new thesis, containing within it more contradictions to be resolved.

Wise mind is itself a dialectical perspective because it considers facts and emotions and allows for the elements of time and uncertainty. By pausing and consulting wise mind when we are deeply uncertain or emotional, we improve our ability to make good choices. Eventually the struggle we are experiencing will resolve enough that we can see our way forward. In the meantime, we need to stay in close contact with wise mind. The following story illustrates wise mind as a dialectical perspective.

• Rose's Story

Rose, forty-five, is a high school teacher who was diagnosed with multiple sclerosis in her thirties. Recently, she has been having problems with fatigue, dizziness, and muscle spasms, and is worried that she won't be able to keep her job. Rose ruminates about what would happen if she couldn't work. She feels emotionally paralyzed and is in emotion mind most of the time because of her fears. These fears are the *thesis* of Rose's argument with herself.

Rose's brother, Jim, tells her not to worry. She should use her disability insurance and then try to get Social Security Disability (SSDI). In Jim's view, all will be well. Rose will adjust to her disability and all that it entails. Jim's solution, reasonable mind, is the *antithesis* of Rose's argument.

Let's look at how these two perspectives struggle with each other. At first, Rose doesn't want to listen to Jim at all. She likes her job and doesn't want to give it up. Rose expresses fears that her disability policy will not pay her an adequate benefit. She is also afraid that applying for permanent SSDI will be difficult. Rose and Jim argue over the phone, each one articulating a position forcefully. Over time, Rose's mental and physical health continue to deteriorate. Jim persuades her at least to apply for temporary disability using her insurance. Rose takes a leave of absence from work and is able to rest and recuperate for six months. During this time, she is less fearful, although she knows that eventually she will have to make a decision about what to do next. This brief time represents a *synthesis*.

Rose's situation continues to change, of course. After a few months her MS has gone back into remission. She has more energy. When she looks into permanent SSDI, she is appalled at how little money she will have each month. She might have to sell her house. The very synthesis—temporary disability—now becomes the new problem, or thesis, because her benefits are running out. Rose decides she doesn't want to take permanent disability if she doesn't have to. She talks this over with Jim, who again presents the antithesis. He reminds her that MS is a progressive disease and she is unlikely to stay in remission for long. Jim encourages Rose to accept her fate. Other people adjust to such a lowered income; why can't she? Rose and Jim battle it out again to find a new synthesis.

Rose finds herself constantly ruminating about what could happen. Her illness could get dramatically worse, and going back to work could become impossible. She could stay in remission. If she applies for Social Security Disability, she might be denied, or she could get SSDI and still feel well enough to work. Rose's worries are ruining her quality of life. She enters therapy and learns about dialectical thinking and wise mind. Rose decides to adopt a dialectical perspective.

With help from her therapist, Rose recognizes and accepts that the dialectical struggle between her health needs and her financial needs will continue as long as she lives. Rose begins to practice the mindfulness skills she is learning and consults her wise mind. Wise mind helps her to stay focused in the present. In the moment her situation is neither as cut-and-dried as Jim (reasonable mind) proposes, nor as dire as she sometimes feels it to be (emotion mind). She begins to recognize that because her situation is changing and evolving, influencing and being influenced by myriad factors, it will always be uncertain. Her quality of life does not have to be ruined by worries about the evolving dialectical struggle, much of which is out of her control. She only needs to accept the moment to feel better in the moment. When she can let go of constant worry and fear, she can also plan and problem solve more effectively. She can feel more in control of her choices. She can prioritize her values.

With her newfound peace of mind, Rose is able to focus on what to do next to preserve her quality of life and work. Rose goes back to work while also investigating what she would need to do to go on permanent disability, should that be necessary. Making use of her reputation as an expert teacher, Rose starts a small tutoring business, which she could expand if she had to quit her job. Most of all, Rose focuses on maintaining her health with stress reduction, including a mindfulness practice, improved diet, and exercise, as well as building in as many positive experiences as possible. She embraces the uncertainty of her life and tries to feel gratitude for each day.

Adopting a Dialectical Worldview

In addition to being a type of argument, dialectics also present a worldview that is useful for understanding wise mind. In a dialectical worldview, everything in the world is connected to everything else in a systematic way. In the 1970s, James Lovelock (2000) and Lynne Margulis formulated the "Gaia hypothesis." This theory holds that all living things on earth and their nonliving support structures form one highly regulated, complex system, which works to maintain stability of life. Dialectic philosophy posited long ago that such a systematic interconnectedness not only pertained in nature but also in human affairs. Everything we do, we do in a context in which we influence, and are influenced by, multiple opposing forces (Buckingham et al. 2011).

A dialectical worldview gives us perspective. When we are emotionally dysregulated or in crisis, we usually have trouble thinking clearly. We tend to catastrophize—that is, see the situation as an insurmountable problem—and to focus so intently on the problem at hand that the big picture is lost. From a dialectical perspective the big picture includes recognition that everything is interconnected, that change is constant, and that nothing is permanent. When we are able to step back from catastrophizing—perhaps after taking a cold shower or running on a treadmill for twenty minutes, or after weeks of tolerating uncertainty—we can see that there is much more to the picture than the narrow, scary perspective on which we have been fixated.

Such awareness has been called "spaciousness of mind" in Zen (Mipham 2006). It allows us to relax, stop clinging, and accept the facts of the situation and how we feel about it. An answer will come, but it might take time for it to arrive. The key is not to give in to impulses, but to wait for clarity. Spaciousness of mind is not resignation or fatalism. It is acceptance of reality *in the moment*. A hurricane may be blowing, but we are in the calm center, awaiting wise mind.

Increasing Your Connection with Wise Mind Through Dialectical Practice

Here are several dialectical practices that will strengthen your connection with wise mind. You may wish to try one or more, regularly checking in with yourself on how the practices are working for you.

77

1. *Keep a gratitude journal.* The mind tends to focus on problems to be solved rather than on what is working. Change this up by starting a gratitude journal. At least once a week write in your journal about the things for which you are grateful. Leave complaining out of this journal! This practice increases the likelihood that you will notice positives in your life, a skill that will reduce your vulnerability to emotion mind.

2. *Track your worries* (Behar et al. 2009). Each week write down the top three worries in your mind and rate them as to how likely they are to happen. Once a month review your list and see how many of the things you worried about did or did not become problems. Chances are you will find a higher percentage of your worries never manifested. Reflect on the usefulness of constant worrying.

3. *Look for ways to make lemonade* (Linehan 1993a). As the saying goes, "When life gives you lemons, make lemonade." Reflect on things in your life that have seemed like lemons at the time (such as a divorce) that ended up being lemonade (allowing you to find a happier relationship). Try to find opportunities in your daily life to make lemonade out of disappointments or reversals.

4. *Inquire into your wise mind values and work to live within them* (Linehan 2014). Reflect on your values and how you have come to feel the way you do. Consider the struggles you have undergone to arrive at your values and the struggles ahead as you try to live more in line with your values. Consult with your therapist or a trusted friend. Look for articles, books, and podcasts on values clarification to help you in this inquiry. The reading list at the end of this book has several helpful suggestions. Knowing and living from your values will improve your sense of self

and your ability to love and accept yourself, which are important for strengthening wise mind.

• *Jennifer's Story*

Jennifer is sixteen and lives in foster care. Her mother has been in prison for four years and her father is dead. She has been with the same foster family for a year. Jennifer attends a DBT skills class with her foster mother and feels it has helped her. She is a junior in high school, has made the honor roll once, and loves running track.

Jennifer's mother, Carla, is getting out of prison in four months and wants Jennifer to live with her on the reservation. Jennifer would like to be near her grandparents, who are getting old and are in poor health, but she doesn't want to live with Carla, with whom she has had a rocky relationship. Jennifer feels Carla wants her to take care of her, and resents that her mother used to tell her more than she wanted to know about her abusive boyfriends. If Jennifer returns to the reservation, she will have to leave her foster parents and change schools for her senior year, and it makes her sad to think about the relationships she will lose. Yet thinking about telling her mother she's not coming back home makes her feel terribly guilty. Jennifer doesn't know which choice to make.

In skills class Jennifer is learning to consult her wise mind about decisions she has to make. Jennifer talks with her therapist about the pros and cons of moving back to live with her mom versus staying with her foster family. The facts indicate that staying put would be better for her, but she keeps thinking of her grandparents and of what her mother will say if Jennifer tells her she isn't coming home. Because Jennifer has learned to identify emotion mind as a state in which she cannot see doing anything but acting on her emotions, she feels she is in emotion mind now.

When Jennifer pictures going back to her mother's place she feels a lot of anger and resentment. Why should she have to move back there now when everything is going well for her? It was just like what was happening when her mother abandoned her to go to jail! Jennifer was doing well in school then and had a few real friends. But that seems like a long time ago now. Jennifer doesn't know if she is more angry or sad, and she doesn't know what to do.

Jennifer tries to consult her wise mind by going for long walks on the river trail near her house. She consults her teachers and therapist but finds herself reacting to whatever they tell her.

One Saturday, Jennifer's Uncle Jerome comes to visit. He is only eight years older than Jennifer and is almost like a brother to her. "Are you going to tell me to come home?" Jennifer says, putting on her sneakers so they can walk together.

"No way. That is not my decision."

"That's what everyone says. They say it is my decision. But I can't decide!"

"Not everyone. Carla says it is her decision, right?"

"Right. She says I owe her this. And she says I owe it to Granny and Grandpa."

"She can't speak for them. Do you think you owe everybody?"

"Sometimes I do, sometimes I don't. "

"That is a sure sign you are confused."

"You mean because I change my mind?"

"That's right. When you know, you know. When you don't, you go back and forth."

"So what do I do now?"

"Take your time. Don't be in a rush. Don't give in to pressure. Just listen inside, like when we used to listen for the owl at Grandpa's, remember? Just listen and you'll hear. And don't make a move until you do."

Jennifer took Uncle Jerome's advice. She noticed how the emotions of sadness, guilt, and anger came and went, and how she felt before and after. She noticed that when she was in her emotions they were convincing, but once the emotions passed the things her mind told her seemed less true. She finished the semester and still had not made up her mind.

Once Carla got out of prison and moved back to her house on the reservation, she began to put more pressure on Jennifer to come back. One day, after Jennifer got her semester grades, Carla called to tell Jennifer that her grandfather was very sick. Jennifer arrived at the hospital and found her grandfather alone in his room. She felt very emotional all of a sudden. "Grandpa, I need to come home and help take care of you."

"Don't you dare!" her grandfather said, looking stern. "I don't want all this fuss. Besides, you need to make your own decision on this." He shook his finger at her, lay back on the pillow and closed his eyes. "When I get well, I'll come to your next track meet," he said as she tiptoed out of his room.

Just then, Jennifer realized that she was trying to please everyone but herself. Everyone she had spoken to and trusted had said, "You have to make your own decision." Everyone, that is, except her mother, who wanted something from her, something Jennifer knew she was unable to give. She couldn't take care of her mother, not now when she was still a kid. And she couldn't take care of her grandparents either. Jennifer knew she had to take care of herself, which meant she needed to stay in foster care and finish her senior year in her current high school.

Jennifer knew her decision was a wise one. At last she knew what she needed to do. It wouldn't be easy to tell her mother she wasn't coming home, at least not until she graduated. But she now felt she had the strength to do it. She knew her own mind at last.

Jennifer's story illustrates some important aspects of knowing one's state of mind. When she talked with her therapist, Jennifer knew that the facts were compelling for her to stay in foster care, but facts alone could not convince her that this was the choice she needed to make. The facts crumbled before the emotions that rose up when she imagined telling her mother she wasn't coming home. Jennifer could distinguish between what her reasonable mind had to say and what her emotion mind had to say, but she couldn't arrive at a synthesis. It took her a long time to reach wise mind.

As Jennifer's story shows, time can be a factor in arriving at wise mind. She used some skillful behaviors to try to come to a decision, including taking long walks on the river trail, talking with her therapist and teachers, and asking Jerome for his advice. She learned to distinguish the changeability and intensity of emotion mind from the quiet deliberation of wise mind. She resisted quick answers and gave herself time and space even as her mother was pressuring her for a decision. Finally, in her grandfather's hospital room, clarity arrived. Jennifer found her wise mind answer and could go forward with her decision.

Strengthening Wise Mind with Daily Practice

Wise mind exists in the moment and for the moment. It is like the manna in the desert that the Old Testament God provided each day for the Israelites. Manna had to be eaten on the day it fell from the sky and could not be preserved, except for that gathered to be eaten on the Sabbath. The Israelites who didn't believe that enough manna would be provided tried to save it, but they quickly found that it became full of maggots. Similarly, we can accept the wisdom of our wise mind only for today. We must access wise mind every day—and luckily, like the manna, it is available every day. Any day our situation might change and the direction from our wise mind might thus be altered, even if only slightly. To be nourished by wise mind, we have to let go of constant worries that we won't have what we need or won't know what to do, that things won't work out. We have to learn to accept the moment of wise mind.

Practices to Strengthen Your Wise Mind Awareness

The following practices and exercises are designed to help you strengthen your experience of wise mind.

1. *Take a mindfulness walk and count your breath.* Instead of letting your mind wander over your problems, take a break and walk mindfully. Find a path where you won't be disturbed, such as a walkway near your home or workplace or in a quiet, safe neighborhood. Walk for about ten minutes, breathing normally and counting your breaths, one on the in-breath, two on the out-breath, and so on, up to ten. Then return to one. If your mind wanders and you lose count, return to one. Focus on your feet and notice what you see with your eyes cast down. Let thoughts come and go, judging nothing, and noticing what your senses bring to your attention. A mindfulness walk will strengthen your ability to observe your own mind, which will help you better access wise mind and prepare you for more formal sitting practice.

2. *Develop a daily meditation practice.* Start with three minutes of "just sitting" (Loori 2002) in the morning (see "How to Sit for Meditation" directions at the end of this chapter). Do it every day until you want to sit for longer, and then go to five minutes. Take it slow and don't judge whatever happens. This practice will help you observe your own mind and body, which is useful for recognizing your state of mind.

3. *Practice a mantra.* Instead of letting your mind wander or getting impatient when you are waiting in line or have free moments, try practicing a mantra, or invocation. You might try "wise" on the in-breath and "mind" on the out-breath, or (from Thich Nhat Hanh) "just this" on the in-breath and "moment" on the out-breath. Not letting your mind wander decreases the tendency to ruminate and worry. It may also improve your mood, reducing your vulnerability to emotion mind.

4. *Check in with yourself every morning and evening.* Before going to bed at night and when you first wake up in the morning, take a few moments to ask yourself, "What is my state of mind?" If you aren't in wise mind, see if you can get there by using one of these methods.

5. *Practice just sitting.* Sit for up to thirty minutes in one of the postures illustrated in figures 6 through 10. Allow thoughts to come and go in your mind. Try not to follow them or push them away. Simply notice thoughts, sensations, and emotions that arise, without judging them. Do not evaluate your practice; just do it, daily if possible. Have no expectations and see what happens!

As we have learned in this chapter, wise mind is the state of mind in which we are in touch with both the facts and the feelings of a situation. We use wise mind in order to reach our own unique inner understanding that allows us to make better decisions. Over time, being in regular contact with wise mind builds a sense of self.

Wise mind is also a skill we can practice by pausing, inquiring within, and then listening to the answer. Wise mind arises out of a dialectical struggle between the facts of a situation and our emotions about it. Sometimes we may have to spend time in wise mind's waiting room before we hear the full answer. Just building in the pause to listen is useful, since while we wait for an answer we are not acting out of emotions in ways we might later regret.

Next we turn our attention to the skills we will use to reach wise mind, the what and how skills. These skills increase our familiarity with wise mind and are each helpful in their own unique ways with regulating intense emotions. Chapters 4 through 6 cover the what skills; chapters 7 through 9, the how skills.

How to Sit for Meditation

The most important qualities of your meditation posture are that you be stable, alert, and reasonably comfortable.

- *If you wish to sit in a chair, find one that supports an upright posture and has adequate padding. Place both feet flat on the floor or on a pillow. (See figures 6 and 7.) If you choose to sit on a mat and pillow on the floor, try to create the stability of a triangle with your knees and buttocks being the three points. If you are very flexible, you can sit in full or half lotus. Or you can sit Burmese style, placing one foot in front of the other so as not to compress the feet, as shown in figures 8 and 9. Don't place one limb on top of another or they will both go to sleep! Be sure to alternate which foot is in front during longer sitting periods. Two postures that reduce pressure on your legs (called sitting seiza) are illustrated in figures 10 and 11. You can use either a firm pillow*

Figure 6

Figure 7

Figure 8

Figure 9

Figure 10

Figure 11

or a stool to support your seat. With all seated postures, let your buttocks push back and your belly rest forward. Allow your spine to assume its natural curvature. Picture how a toddler sits on the floor. Rest your hands on your knees or in your lap, perhaps supported by a small pillow. Find the sweet spot for your head to balance gently on your neck and let your shoulders relax. Now hold as still as you can while practicing.

- You may practice with your eyes closed or open. Open eyes are cast down to the floor and remain still, as much as possible, but not fixed, which will make them water. Open eyes can help you stay awake and present and make it harder to dissociate. Closed eyes may make you more likely to fall asleep or allow you to focus on your practice better. Try both methods and see which works for you.

Chapter 4

SEE REALITY AS IT IS: OBSERVING

My biggest problem is my anger. I used to get so angry I would do and say really hurtful things, especially to people I love. I didn't notice the anger building up until I exploded. I remember the day I knew I had to learn how to see my anger coming. I was getting ready to take the baby for a checkup and my four-year-old was being impossible—whining and dawdling, making me late. I shouted at her to get dressed right away. She kicked me! Suddenly I smacked her face and called her "a little f—g brat." She fell down and began to scream. I will never forget the look on her face. I would have given anything to take that moment back. Anything. But I hadn't seen it coming. Now I know better. I've learned to observe all the signs that I'm getting angry and to take steps to calm myself before I act.
—Mary, 27

To practice recognizing her anger in the moment, Mary learned the skill of observing, the first of the what skills and the topic of this chapter. The what skills tell us *what to do* to access wise mind (Linehan 1993a). The other two what skills are *describing* (chapter 5) and *participating* (chapter 6).

Before we turn to the skill of observing, let's start with an overview of how these three skills work together. Each of the what skills describes a simple behavior that is done in a single-minded way, and each works in sequence with the next. For example, when you observe, you only observe. When you begin to describe what you have noticed, you stop observing. When you participate, you put aside both observing and describing, and flow into your experience (Linehan 1993a).

Imagine you are taking a dance class. The dance instructor performs the moves of the Texas Two-Step, his boots shuffling across the floor in a pattern you have yet to fathom, while he holds his partner firmly by the waist, his right arm raised to shoulder height, her hand in his. You stand to the side and observe them, not putting any words to what you are watching. After a while you start to talk to yourself about what you see, putting words to what you are trying to understand. This is the skill of describing. "Quick, quick, slow," says the instructor, "on the balls of your feet." He describes each step in succession: how to maintain the proper dance space, how to lead or follow, how to turn your body. You listen to the description of what you have noticed. Then you try it out with your partner, describing to yourself over and over: "quick, quick, slow," or "now we turn," delineating the process and attempting to replicate what you've been shown. And when you get lost or step on your partner's feet, as you inevitably do, you go back to observing your own movements, and then to describing to yourself what you are doing.

Meanwhile, the instructor, who is dancing with an advanced student, models perfectly the skill of participating. He is smiling and dancing without looking at his feet, talking to himself, or stepping on his partner. They are having so much fun, and they look terrific, fully flowing in the activity of two-stepping. This is exactly where you want to be, and will be if you practice. Eventually you will dance the two-step with ease and enjoyment. The more you practice and gain mastery, the longer you are able to stay in the flow state.

Let's say you become distracted or you or your partner makes a mistake. Immediately, the flow is lost and you return to observing and describing. When you get back in the groove, you return to participating. In this example, one might say that the goal of the what skills is to arrive at participating.

It is equally true that the what skills are ends in themselves. Much of contemplation or meditation, for example, is observing practices. When we teach or write we mainly use describing. And when we are in pure participation, paying attention and fully present to our wise minds, we are most able to enjoy our favorite activities, such as playing sports, eating, visiting with friends, or making art. The key factor with the what skills is that you use each one as needed and move among them seamlessly.

Now let's turn to the skill of observing. Just why is this skill so important?

The Problem: Inability to See What Is

When I worked with female veterans at a VA medical center after the first Gulf War, I participated in a research study that found that women who were sexually abused as children were almost five times as likely to be raped on active duty as those who had no previous sexual trauma (McIntyre et al. 1999). This research was in line with what we knew in general about sexual abuse in childhood and how it makes women more vulnerable to adult victimization. Why were women who had been abused as children so much more likely to be raped on duty? One hypothesis was that women who have been traumatized might find it harder to observe and recognize certain kinds of dangers in the environment, especially the possible threats posed by their fellow soldiers. In the stressful environment of military deployment, it is challenging to see and prioritize the many potential threats. And, for all of us, it is much harder to observe well in the presence of intense emotions.

Whenever you feel angry, sad, or afraid, your attention dwells on what is prompting those feelings (Ratey 2001). It seems like your mind will focus only on how bad you feel or how much you want to escape that feeling. Your attention is taken hostage while crucial things going on around you go unnoticed. This is exactly where the skill of observing is so helpful.

The Solution: Observing

Observing uses the senses to notice, quite intentionally, what is outside of you—such as a car crossing into your lane—or inside, such as a sensation of hunger. To observe, you must first step back from thoughts and emotions and come into the present moment with alertness and purpose. This skill takes a great deal of practice. Here are some examples of how observing works with sensations, thoughts, and emotions. (Audio versions of certain observing exercises in this section are available for download at http://www.newharbinger.com/33001.)

Observe Sensations

When we simply take in an experience through our senses without categorizing it, we get as close as we can get to perceiving reality without interference from our concepts. No matter how many times we have eaten oatmeal or taken a shower or answered the phone, we approach the activity in the moment with openness and eagerness, to experience it *as if for the first time*. This is called "beginner's mind" in Zen (Suzuki 2006).

Sensory experiences can be quite vivid when approached this way. We smell just this rose, hear just this bell ringing, see just this cloud, touch just this stone, taste just this peach. Everything is experienced as a feeling: the *sweet tickle* of smelling the rose, the *vibration* of hearing the bell, the *sensation* of observing a cloud, touching a stone, or eating a peach. Words don't characterize the experience; at least they are not front and center. Words come and go but our attention is on the sensations.

Observe Thoughts

Moving from the level of pure sensation, we can also observe our thoughts. Thoughts are constantly forming in our minds as we move through our day. Observing thoughts is different from thinking. When observing, we notice types of thoughts without getting caught up in their content. *I just had a worry thought,* for example, rather than *I am so worried about my sister, who always makes bad choices.* We don't follow one thought down the path to another, but maintain an observing position as thoughts come and go.

Zindal Segal, Mark Williams, and John Teasdale (2002), the authors of *Mindfulness-Based Cognitive Therapy for Depression,* use a wonderful image for the practice of stepping back from thoughts when observing thoughts. They suggest that behind the waterfall of thoughts is a place to stand, perhaps a little cave or indentation, that allows us to remain dry while viewing the thoughts like water flowing over our heads and pouring into a river of thoughts traveling downstream and away from us. We observe the waterfall of thoughts, but don't get washed downstream by it.

Observe Emotions

To observe an emotion we have to bring our intention to the effort. We are not the emotion itself; we are a person having an emotion (Linehan 1993a). An emotion is an event in the body; it physically impacts us. We can identify its sensations: heart rate rising, sweat breaking out, stomach churning, jaw clenching, and so forth. We can notice how the emotion comes and goes in intensity. When the thoughts associated with the emotion appear, we can also step back from them, noticing them as emotional thoughts. By the time action urges arise we already have a little distance between the emotion and ourselves. Do we want to respond to the cue and walk into the drama? When we use observing, it is our choice.

Below are exercises for practicing observing. They are broken into the following categories: observing externally, observing internally, observing thoughts, and strengthening observing. Each section offers several options to choose from while you work on this important skill.

Practice Sensory Focus Externally

1. *Take an observing walk.* Find a safe and pleasant place to walk, such as a quiet street, a park, or a trail in the woods, and practice observing for about twenty minutes. As you walk, look around at everything you see in the present moment. Notice the trees, the sidewalk, cars passing by, the sounds, smells, and the breeze on your face. Notice everything but don't comment to yourself on any of it. When you start to comment, bring your attention back to observing. Notice how you feel as you walk and observe sights, sounds, and smells. When your mind wanders, simply bring it back to the present moment, the feeling of your body moving through space, and all that you see, hear, smell, and touch. If you don't have a good place to walk or don't have time in your schedule, do observant walking with an activity that you do daily, such as walking your dog or going from your car to your workplace,

school, or the grocery store. For those few moments practice walking slowly and deliberately, breathing in and out, and
noticing everything.

2. *Listen to ambient sounds.* Go outside to a natural spot, in
    your backyard, in the park, or in some woods, and find a safe
    place to sit. Allow your gaze to rest quietly on the ground in
    front of you and listen to the ambient sounds around you. You
    may hear traffic, birds, people talking, dogs barking, wind in
    the trees. It doesn't matter what the sounds are or whether you
    like them or find them annoying. Simply sit and listen without
    commenting to yourself, without judgment, for at least five
    minutes. Resist the urge to end early.

3. *Listen to music.* Select an unfamiliar piece of music. Longer
    instrumental pieces (seven to ten minutes at least) are espe-
    cially good for this practice. Find a quiet place to sit and begin
    listening, with earphones if possible. Listen to the instrumen-
    tation and the tempo of the music without describing it to
    yourself. Let go of whether you like the music or not. Resist
    the temptation to drift away in thoughts. If you do drift away,
    return to the simple sounds of the music as soon as you notice
    you have drifted.

4. *Observe clouds.* Spread a blanket on the grass. Lie on your
    back and find a cloud to observe. Notice the cloud for about
    five minutes as it naturally changes shape or even disappears.
    If it disappears, find another one. When your mind starts to
    describe what you are seeing or begins to talk to you about
    anything, bring it back to just observing. You may need to
    bring your mind back many times. Do not judge your efforts
    and don't be alarmed by your wandering mind. Simply return,
    again and again, to observing.

5. *Watch fish.* Find a fish tank in a restaurant, pet shop, or aquar-
    ium. Get comfortable and watch the fish swim into and out of

view. Try not to comment to yourself. Simply watch them for at least ten minutes and notice everything you can about the ones who swim your way.

Practice Sensory Focus Internally

1. *Taste fruit.* Cut a piece of fruit into bite-size pieces and arrange them on a plate. Any fruit will do, even raisins. Take the plate and sit in a quiet place. Pick up each piece of fruit and examine it. Smell each piece and notice its fragrance. Place each piece in your mouth and let it rest on your tongue until saliva flows a little. Then begin to chew it slowly and carefully, fully masticating each piece before you swallow. In between pieces take one full breath, inhaling and exhaling fully. Allow thoughts to arise but do not follow them.

2. *Taste water.* Fill a glass with eight ounces of pure water. Sip enough water to cover your tongue but not so much that your cheeks bulge out. Allow the water to rest in your mouth for five seconds before you swallow it. Feel the water descend down your throat and into your stomach. Take a full inhalation and exhalation and repeat with another sip. Continue until the glass is empty.

3. *Notice fragrances.* Take a little of your favorite herb, flower, lotion, essential oil, perfume, or incense. Choose a scent that is not too strong or complex, such as lavender, coconut, or lemon rind. Sit in a quiet, safe spot where you can close your eyes. Slowly bring the fragrance to your nose. Inhale deeply. Notice the different notes in the fragrance but do not describe them. Breathe normally. Repeat when ready. Do this for five minutes.

4. *Massage your hands or feet.* After showering, apply your favorite lotion to your hands and feet, slowly, carefully, and

deliberately. Notice the sensations as you rub the lotion into each finger and toe, smoothing it onto every surface with the level of firmness you find comfortable. If the lotion has a fragrance, allow yourself to drink in the smell while also noticing the feeling on your skin. Note any sore or tender places and observe how it feels to touch them. Notice how the soles of your feet feel to your hands and vice versa. Do this for ten to fifteen minutes. Notice thoughts and emotions that arise and let them go. Return to observing the sense of touch.

5. *Observe the sensation of touching objects.* Collect some smooth stones, shells, nuts, beads, or other objects that feel good in your hand. Put one in your pocket. When you are standing in line or waiting, take out the object and run your fingers over the surfaces, noticing how they feel. Close your eyes and focus on the sensations in your fingertips, the temperature of the object, any ridges, curves, or indentations. Allow thoughts to come and go but do not dwell on them. Put all your attention on observing the feel of the object in your hand.

6. *Take a morning stretch.* Before getting out of bed, take a deep inhalation and exhalation and notice any sensations in your body. Stretch your arms over your head and your legs as far as you can in the opposite direction and notice how it feels. Scan your body from head to toe for any aches, pains, tender places, tension, or stress. Continue to breathe deeply and notice any feelings of wellness or illness without comment or judgment. Experience the feelings in your body without commenting to yourself for a few breaths.

7. *Scan for sensations in your body.* Sit quietly in a chair for a few minutes and scan your body, noticing all sensations. Starting with the toes on one foot, move up through your leg, then into your groin, to your chest and shoulder, down your left arm to your hand, then all the way back to your foot. Repeat

on the other side. Notice sensations in your neck, jaw, lips, face, and scalp but do not describe them; simply observe. Pay special attention to any area where there is tension or discomfort. Create space for the tension or discomfort to be present without avoiding it or intensifying it. Simply allow it to be. Continue scanning first one side, then the other, simply noticing any sensations. Do this for five to fifteen minutes. When your mind wanders, notice it and then return to scanning the body.

8. *Observe the presence of contentment.* Select some times when you are most likely to feel contentment, such as sitting down with your coffee in the morning, taking a hot shower, watching your favorite show on television, being greeted by your pet when you return home, watching the sunrise or sunset. List as many such routine moments of contentment or pleasure as you can think of. Post the list on your refrigerator door. When these occasions arrive, practice observing the subtle sensations associated with contentment. Notice how this feels in your body. Notice the gentle urge to have more contentment, but do not rush past the contentment that you are already feeling. Feel the contentment in the moment and watch to see if gratitude also appears.

Practice Observing Thoughts

1. *Scan your mind for thoughts.* Take five minutes in the middle of your workday or when you are traveling, visiting friends or family, or otherwise occupied with people. Find a quiet, peaceful place where you will not be disturbed. Sit comfortably. Let your gaze rest on the floor in front of you and begin to notice your thoughts. At first your mind may be completely blank, but gradually thoughts will begin to form and dissolve, like waves in the ocean. Be an observer on the beach where

the thoughts arrive. Do not allow them to pull you into the water, not even to wet your feet. In other words, do not follow the thoughts; just notice them. When patterns of thoughts emerge, do not comment on the patterns; simply notice them.

2. *Practice free writing.* Get paper and a pen, a journal, or a computer at a time when you won't be disturbed. For a few moments simply observe your breath coming and going. When you are ready, begin writing, and do not stop for five minutes. Write whatever comes into your mind without censoring or editing. Freely write without commenting on what you are writing.

The Obstacles: Autopilot, Emotional Avoidance, and Dissociation

We might think that observing would come naturally, as it is such a simple and direct way to interact with the world. Unfortunately many habits directly inhibit our ability to notice what is going on around us and within us. Some of the most common problems that interfere with observing are going on autopilot, emotional avoidance, and dissociation.

Autopilot

Our awareness has many levels. We can be in full limbic alert (such as when we are in an airplane experiencing turbulence) or deeply asleep and unaware of anything going on around us, or many levels in between. For many of us, much of our time awake is spent in a type of awareness called "autopilot." Autopilot has been linked to daydreaming and self-referential thought and is also called the brain's "default mode." Autopilot is the opposite of observing (Paulson et al. 2013).

Autopilot is characterized by a wandering mind, a diffuse focus, and automaticity of behavior. It is most likely to occur when we are engaged in routine activities such as grooming, cleaning house, preparing or eating food, or driving to a familiar place. Autopilot can also occur when we are with familiar people doing familiar things but our minds are not engaged with what we are doing. Instead we are lost in thought while "going through the motions."

According to cognitive scientist George Mandler (1984) three things are most likely to take us off autopilot automatically. The first is learning a new task. We concentrate when we want to learn something new and we continue concentrating until the task is fully learned. Once the task is learned, it can be done on autopilot. Consider how attentive you were when you were first learning to drive. You were riveted to the moment, observing and describing every activity with the profound sense that you were *driving a car!* But eventually you find yourself able to drive a car, engage in a heated conversation, and eat a sandwich. (Or so you might think.)

Needing to make a decision about something immediate is the second thing that causes us to go off autopilot. Perhaps we are confidently driving through a familiar part of town, listening to reggae music, and thinking of our upcoming trip to Jamaica. Suddenly we realize we don't know where we are. Immediately, our autopilot shuts off. We return to present mind and say to ourselves, *What was the name of the street this place is on? Is it a right or left turn?* The need to decide quickly takes us off autopilot.

The third thing that is likely to shake us out of autopilot is an unexpected or unusual situation. Say you are driving at night on a stretch of familiar but deserted road. You are tired. You are thinking about getting home. You are on autopilot. Suddenly, you see a figure in your headlights. A woman standing on the side of the road is waving her arms at you. Immediately, you go off autopilot. You are now fully alert and beginning to observe this complex situation.

When we go on autopilot during routine tasks our minds wander. As discussed in the introduction, allowing our minds to wander exposes us to more worry thoughts, ruminations, and fantasies. (See "Identifying Unwanted Thoughts" in chapter 5 for more about rumination.) When we are on autopilot we are at greater risk for making mistakes, both minor and serious. We may not notice important information or events in our environment. Consistently being on autopilot contributes to feeling cut off from life (Paulson et al. 2013).

Emotional Avoidance

Going on autopilot can be a habit, but it can also be a strategy for avoiding emotions. Avoidance is the opposite of observing, because while we are avoiding we are not noticing our own inner experience. Because painful emotions are accompanied by unpleasant bodily sensations, thoughts, and urges, it is understandable that we want to avoid them. Although avoiding emotions may provide some relief in the short term, it has destructive long-term consequences.

Emotions don't just go away; by avoiding we simply go numb to them. At first, numbness is a relief. Perhaps we've been worried about paperwork we need to do but don't want to face. *Crack open a beer, turn on the game, and forget your troubles*, we say to ourselves, feeling momentary relief as we avoid. That relief has just *reinforced* avoiding the paperwork and our worries, making it more likely to become a habit. Reinforcement is the tendency of behaviors to increase when they produce pleasant or relieving consequences, such as an afternoon watching the game while avoiding tedious work. But after hours of TV and beer, we are probably numb as well. The emotions are still there, but we don't feel them. Instead we feel flat and empty.

If a pattern of emotional avoidance gets established early, it can be difficult to change. Emotional avoidance is often learned as a coping mechanism in environments where expressing emotion is punished, equated with weakness, or not tolerated, and often is a response in an environment where emotional neglect or abuse is accepted as normal (Linehan 1993). Depending on a person's temperament, emotional avoidance may take the form of denying emotions or of alternately suppressing emotions and becoming overwhelmed by them. A pattern of emotional avoidance often is accompanied by powerful distractions like addiction (Bowen et al. 2007). It is easy to see why observing is not often practiced in these environments.

Avoidance of emotions can lead to behaviors that serve to distract from emotions but end up being problems themselves (Linehan 1993a). Examples include excessive eating, drinking, sleeping, working, exercising, web surfing, video game playing, and television watching, or distractions such as "retail therapy" or gambling. These behaviors take center stage while your emotions retreat to the wings. Eventually, the drama becomes all about the problem behavior. The emotions themselves are almost forgotten.

Often people do not recognize when they are avoiding their emotions. Imagine that your elegant, slim mother often teases you about your weight and appearance. You find this irritating but have learned to ignore it. One day she does it in front of your new girlfriend over cocktails before a family dinner. Privately, your girlfriend tells you how appalled she is at your mother's comments. "Oh, it's no big deal," you say. "She does it all the time." You find yourself embarrassed and a little irritated at her for noticing and commenting on your mother's behavior. You proceed to overeat and drink three glasses of wine. Later, talking it over with your therapist, you realize you've been angry with your mother for her criticism of your body since you reached puberty. But because she would berate you further for standing up to her, you learned to tolerate your mother's criticism by suppressing your anger, first with food and then with alcohol. By observing, you see the pattern and acknowledge your anger. The more you observe the less you avoid, and the more clearly you can face how you feel and make necessary changes.

Dissociation

Dissociation is a behavior that we learn, primarily during traumatic experiences, which acts as a coping mechanism for abuse, neglect, torture, and other life-threatening experiences (American Psychiatric Association 2013). It is characterized by losing track of ordinary consciousness for a period of time, from a few minutes to hours, days, or even weeks. During dissociation normal awareness of what is going on in and around us is greatly diminished and may be altogether absent. While dissociating we may go through the motions of doing activities or we may sit quietly vacant. We may or may not be aware of our behavior.

Dissociation can become so habitual that it interferes with our lives in major ways. If you dissociate you may become fearful of having contact with anything that might prompt an episode, including your own inner experience of bodily sensations, emotions, or thoughts. Having flashbacks, painful memories, intrusive thoughts, self-loathing, and deep sadness trigger feelings of wanting to escape. Such fears can cause us to dread being alone and to avoid solitude and silence at all costs. These fears can also get in the way of participating in mindfulness activities. The more you avoid contact with your inner experience, the less likely you are to have the corrective experience that contacting your inner resources is not actually dangerous. This is why even brief daily exercises with the skill of observing can be so helpful. They provide direct learning so we can see that it is possible to tolerate, and eventually become comfortable inside of, one's own experience.

We can overcome the problems of going on autopilot, emotional avoidance, and dissociation by gradually learning to practice observing with unpleasant sensations, complex thoughts, and painful emotions (Paulson et al. 2013).

Overcoming Obstacles with Observing

Observing is a useful skill to block avoidance and dissociation, even when we are forced to endure unpleasant physical sensations (such as a dental procedure), sensations of a persistent negative emotion, or complex difficult thoughts. We focus our attention on remaining present, trying not to distract ourselves or escape, and noticing everything without commenting on it or recoiling from it.

Observe with Unpleasant Sensations

Observing sensations we deem unpleasant is tricky, because unpleasant sensations prompt very strong reactions, including judgmental thoughts and emotions. The purpose of observing is to remain present, accept the sensation in the moment, and avoid slipping into emotion mind. In fact, research tells us that we cope better with both physical and emotional distress when we bring a focused attention to observing rather than resisting our experiences (Zeidan et al. 2011, Paulson et al. 2013). Rather than tensing against an unpleasant sensation, we can relax around it, using deep breathing to reduce its intensity.

Observe Complex, Difficult Thoughts

We can never stop thoughts entirely, because the mind secretes them constantly. Complex and difficult thoughts are often connected with intense emotions, so they will frequently be worry thoughts or ruminations. Because they have strong emotional content we find them compelling. The key to observing complex and emotionally intense thoughts is first to label them as thoughts rather than facts. Labeling thoughts as thoughts allows us to detach from them a little and return to the present moment (Linehan 1993a). We don't have to attend to all the thoughts our minds serve up. We can return to the present moment and leave problem solving to when our minds are less troubled and we can access wise mind.

Once we have detached a bit from our thoughts, we can begin to notice our personal thinking patterns. We may notice automatic thoughts that arise in social situations and increase our anxiety—thoughts such as *I won't know what to say* or *They won't like me*. We start to notice judgments and negative self-talk that go on in the background and make us feel sad or ashamed. Perhaps we notice a tendency to get distracted by worry thoughts when someone is showing us how to complete an important task, or by our to-do list when our children are telling us about their day at school. Observing these habitual behaviors can increase the likelihood that we can observe difficult, complex thoughts without becoming trapped in them.

Some thoughts can be as repetitive as film footage running in a continuous loop on a cable news show. But when we use observing, we stop clinging to their content and recognize them for what they are—intrusive thoughts. We can say, *Oh, there is that particular thought again,* and turn our attention away from it, perhaps noticing that it is a beautiful spring afternoon and the trees are just starting to put out their tender green leaves. How different it is to notice reality rather than being trapped in thoughts! This practice is not easy to do but it is effective when done diligently, due to the neuroplasticity of the brain (Lazar, Kerr, and Wasserman 2005).

Observe Strong or Painful Emotions; Notice Subtle Ones

Strong emotions definitely get our attention, but not usually our mindful attention. When a strong emotion arises, it often throws us into emotion mind. We *become* the emotion (Linehan 1993a). Before we notice what is happening, everything in our mind and body is organized to *act* on that emotion.

Many people find subtle emotions—such as contentment, relief, or liking—difficult to observe. Since our survival does not depend on reacting strongly to positive emotions, we do not experience joy with the same intensity with which we experience fear (Ratey 2001). Many positive emotions do not scream for our attention with intense bodily sensations and action urges. Even love, which can be quite powerful and important to our survival, is usually not experienced as intensely as is anger. Emotions related to joy (such as amusement, satisfaction, peace, and contentment) and those related to love (such as tenderness, respect, and caring) may fly under our radar, especially if we're more used to painful emotions (Reed and Zanarini 2011). Are we missing our joy, overlooking our tender feelings? Observing helps us to notice and identify pleasant emotions, however subtle.

Painful emotions that are not strong may also get overlooked. When we overlook the subtle feeling of emotion we may be vulnerable for a more intense feeling later. For example, not paying attention to how much something is annoying or frustrating us may make us more likely to experience rage later when the stimulus upsetting us persists or intensifies.

Perhaps we have not cultivated the skill of identifying our emotions, naming them for what they are. Practicing observing with subtle emotions is similar to bird-watching. You have to be patient and still, and it helps if you have some idea of what you are seeking. We can get more adept at identifying emotions by what typically prompts them, and by their sensations, urges, and accompanying thoughts, the way an expert birder can identify a bird by its location, song, and habits. Practicing the skill of observing with emotions leads to a deep appreciation of how complex our emotional lives truly are. Below are some exercises that will help you cultivate the skill of identifying painful emotions.

Practice Observing Painful Emotions

1. *Observe frustration.* The next time you are caught in traffic, put on hold on the phone, or waiting on someone who is late, notice the sensations of frustration as well as the associated thoughts and urges. Do not follow or dwell upon the thoughts or suppress them. Notice the intensity of the action urges, how they build and subside, but do not act on them. Breathe deeply and fully while noticing the frustration until it passes. Do not cling to the frustration. Let it pass as it naturally will, or breathe it out with your exhalations. If anger is difficult for you, this is an especially useful practice. Be kind and patient with yourself as you do it, as well as before and after.

2. *Observe sadness.* Whenever a feeling of sadness arises in you for any reason, notice it as a sensation. Notice where you feel it in your body and what kinds of thoughts go along with it. Step back and observe the sensations of sadness, such as tightness in your chest or pressure in your throat. Notice how it builds and subsides. Notice the feeling attended by certain thoughts, desires, and action urges. Allow space for the sadness to be. Do not try to either make it go away or hold onto it. If it goes away, let it go. If it stays, breathe it in and out. Allow it to be present within you, but don't dwell on the thoughts associated with it or act on its urges. Watch what happens. If sadness and depression are problems for you, consider this an especially important practice. Be compassionate with yourself as you do it, as well as before and after.

3. *Observe aversion and disgust.* Whenever you face a task that you usually hate doing, such as cleaning the cat's litter box or washing pots and pans after a big meal, use observing to step back from your aversion. Empty your mind as much as possible of negative or judgmental thoughts. Observe each thing that needs doing, one thing at a time, without judgment or comment. If disgust or anger arises, notice the emotion but do not act on it. Complete each aspect of what you must do with full energy, staying present by saying to yourself, *I am observing myself doing this task,* until the task is complete. Practice many times and always reward yourself with a word of self-encouragement or praise: *Good job!*

4. *Observe rumination or worry.* As soon as you notice that you are ruminating or worrying, step back and observe how it feels in your body. Notice the emotions that arise. Gently disengage from rumination by saying to yourself, *I am letting go of ruminating and coming home to the breath.* Gently step aside from worry thoughts by saying to yourself, *I am letting go of worrying and trusting the moment to my breath.* Repeat many, many times.

5. *Observe fear.* Notice when you feel fear, anxiety, or apprehension. Notice how fear and anxiety feel in your body. Breathe into those sensations and ask yourself, *What am I afraid of and is it truly a threat to me now?* Listen carefully to the answer. Observe how your fear changes as you observe it.

• *Julie's Story*

Julie entered DBT when she was nineteen. She had just gotten out of the state hospital, where she had been since she was diagnosed with severe BPD at age eighteen, during her freshman year of college. In addition to BPD, Julie also had PTSD from an early childhood spent in an orphanage in Russia, where she had experienced profound neglect and possibly abuse. Her adoptive parents, who were both high school teachers, referred Julie for DBT. They were afraid she would kill herself and were desperate for Julie to develop skills to manage her behavior.

Before being hospitalized, Julie had been a diligent student who was especially gifted in languages. She was fluent in Spanish and said she was interested in working for the United Nations. During the first month of her second semester in college, she began to have problems with depression and had started to self-harm again, something she hadn't done since high school. She disappeared from school and was found wandering along a road in a nearby city. She had cut herself severely and had lost a fair amount of blood. Julie had no memory of what started the episode, but said that her parents thought she began having severe problems when she started studying the Russian language that semester.

Since Julie was a little child, whenever she was very upset she would go off by herself, curl up with her stuffed animal toy, and go into what she called "the fog." Julie described the fog as a "blank, empty space" and "like being dead." She could spend a lot of time rocking back and forth, stroking her teddy bear, almost completely unaware of what was going on around her. Her mother and father had sent Julie to several psychiatrists since they brought her home at age five. The psychiatrists had identified the behavior as dissociation, but none of them had been able to help her stop doing it.

Julie remembered little about her time in the orphanage, but over the years she, her parents, and her doctors had developed some theories about how Julie began dissociating. In the orphanage, where she lived from the age of fourteen months until she was adopted at age five, Julie had spent a great deal of time either alone or with many other children attended by one or two caregivers. Her efforts to get extra attention were largely unsuccessful, so Julie learned to withdraw into her own world of rocking and stroking a blanket to self-soothe. The best guess was that the dissociative state allowed her to avoid the sadness and loneliness she felt.

After several weeks of orientation, Julie committed to therapy, which included enrolling in skills class and being willing to work on giving up self-harming behaviors. The problem for Julie was that sometimes her self-harm took place when she was dissociated, and she was not sure how to give up going into the fog.

"It just comes over me," she said. "I never seem to get any warning. The next thing I know I've been gone for I don't even know how long." By analyzing many episodes of the behavior, she and her therapist were able to determine that Julie was most likely to hurt herself when she experienced a loss of some kind, such as a friend rejecting her. Most often the behavior seemed to be an escape from the emotion of sadness, but this was a guess because Julie had little or no awareness of her inner experiences. She had few associations between things that happened to her and the emotions they were likely to trigger. In fact, Julie could almost never label her emotions. She also had little or no awareness of bodily sensations, and not just when she dissociated.

Julie was capable of ignoring many sensations, including hunger, thirst, and physical pain. Her memory for interpersonal interactions and other events in her life was extremely limited. She didn't remember things she had talked about the previous week in therapy, where she had gone with her mother on the weekend, or events from her childhood either before or after the adoption. Julie spent almost her entire life in avoidance of her own experience. Her grasp of Spanish vocabulary and grammar was extraordinary, so clearly this was not simply a memory problem.

Julie had a breakthrough when she began to grasp observing. When Julie started to learn mindfulness skills, she said they were so abstract she couldn't comprehend them. In sessions her therapist began having her try to use observing for sensations such as how her feet felt in her shoes and on the floor, and how cool the surface of the leather couch was under her hand. At first the therapist needed to talk her through these exercises because of her anxiety about them. Julie told her therapist she had spent most of her life completely numb to her body. Paradoxically, even though she was profoundly afraid of being in touch with simple sensations, Julie said that self-harm made her feel alive, because the numbness went away. Still, she was willing to try to use observing in hopes it would reduce her problems with dissociation and self-harm.

Gradually Julie was able to observe the sensations in her jaw, throat, and stomach. Her therapist coached her through repetitions of the practices and then had her do them in silence. She was assigned homework to practice observing bodily sensations on her own, but for months she was unwilling to do the homework. Months later she was able to admit to her therapist that she did attempt the exercises at home but dissociated every time she tried.

Whenever Julie had an emotion during one of the sessions, her therapist directed her to observe her bodily sensations and the thoughts that arose. Her urge to avoid experiencing what she was feeling was extreme. Sometimes she would get angry with the therapist and refuse to try. Sometimes she would try but would begin to rock and wring her hands; at other times she would sit and stare blankly. When she dissociated in session, her therapist got her to hold an ice-cold washcloth on her face to help her calm down and return to normal consciousness. Slowly she became better at staying present when she was emotional. Every time she was able to observe and remain present during an emotional experience, Julie's brain received the information that she could handle emotions without real harm coming to her. She began to become accustomed to the sensations that accompanied her emotions.

As she progressed, Julie observed a pattern that happened immediately before she went into the fog. The first thing she noticed was a painful sensation in her stomach that she interpreted as "gnawing." The day she identified this sensation she wept. That sensation had all the power of a memory even though she couldn't remember when she first felt it or what had prompted it in her life. She described it as a profound loneliness and emptiness, which she interpreted as a feeling that could never be filled. While she sobbed her therapist imagined her sitting in her little crib in Russia desperately wanting to be loved and nurtured without even knowing what that actually was.

Julie had believed she would never be able to give up dissociating. By observing, however, she learned that when she became very upset there was a clear moment of choice she could now recognize. In that moment, she could choose to focus her mind and weather the emotional storm or she could choose to go into the fog. The moment of choice, Julie saw, was when she felt the gnawing. When she felt it, Julie practiced grounding herself by feeling the sensation of her feet on the floor and saying to herself, *This is now.* As she learned to tolerate the gnawing sensation, she could remain present and resist any urges to dissociate or self-harm. As she practiced observing the feeling as just a feeling and not something she had to escape at all costs, Julie gained more confidence in herself. She became strong enough to stop cutting herself and felt a great deal of pride at her accomplishment.

By practicing observing diligently, Julie was also able to pretty much eliminate dissociation. "That feeling I feared the most, the gnawing," Julie told her therapist one day late in her treatment, "has become a sort of friend. Now it reminds me to focus and observe. It reminds me I'm alive."

Julie mastered the skill of observing. She learned to identify all her emotions and be in touch with her bodily sensations. She recovered enough to return to university, graduating with a degree in Spanish and a teaching certificate. Julie's therapist got a Christmas card from Julie three years after she completed therapy. "I hardly ever feel the old pain anymore," Julie wrote. "It seems like whatever comes up I can handle. At least so far. I feel like I have come out of the fog once and for all."

Observing, the first of the what skills, is a powerful antidote to emotion mind. When we observe, we become present to what we notice around us and within us, fully experiencing whatever it is without judging it or trying to avoid it. We can also observe our thoughts and our emotions. The more we practice observing, the less time we spend on autopilot with our minds wandering, avoiding our emotions, or dissociating. Learning the skill of observing is key to how we can begin to unlearn dissociation.

When we observe, we automatically start to use words to talk about our experience. In the next chapter, we will learn the skill of describing, a skill that teaches us the mindful way to put words with our observations.

Chapter 5

CHOOSE YOUR WORDS: DESCRIBING

My older sister called me "Bratty" as early as I can remember, and sometimes even my parents did. When I objected, everyone teased me, saying I was "too sensitive." My mother would say that "Bratty" was a term of endearment, but I always felt it was a hurtful nickname. Years later, when I started practicing mindfulness skills, I realized I called myself that whenever I was embarrassed or disappointed in myself. When I tuned in to my own self-talk I was shocked at the awful things I would say. The worst was calling myself "Bratty," because it felt like such a betrayal. —Sharon, 42

In spite of the nursery rhyme about sticks and stones, everyone knows that words can hurt us. Most religions, laws, and ethical codes reference aspects of speech as part of moral behavior. "Bearing false witness" is against the ninth commandment in the Judeo-Christian tradition; in Buddhism people are cautioned to use "right speech"—that is, to avoid abusive language and communication meant to divide people; in Taoism, the fourth basic precept is to forgo "false speech," which is not only lying but also speaking about something one did not hear, see, feel, or realize for oneself (Morgan and Lawton 2007).

In Western culture we are frequently exposed to emotion-laden language, especially in the media. Conceptual distortions bombard us in advertisements and political talk. We can become desensitized to and influenced by the diction of emotion mind. And if we grew up in an environment of emotional abuse and invalidation, we may have learned to save the cruelest words for ourselves.

The Problem: Words Can Hurt

It is much harder to express ourselves well when intense emotions are on board. We are more likely to use emotion-laden words, distort the facts, infer things that are not true, or jump to conclusions. Our audience is more likely to hear the emotion than the other content we hope to convey. Even people predisposed to help us may not be able to figure out what it is we really want or need. In a disagreement, emotional speech can result in intensified conflict (Knapp and Daly 2002).

Certain types of communication tend to create disharmony (Rosenberg 1999). These include making moral judgments, issuing demands, denying our own responsibility, making comparisons between people, and focusing on deserving versus undeserving. These types of communication short-circuit our audience's ability to respond nonjudgmentally and compassion-ately to what we have to say.

Intense negative emotions also prompt critical self-talk. We may begin blaming and shaming ourselves in ways we would not tolerate from another person. Sometimes this self-talk sounds like the voice of a hypercritical parent or abusive spouse. The more we listen to this brutal monologue the more emotionally dysregulated we become (Linehan 1993). We need a powerful skill to help us step back from the inner hate speech of self-invalidation.

The Solution: Describing

Describing, the second what skill, teaches us to pay attention to how we speak to ourselves and to others. How we verbalize our wants, needs, and feelings can either thrust us into emotion mind or help us come closer to wise mind. When we use describing we put into words *in the moment* whatever it is we are noticing *in the moment*, sticking with just the facts and without judging. We can use this skill to talk to ourselves and to others about what we observe in the external world and about thoughts, emotions, and bodily sensations we experience internally.

Describing Bodily Sensations

The statement "I am noticing my stomach is full because I ate a lot of food" uses describing. Describing here focuses on a sensation and a fact in the moment without judgment or blame. Contrast this with "I feel like I am going to burst because I ate like a pig!" This expression includes self-judgment and doesn't stick to the facts—unless, of course, you actually ate from a trough! Notice the difference between "I have a headache that really hurts" and "My head is killing me." Describing can tone down unnecessary emotion about body sensations.

117

Describing Emotions

We can use describing to talk to ourselves about our emotions as they arise. "A tingle of joy in my chest," "a sensation of sadness and my eyes filling with tears," "irritation and an urge to say something hurtful" are statements that describe emotions as they enter our awareness through observing. The practice of describing emotions as sensations and urges can ground us in the present moment and make whatever is happening more concrete. Describing allows us to preserve a sliver of distance between our self, which is watching the emotion unfold, and the emotion itself. It can help us sidestep the emotion mind experience of becoming stuck to the emotion.

Research has shown that creating a self-critical, deficit-focused narrative about our painful experiences contributes to decreased coping (Pennebaker and Seagal 1999). Describing keeps us from constructing a narrative that assigns blame for the emotion or judges us and our emotions. Describing allows us to notice and narrate our experiences as they unfold in the moment, without forming a concept about the experience. To help you understand better how describing works with emotions, practice the seven steps below.

Practice Describing Emotions

1. Ask yourself, *What do I feel in my body?* Locate the sensations in the part of the body where they are felt. For example, *I feel a dull pain in my chest and a lump in my throat.* Use concrete language.

2. See if you can name the primary emotion you are feeling. *I am feeling sadness.*

3. See if you feel any action urges associated with the emotion, such as *I feel like lying down on my bed.*

4. Ask yourself whether you feel any secondary emotions about feeling the primary emotion, such as *I feel angry about being sad.*

5. Ask yourself, *Can I describe why I am sad?*

6. Ask yourself, *Is there anything else I need to describe, such as what I should do about this emotion?*

7. Ask yourself, *Am I accessing my wise mind right now?*

Describing Thoughts

Thoughts arise in the mind ceaselessly, like waves on a beach. Usually we take our thoughts seriously, as if they are crucial to our understanding of reality. Often we become completely lost in our thoughts, not even realizing how much they are influencing our moods and emotions.

We cannot stop thoughts but we can step back and notice them. Are they quiet and in the background while your experience in the moment stays in the forefront? Or are your thoughts agitated and racing, obsessional or chaotic, blocking out whatever else is going on? When we use describing to label the content of thoughts and their qualities, we become more able to step outside of them and get a fresh perspective. We can say to ourselves, *I just had a thought that I should call up my old drinking buddy. Am I in danger of a relapse?* We might notice, *I keep thinking something bad is going to happen. Is there a reason why that thought keeps arising?* Using describing in this way can save us from following our thoughts into a relapse or a depression. When we can describe thoughts *as events in the mind only,* we create a sense of freedom about what to do about them. They are not urgent imperatives, even though they might sometimes feel that way.

Exercise for Categorizing Thoughts

When we practice mindfulness it can be helpful to categorize our thoughts as they arise because, especially at first, thoughts seem to encroach on our very ability to practice.

Here is a helpful technique I learned from Pat Hawk, Roshi, my Zen teacher. (An audio version of this exercise is available at http://www.newharbinger.com/33001.) When you find yourself thinking, you can notice the type of thought that is arising. Is it a thought about work, a thought about other people, or some kind of pleasant or unpleasant fantasy? Many thoughts that arise in meditation can be placed in one of these three categories.

"Working" thoughts would include thoughts about projects you want to do, problems you need to resolve, your to-do list, or concerns about your performance at work, about money, or about other details of daily life. The moment you notice these thoughts arising or you become lost in these thoughts, say to yourself, *I have been out working; I will come home now*, and let go of the thoughts. Return to the present moment.

Thoughts about other people include imagining being with someone you love, missing loved ones, reliving shared experiences, worrying about loved ones or about conflicts with people, ruminating about people you dislike, and so forth. When you notice yourself thinking of others, say to yourself, *I have been out visiting; I will come home now*. Let go of the thoughts about others and return to present moment awareness.

Fantasy thoughts are often about the future and include thoughts about pleasant activities—such as going for a walk on the beach or planning a vacation—or dwelling on some daily activity you enjoy, like cooking dinner or having sex. Unpleasant fantasies include anticipating future events you are dreading, such as having a medical procedure or going on a difficult journey. As soon as you notice you are thinking about such activities, step back and let go of these thoughts. Say to yourself, *I have been out playing; I will come home now.* Rather than being lost in pleasant or unpleasant fantasies, come home to the present moment and the breath.

Finally, here is a part I added for people who are going through a difficult time. When you lose yourself in painful thoughts or emotions of shame, guilt, or anger, and these thoughts and emotions are taking you away from your practice, step back as soon as you notice them and say to yourself, *I have wandered and become lost. I will find my way back home now.* Then return to your practice of mindfulness. The thoughts and emotions will not go away, but your focus will be on your practice and on the comfort of finding yourself back at home in the moment.

Coming home means returning to awareness in the moment. Don't worry if you sometimes cannot categorize which thoughts you are having. Just practice *I will come home now to the breath* as much as you can.

The Obstacles: Not Sticking to Facts, Not Labeling Emotions

First we observe something, and then we describe it. The first obstacle to describing effectively is trying to describe what we cannot observe. Since we cannot observe someone else's emotions, thoughts, sensations, or motivations, neither can we effectively describe them. Instead, we can only make assumptions about the private experiences of others. As soon as we start talking about someone else's thoughts or emotions, we leave the realm of describing and enter a world of inference and conclusions about our own experience—a world that lies close to emotion mind. For example, after a painful argument with a friend has left us feeling angry and confused, we might say, "She doesn't give a damn about me." But unless she actually told us that, we would be making an inference about her feelings that could be incorrect. Such an inference only increases our anger and sadness.

To use describing correctly we are required to stick with the facts, making sure our facts are correct. We can describe our feelings about the facts and label feelings as feelings, not facts. If new facts become available we remain open to hearing them.

Making Inferences and Drawing Premature Conclusions

Describing does not include any inferences or premature conclusions about the facts. To infer is to "conclude or judge from a premise." Thus if we take the premise that not as many women as men enter the engineering field and infer that this must be because women lack the interest in or aptitude for engineering, we are drawing a premature conclusion. Drawing premature conclusions based on unproven premises puts us at the mercy of our biases, making us less wise. If we want to describe *why* more women do not enter the engineering field, we need to do some research.

An example of an emotional inference is, "When I first saw her I *knew* she was disappointed in me." We cannot really know this, of course, unless she told us. Instead, the skill of describing would have us say, "When I first saw her I noticed she was not smiling and not making eye contact. I had the thought, *She is disappointed in me*." The inference in the first statement leads to a premature conclusion ("She *is* disappointed in me"). The second statement, which sticks with the facts, leaves the mind open to other possible causes for her behavior.

The second statement also carries less emotional charge. Here the speaker has already begun to step back from the emotion/inference problem and is focusing instead on describing, separating the facts from his reaction to them. Because emotion mind only attends to the facts *when they are congruent with the felt emotion*, speaking in emotional terms puts us at risk for overlooking information that doesn't match how we are feeling. Describing helps us avoid this trap.

Evaluating from Emotion Mind

An evaluation is an appraisal of something's worth based on facts and opinions. Evaluations do not necessarily lead to judgments, but they can put us in their vicinity. For example, in the airport we rush to the gate to board our connecting flight. We are dismayed to find our flight not listed among the departures. If we stick with the facts, we say, "The airline has cancelled my flight." As we stand in a long line at customer service with other unhappy travelers, we may say, "This airline is incompetent." This evaluation may or may not be based on facts. Maybe our flight was cancelled due to a blizzard at our destination. Or maybe a plane is unavailable due to administrative or mechanical errors. If we don't have the facts (or if we choose to ignore them), any evaluation we make is suspect. As we descend further into our anger, we may assert, "This is a crappy airline run by idiots." In this sequence, "cancelled my flight" is the skill of describing, "incompetent" is an evaluation that may or may not be correct, and "crappy airline run by idiots," obviously, is a judgment. Describing uses only evaluations based entirely upon facts. Instead of creating a narrative, we can note our reactions: "The airline cancelled my flight and I feel exasperated about it." Describing lowers the emotional charge by staying focused on the facts and our reactions to them without making inaccurate evaluations.

Difficulties Identifying and Labeling Emotions

Another big obstacle to using the skill of describing arises out of difficulty in identifying or labeling our internal experiences, a condition called *alexithymia*. Alexithymia is not a mental disorder but is often seen in mental disorders. It may be a personality trait that appears relatively constant, such as in persons with

123

Asperger's Disorder, or it may be a state that comes and goes when a person is depressed or traumatized (Bermond et al. 2007).

Sometimes, people with pervasive emotion dysregulation also have alexithymia. By observing the bodily sensations and urges, people can learn to identify which sensations and urges go with which emotions. This information can then be used to describe their emotions to others. When others can understand what we are feeling, it makes it easier to communicate effectively. Below is a story about someone who found words for his feelings as he recovered from a painful divorce and an accompanying depression.

• Sam's Story

Sam, a fifty-seven-year-old surgeon, came to therapy because he was experiencing severe depression. He had just separated from his wife of twenty-six years. The couple had one son, Jack, who was on active duty in the military overseas. Sam grew up in a family that valued keeping a "stiff upper lip" and avoiding "self-pity." This stoic attitude had mostly worked for him, especially in his work, but it caused profound problems in his marriage, where his wife longed for more intimacy and communication. Sam's depression was particularly severe because he couldn't really feel or identify his own emotions, having been brought up to see emotions as a weakness.

Sam arrived early for his first appointment, with his paperwork and copay in hand. A trim man with short gray hair and a square jaw, he smiled ironically. "Well, Doc," he said. "This is a role reversal."

He described his sleep problems, lack of appetite, agitation, inability to experience pleasure, and suicide ideation in crisp, clinical terms. He said he felt hopeless about the future.

"I don't even know what I feel!" He covered his face in his hands. "I can't go home from work. I get takeout and sleep on the couch in my office. I only go home to shower in the morning. I am…lost." He seemed to choke back tears. "I can't talk to anyone about Meredith leaving. I've even considered killing myself. I would, except it wouldn't be fair to Jack." He sat in silence for a few moments. He straightened up in his chair and resumed his mask. Sam had still not identified a single emotion. The closest he came, feeling "lost," was more of an evaluation than an emotion.

Then Sam took a deep breath and closed his eyes. "I think what I feel is scared." Over the next year Sam learned and practiced mindfulness skills. He started to engage purposefully in recreational events, which at first he described by emphasizing how little enjoyment he experienced. Gradually, he learned to describe more of what he felt and to stop avoiding his emotions. He stopped the jaunty banter and started talking seriously about how sad and angry he felt about his wife leaving. He described in detail his role in the dissolution of his marriage and his regret that he hadn't been able to make her stay.

After about six months, Sam stopped wishing he were dead. In sessions, he frequently referred to his emotions by name, including love and joy. Even though he continued to live alone and eventually got divorced, his anxiety and depression decreased. When he'd been in therapy for two years he had a daily practice of mindful walking and was referring many of his patients to mindfulness-based stress reduction classes. Sam no longer made fun of himself for his feelings. He talked about wanting to find more meaning in his life than doing the procedure surgeries he'd excelled at for twenty-five years, which had made him a lot of money but left him feeling unfulfilled.

When he completed therapy after three years, Sam was on his way to work as a volunteer for a medical charity near where his son was stationed. "How do you feel about going overseas?" I asked as he was headed out the door. "Scared, but also excited. I've learned that for me those two feelings are a lot alike, almost like twins. I feel them both here," he said, touching his chest. There was no irony at all in his smile.

Facial Expressions, Bodily Sensations, and Attentional Foci of Emotions

One way to increase the likelihood that you will be able to identify and label your emotions is to describe the facial and bodily sensations of emotions. Here is a quick reference for describing the characteristics of six basic emotions (Linehan 1993a; Hatfield, Capaccio, and Rapson 1994).

Anger. The facial expression for anger is a grimace. The posture includes tensed muscles. The bodily sensation is feeling flushed, jaw clenched, and an increased heart rate. The attention is focused.

Sadness. The facial expression for sadness is a frown or a blank face. The posture is drawn and limp. The bodily sensations include a dull pain in the chest moving up into the throat and eyes, and a slowed heart rate. The attention is diffused.

Fear. The facial expression for fear includes wide eyes and an open or slack mouth. The posture is tense and frozen. Sensations include trembling of the limbs, intense feeling in the pit of the stomach, and an increasing heart rate. Attention is focused.

Shame. The facial expression for shame includes flushed skin and eyes either cast down or shifting. The posture is collapsed and limp. The bodily sensations include a hot face, queasiness in the stomach, and heart rate increasing. Attention is diffused.

Love. The facial expression of love includes gazing eyes and a soft smile. The body posture is relaxed. Love's sensations are warmth throughout the body, especially in the upper chest and face, with a normal or slightly elevated heart rate. Attention may be focused or diffuse.

Joy. The facial expression of joy is a smile with merry eyes. The body posture is collected but not tense. The sensations include a tingling in the upper chest and throat with the heart rate slightly elevated. Attention is diffused.

Overcoming Obstacles by Describing Inner Experiencing

Naming emotions is one of the most important uses of describing. We can also use describing to notice the content of our thoughts and to reduce rumination and negative self-talk. By first observing our inner state and then describing it to ourselves, we delineate options for how to proceed to wise mind. Thus we can restructure the assumption, *She doesn't give a damn about me,* into *I feel angry that I didn't get what I wanted, and sad that my friend didn't seem to understand what I was feeling.* Describing in this way might lead to a decrease in anger and an increase in self-compassion for our sadness. It also might result in a more effective conversation with our friend should we choose to approach the topic with her.

Identifying Unwanted Thoughts

Unwanted thoughts include worries, ruminations, obsessional thoughts, and judgments of others or ourselves. Describing allows us to step back from making unhelpful and inaccurate narratives about these kinds of thoughts. For example, perhaps you worry, *My boss doesn't like me*. Describing encourages us to step back and say, *I just had the thought* My boss doesn't like me. *It is just a thought. I don't know if it is true. I am going to let it go!* Over time we may notice a pattern. For example, we may describe, *I have frequently been anxious in the presence of my boss, and anxiety often makes me think people don't like me.*

Rumination, a thinking behavior associated with depression, is defined as an obsessional focus on one's distress, including the distress's causes and consequences (American Psychological Association 2013). It usually involves evaluations of the self and others. Describing is useful in first identifying rumination: *I notice I am ruminating. I am now going to turn away from this rumination and distract myself.* Describing is also useful in identifying patterns of rumination: *I notice that when I start thinking a lot about how I ended my first marriage I am probably starting to get depressed. Maybe when I notice this I can "change the channel" in my brain.*

Obsessional and chaotic thoughts create agitation and intense distress. Identifying thoughts and labeling them can be part of effective treatment. I once worked with a woman diagnosed with obsessive-compulsive disorder who was troubled by the thought that she would stab her husband in the middle of the night. She and her husband had an affectionate marriage, but Doria, who had suffered from previous similar obsessions, was so afraid she would murder her husband that she tried to check herself into the state mental hospital.

I taught Doria the skills of observing and describing. She learned to observe the obsessional thoughts and images and to describe them to herself as *obsessional thoughts and images, not actual plans*. She went on to describe, *I have had these thoughts in the past and will likely have them in the future. I do not need to fear them.* This allowed Doria to release the thoughts, knowing they would return to be released again and again. Previously she had focused on trying to reassure herself that she would not follow through on the images. Oddly, Doria felt that this actually made the thoughts stronger. Instead of trying to counter her thoughts, Doria learned not to argue with them, only to describe them (and not act on them).

Using "Teflon Mind"

I also taught Doria the DBT skill of "Teflon mind" to help her let go of the obsessional thoughts. I used Linehan's (1993a) image of thoughts sliding off her mind the way a fried egg slides off a Teflon pan. Doria's therapy involved a great deal more than practicing Teflon mind, but this skill definitely helped reduce her agitation.

When we use Teflon mind, we observe the thought, describe it as an unwanted thought, and then let it slip out of our minds. We may need to do this many times within a short time frame, especially at first. The less we entertain unwanted thoughts, the more likely it is that the frequency of the thoughts will diminish. By using Teflon mind we actually "rewire" our brains away from unwanted thoughts; research has shown that due to the neuroplasticity of the brain, such changes, which include an increase in cortical thickness, can last over the long term (Lazar, Kerr, and Wasserman 2005).

Reducing Self-Invalidation

Describing is also useful in reducing negative self-talk, including self-invalidation. The more emotionally upset we become, the more we tend to blame and shame ourselves. This becomes a downward spiral that "circles the drain" of emotion mind.

For example, a friend cancels a much-anticipated date. We go from feeling disappointed and even irritated with our friend to the thought *No one wants to be friends with me*, and finally to *I am such a loser. I am bound to be a miserable, lonely person.* When we notice what we are doing, we can step back and use describing to reframe our experience. We can say, *Right now I feel disappointed and discouraged. I am having lonely feelings and I am also angry at my friend.* This reframing reduces our distress. We are then free to offer ourselves encouragement instead of blame.

Strengthening the Skill of Describing Inner Experiences

You can strengthen your ability to describe your thoughts and emotions with the following activities.

Keep an emotion diary. Each day write a line or two about the thoughts, sensations, and emotions you experienced during the day. Describe thoughts as thoughts, sensations as sensations, and emotions as emotions.

Use precise language. Learn as many words as you can for the emotions you experience and use them accurately. When you feel anger, for example, is it pique, frustration, annoyance, bitterness, wrath? When you feel fear, is it worry, nervousness, apprehension, dread? Use the precise word that best describes what you feel.

Pay close attention to how you feel in your body. Describe your sensations to yourself. Do you feel hot or cool? Notice how your belly feels, how your jaw feels, the sensations in your throat and chest, and so on. Practice many times during the day.

Step away from inferences. Establish a habit of noticing inferences and stepping back from them. Describe facial expressions rather than attributing emotions to people based on your assumptions. Describe events in sequence rather than drawing conclusions. Whenever you are about to make an inference, stop and ask, *Is that an inference?* If it is, drop it and return to describing the facts only.

Be the camera. Write a description of an emotional event as if you were writing directions for a screenplay. Stick with the facts, as if writing directions ("Maria enters, carrying a notebook"). Let your "camera" zoom in for a close-up of facial expressions and body postures or gestures, and describe them as if for a storyboard. This kind of describing can give you perspective and help you to step back from an intense event. Be careful not to let emotion mind write the directions!

Practice "right speech." Notice urges to stretch the truth, exaggerate, betray confidences, make judgments, or use divisive speech. Step back from emotion mind and destructive speech and use describing instead.

Overcoming Obstacles by Using Describing to Communicate

Because emotions are contagious, people tend to respond to highly emotional communication with emotions of their own, sometimes congruent and sometimes opposing (Hatfield, Capaccio, and Rapson 1994). Whenever we communicate out of emotion mind we run the risk of increasing interpersonal communication mistakes and conflicts. Describing helps us avoid vague, emotional, and unclear communications; helps us ask for what we need; and helps us say no more effectively (Linehan 1993a).

When we communicate with others it is important to stick with the facts and own our feelings as feelings. Here are two useful models for how to practice describing to improve interpersonal communication.

Nonviolent Communication

Nonviolent communication (NVC) has a four-step process for communicating with others about our needs (and for receiving another person's communications): what I observe, how I feel, what I need or value, and the actions I would like taken (Rosenberg 1999). Let's use NVC to look at a situation in which we were passed over for a promotion and we want to speak to our supervisor about it.

First, we establish a context by sharing our observations about the situation we are in, without falling into evaluations or generalizations: "I notice that you gave Mike the promotion to assistant manager." Second, we express our feelings, without creating a story or drawing conclusions: "I am disappointed I was not chosen." Third, we express our needs with as much self-compassion as possible: "I want to feel like my contributions to the company are appreciated and acknowledged." And fourth, if we decide to make a request, we recognize that this request is not a demand and that the other person is entitled to say no: "Would you consider giving me a promotion or a raise within the next six months or year?" (We might decide that what is important to us at this time is only that our feelings be heard, in which case we might ask, "Would you be willing to listen to me about how I feel about not receiving a raise or promotion?") In any case, we express our feelings honestly.

If the answer to a request is no, we will not necessarily give up on it. We will try to receive the answer with compassion for the person who says no, however, and try to understand the point of view or circumstances that made that person deny our request. Nonviolent communication is based on the premise that all human beings have the same needs and capacity for compassion, so that when needs are clearly expressed it is more likely that they will be met (Rosenberg 1999).

The DBT Interpersonal Effectiveness Skills

In the DBT Interpersonal Effectiveness Skill Module (Linehan 1993a), we begin by observing that there are three important aspects to all interpersonal interactions. The first aspect is what we want, called our objective. This could be asking someone to do something for us, take our feelings seriously, or accept a "no" answer from us. The second aspect is to try to ensure that our relationship with the other person will remain on a stable footing as we make our request or say no. The third aspect is to feel good about how we conducted ourselves while making our request or saying no, thereby keeping our self-respect. We must access wise mind to know which aspect is most important for us in each specific interpersonal interaction and what, if any, conflicts exist among the aspects. Thus we prepare a plan for our communication, especially about matters of great importance to us.

Within the DBT system is a sequence of four steps: describe, express, ask, and reinforce (DEAR). We execute our plan by first describing to the other person the context in which we are going to make a request, the context that is most relevant to what we want. Next, we express our thoughts and feelings about making the request. Third, we ask for exactly what we want or we explicitly say no. Finally, we specify how responding positively to our request will benefit the other person. How we deliver this sequence of steps allows us to emphasize one or more aspects of our goal: getting our objective, keeping the relationship, and maintaining our self-respect.

Let's practice the DBT Interpersonal Effectiveness Skill sequence, using the example of your wanting to ask a friend for repayment of a loan (Linehan 1993a).

> **Describe** the framework within which you want to make the request. "It has been six months since you borrowed money from me, and we agreed you would start paying me back by now."

> **Express** how you feel about the request itself or about making the request. "I would like to have the money now to cover other expenses."

Ask clearly for exactly what you want. "Can you pay me what you owe me by next week?"

Reinforce by telling the other person why it is good for him or her to give you what you want. This may be as simple as "I would really appreciate it" or as detailed as "If you cannot I will be disappointed because that is what you promised to do."

Let's look at a longer example of using DEAR. Brittany, 33, was struggling with depression. Her psychiatrist, Dr. Bly, was unable to find a medication that helped without causing difficult side effects. Recently, Dr. Bly started Brittany on her third new medication in six months. At first Brittany felt better, but she gained seven pounds in six weeks. Brittany knew that gaining weight would make her depression worse, but she dreaded asking Dr. Bly for yet another change. She decided to use the interpersonal skills she had learned and practiced with her therapist to discuss this with her psychiatrist. Brittany thought about what she wanted to say. She realized that the most important aspect of her communication was to get her objective—that is, to get her medication changed. Second in importance was that she maintain self-respect while asking for what she needed. And finally, she did not want to harm her relationship with Dr. Bly by how she asked.

Describe. "Dr. Bly, medication X has reduced my depression. I am sleeping better and feel less agitated. However, I have gained a pound a week since I started on X."

"I am glad to hear that you are doing better on the medication," Dr. Bly says. "A little weight gain is expected with X, of course."

Express. "Gaining a pound a week is a side effect I really can't tolerate," Brittany replies.

Dr. Bly frowns. "You are so sensitive!" he says.

Ask. Brittany ignores this comment and replies, "I want to discontinue X and try another medication. I would like to find one that works as well as X but doesn't cause so much weight gain."

"This will be the fourth medication you will have tried in six months," Dr. Bly says, rolling his eyes. Again, Brittany ignores this nonverbal comment in service of her goal.

Reinforce. "I know we have tried three medications thus far. If you will stick by me until we find a medication I can tolerate, I will be very appreciative."

Although he wasn't thrilled about making the change, Dr. Bly was willing to help and made no further disparaging comments or facial expressions. By focusing on describing what she needed, Brittany was able to communicate her objective without being distracted or getting off track. She rightfully felt proud of herself.

The skill of describing helps us choose our words wisely, whether we are speaking with others or to ourselves. Describing teaches us to stick with the facts of what we actually observe and to avoid assumptions and inferences. When we use describing to talk to ourselves, we gain more understanding of what it is we are actually feeling and thinking, which can help us regulate emotions and decrease unwanted thoughts. By using describing with others we increase the likelihood that we can communicate effectively. Words might still hurt us, but when we use describing, at least we are not using words to hurt ourselves or others.

Chapter 6

JOIN THE DANCE: PARTICIPATING

I've always been painfully shy. The older boys bullied me on the school bus in elementary school, calling me "queer" and "faggot." I was so ashamed I never even told my parents. I had no friends in high school. I began to think of myself as a loser that no one would ever want to talk to, let alone be friends with. The one time I went to a mixer I had a panic attack. In college I was really lonely and confused about my identity. I often felt suicidal. I wanted to go home every weekend. I focused so completely on academics I hardly went out of my room. I kept a 4.0 GPA but I had no life. Finally, my senior year, my mom convinced me to see a counselor. He's the one who helped me realize I had to face my social anxiety and start participating in my life. If I didn't I was going nowhere but into depression. —Jake, 21

Many people with intense emotions also experience severe anxiety in social situations, a problem called *social anxiety*. People with social anxiety try to avoid experiences that expose them to rejection by others. Whenever a situation arises in which we will encounter peers, especially unfamiliar ones, fear of rejection mounts, prompting automatic self-critical thoughts such as *You'll make a fool of yourself* or *Everyone will think you are a loser*. The more anxiety we feel, the more we are likely to avoid others. And when we cancel our plans and stay home, relief floods us, a reinforcer that makes it more likely we will avoid similar situations in the future. Before long we have established a pattern that keeps us isolated and alone (Hope, Heimberg, and Turk 2006).

Even if we are naturally outgoing, enjoying friends and acquaintances with whom we share activities, we may withdraw or isolate because of a divorce, job loss, decline in health, or period of depression (Segal, Williams, and Teasdale 2002). We might avoid getting together with friends after work, stop attending church or synagogue, and even quit talking with acquaintances at the grocery store. Whenever painful emotions consume us, we tend to turn inward, diminishing our social interactions and pleasurable activities. We may find ourselves losing connections even to close family members as we hunker down in isolation. We "go through the motions," barely noticing the lack of spontaneity in our lives. We may feel that we have never really been connected to others at all, but have always been on the outside looking in (Williams et al. 2007).

The Problem: Feeling Outside the Circle of Life

As social animals, humans have a profound need to be with others. The more close human connections we have, the better we can withstand times of difficulty and loss. Without human connections we are more vulnerable to loneliness, which is correlated with lower life expectancy and poor overall health (Caccioppo and Patrick 2008). In short, we need others to survive emotionally and physically.

If we're living in fearful isolation and unable to enjoy activities or function at work, we need a powerful skill to break the pattern of avoidance. We need participating.

The Solution: Participating

Participating is the third what skill. Usually participating happens spontaneously when we join in an activity with others such as making a meal, playing a game, or dancing. We can also make a conscious choice to participate in an activity, either alone or with others, such as walking the dog, singing in a choir, or cleaning the house. When we participate, we let go of observing and describing and enter fully into the moment, awake and aware and open to whatever is coming toward us.

Participating is fundamentally different from acting impulsively, being prompted by emotional urges. When we participate we access wise mind so that our actions are consistent with our values. When we act from emotions we may have spontaneity at first, but eventually, acting on urges traps us in emotional sensations, further urges, and confusion. When we stand back from participating altogether we find ourselves living in self-doubt, self-consciousness, and feelings of disconnection. At the very least, participating stops us from avoiding and helps us experience our lives. Sometimes, by being in the moment and fully present, participating can even bring us into contact with peak experience, flow, and connectedness.

For example, let's say we love horses but know little about them. Horses are powerful, beautiful animals with highly sensitive natures, but they are also unpredictable and thus dangerous. Interacting with horses is a process that involves a lot of learning and some risk. If we approach a horse impulsively—jumping on a strange horse bareback, for example—we might get thrown off. On the other hand, if we hang back and never approach for fear we will do something wrong, we will never learn enough to enjoy horses safely.

The four steps of participating are making an intention, accepting risk, practicing, and letting go of the outcome.

Make an Intention

The first step is to make an intention—that is, to commit to a plan to undertake an action and to follow through on that plan. First we analyze the task and anticipate any problems that might arise. Next we break the task into small steps and prepare for action. As we begin to execute our plan, fears may arise, and we may want to avoid the challenge we have set for ourselves. Our intention and commitment to follow through, however, remind us to face those fears and proceed with our plan.

Whether our goal is to show up at a party or present a closing argument to a jury, intention allows us to let go of everything but the moment. The intention includes a willingness to let go of distractions, self-consciousness, and fear. If you've ever watched a competitive figure skater standing poised and smiling before the music starts, gathering all of herself into the moment before launching her body into a series of acrobatic leaps and turns on the ice, you have seen intention.

Accept Risk

The next step is to accept the risks involved. When we analyze the task at hand, we will always see potential pitfalls. Chances are we will make mistakes. We could fail at our goal, be criticized, even get hurt. People will see our mistakes and perhaps they will judge us. We may judge ourselves. In fact, anything can happen when we participate because we are now *in the game*. To stay in the game we have to give up the safety of the sidelines and accept the risks inherent in playing.

Practice

Full participation requires practice. We may believe that other people engage effortlessly and wonder why it is so hard for us. It is true that it is easier for some, due to their temperament, upbringing, culture, or genetics. But most flawless performances are the result of years of intensive practice, including a willingness to make mistakes and sometimes fail. The intricate footwork of an Irish step dancer is the result of years of practice so that the performance appears effortless to the audience.

To improve our interpersonal spontaneity, we have to seek out opportunities to practice being spontaneous. We have to find situations in which we are willing to make mistakes as we interact. It is a good idea to start with activities to which you can easily belong, such as a beginners' class at something you'd enjoy, volunteering at church, or offering to help at a local community activity—any place where people are likely to be inclusive and tolerant. Practicing in such "safer" environments increases our ability to tolerate feeling anxious or awkward (Hope, Heimberg, and Turk 2006). If we lose confidence and suddenly feel foolish participating, we can quickly return to observing and describing to get our bearings again. The more we practice, the sooner we can get back into the flow.

Let Go of the Outcome

The ultimate goal of participating is to enter the experience of flow, in which intention, risk assessment, and practice fall away, and what is left is the moment and our experience. Tim Gallwey, author of *The Inner Game of Tennis* (1997), calls this "the art of relaxed concentration." Gallwey encourages his tennis students to quiet the mind on the court and "see what actually is." The "inner game" is all about letting one's natural abilities, whatever they are, take over and avoiding punishing self-talk that causes muscles to tense and strokes to go awry. This is what happens in a "hot streak" on the tennis court or when we find ourselves fully engaged in any activity (Gallwey 1997). This kind of flow experience is usually quite pleasant and reinforcing for most people.

Participating enhances every aspect of living, including relationships, sensual experiences, work, play, and rest. The goal of participating is to live intentionally and freely in contact with wise mind.

The exercise below offers four steps to strengthen your ability to participate. To practice, select an activity you are willing to try. This could be volunteering at Habitat for Humanity, taking a free dance lesson, agreeing to make coffee at an Alcoholics Anonymous (AA) meeting, or going to a meetup for new mothers. Select an activity that doesn't make you *too* anxious but that stretches you a little. See the activity through all four steps.

Exercises to Strengthen Participation

1. *Select an activity for practice.* Form an intention to use the activity as a mindfulness exercise. Consider all the aspects of the activity and resolve to remain present for each. Carefully consider any problems that might arise with your plan and consider how to manage those problems should they arise. For example, at your local AA meeting, watch the person who makes coffee for a few weeks and notice all the steps involved. Then make an intention to volunteer to make the coffee, and speak to the person leading the meeting about what steps you need to take to do so.

2. *Anticipate possible discomfort.* Let go in advance of the idea that everything should go perfectly. As you prepare for the activity, consider the possibility that things won't go perfectly and make a plan to accept imperfection. Let go of catastrophizing about a possible mistake. Commit to remaining nonjudgmental of yourself and others. For example, say to yourself, *I will do my best to make decent coffee and make sure there are enough cups, spoons, creamers, and sugar. I will let go of expecting any particular reaction from anybody.*

3. *Stay mindful.* Once you are engaged in the activity, remain mindful. This is a practice exercise! If a problem arises, observe and describe it in the moment and correct it as best you can. As soon as you can, let go of observing/describing and problem-solving mode and return to experiencing mode. Step back into the flow and stay present. Don't go on autopilot. Notice people coming by and pouring coffee and greet them.

4. *Join the dance.* As best you can, enjoy your experience. Engage all your senses and focus on the moment. Be mindful of any pleasure you experience. Notice how people are pouring the coffee you made into the cups you set out. Breathe and experience being part of the meeting as a whole. Feel yourself inside the circle.

Ultimately participating is like walking out on a dock over a deep, clear lake on a warm summer morning and resolving to dive into the water. You know it will be cold at first, but it will also be exhilarating. You will swim to the floating platform, climb out, look around the lake and at the cabins where people are just waking up, dive back in, and swim back to the dock. Then you can have that cup of coffee on the porch, refreshed and tingly, and feel a sense of pride for having had a morning swim. But you've got to dive in first.

• *Miriam's Story*

Miriam, a forty-eight-year-old woman, was referred to DBT for treatment-resistant depression, which she had had off and on since the birth of her son, Ari, now fifteen. Her husband David, an accountant, drove her to her appointment, walked her into my office, and made sure she was comfortably settled on the sofa. Before he left my office to wait for her, he handed me her copious medical and psychiatric records.

In addition to depression, Miriam had also had cluster headaches, migraines, and fibromyalgia for at least ten years. She spent most of every day in bed and rarely left the house. She sometimes read novels or watched television. Her husband brought her breakfast in the morning and left lunch on the kitchen table. He drove their son to school and himself to work. Ari got rides home from school, and when David came home he made dinner and did the household chores. This routine had been in place for seven years.

Miriam's headache pain was often debilitating, and her fibromyalgia caused muscle pain and flu-like symptoms. She had spent many years undergoing tests and trying various treatments. None of her physical problems responded to medications other than opiates, to which she feared becoming addicted. Most days, she felt guilty, hopeless, and alone. Sometimes she had thoughts of killing herself, although she said she would never act on them. Antidepressant medication helped only a little. Miriam's doctors did not know how to help her, and she believed they had started to blame her for her problems.

Though she had trained as a speech pathologist and once owned her own practice, Miriam had not worked in ten years. "I have no life," she said in a voice that barely rose above a whisper. "I can't do the laundry. I can't go grocery shopping. I couldn't go to services if David didn't take me. He had to drive me here even though we live only four blocks away." Miriam was so afraid of being caught away from home by a headache that she had given up driving.

It took a long time for Miriam to commit to attending skills group each week no matter how bad she felt. At first she would come only if her husband drove her and picked her up, but eventually she agreed to take a taxi. For months she would call a few minutes before group started and say she was too ill to come. At least half the time, with some coaching, she would make it, albeit late. Over time, her attendance at appointments improved, and Miriam began to learn and use skills.

Once, Miriam felt ill during group. At break she called a taxi and got home on her own. After class I called to check on her. "I'm all right now," she said. "I didn't even call David. I didn't want to worry him. Six months ago I never could have done that. This is big for me."

Miriam often talked about her desire to participate in the life of her family. "David and Ari sometimes act like I don't exist," she said. "They don't seem to need me. And when I join them in the living room to watch television, the conversation stops. I feel completely irrelevant to them. I want to be in their lives more. I want to be more in my own life."

After this realization, Miriam decided to work on reentering her life by participating. Instead of staying in bed and waiting for her breakfast to be brought to her, she started getting up and coming to the table, even when she didn't feel well. A few times she even got up before David, made coffee, and packed a lunch for Ari. While they seemed uncomfortable with this at first, gradually Ari and David responded positively to her efforts to interact in the mornings.

Miriam decided to throw herself into the mornings using the skill of participating. It became her intention to be as engaged as possible. When she felt really bad she could always go back to bed once they left for work and school. Her efforts paid off. Mornings became a special family time for the three of them, and more often than not Miriam was making coffee and Ari's lunch.

Throughout the first year of therapy, Miriam worked on increasing her participation by acting opposite to her urges to withdraw, go back to bed, and avoid. She began to do the laundry when she felt well enough. She started clipping coupons from the circulars and going to the grocery store with David on the weekends. Not only did she attend synagogue with David and Ari, but she also made herself stay for coffee and conversation. I asked her how she got herself to do these things. She smiled. "I say to myself, 'Get in the game, girl,' and then I do!"

Miriam got approval from her doctor to do physical therapy to strengthen her functionality. She started walking twenty minutes a day, every day. Eventually, she was able to take a driver's education refresher course and renew her license. This was a huge step forward for her, and it opened other avenues. Headaches came and went, but Miriam continued to engage more in her life. Her depression remitted for the first time in years. She was most proud of her ability to drive Ari to his debate team meets. "In the past I wouldn't even have been able to attend. Now I'm driving him there!"

Miriam had some recurrences of her depression after therapy, and sometimes she would come back in for a "tune-up" of three or four sessions. "I've figured out I have to manage my depression like some people manage their weight. I have to get active and stay active as much as I can. I find that if I catch it early, the depression never gets as bad. For one thing, I don't go back to bed anymore. I actually now have a life and I have to live it. Participating keeps me from falling back into where I was when I first came to DBT."

Miriam created a new life for herself that included relationships, activities, and commitments. Research shows that even a few weeks of engaging in activities that reconnect us with others can build positive experiences, improve mood, and make us less vulnerable to negative emotions (Godfrin and Van Heeringen 2010). The skill of participating helps us throw ourselves into life by engaging in activities, attending events, reaching out to others, and being fully present in any interaction.

The Obstacles: Avoidant Behavior and Impulsive Behavior

The first obstacle to participating is avoidance. It is natural to want to avoid situations we find unpleasant, and every time we avoid we are rewarded with a little feeling of relief. The relief, as mentioned earlier, acts as a reinforcer, making it more likely that we will avoid again. This establishes a pattern that damages us in the long term with failed relationships, lost jobs, and diminished trust in ourselves. The more we avoid, the more our brains get the message that it is intolerable to go to work, have a friend over for lunch, or even open our mail.

We may have learned in childhood how to avoid as a way to escape criticism and humiliation. Perhaps we weren't taught how to tolerate making mistakes or how to keep trying and reward ourselves for progress. We begin to feel that if we can't do some-thing perfectly there is no point in taking the risk of trying. Somehow we learned to fade into the background and play it safe. This pattern leads to emotion mind telling us it is better to avoid even if we have to give up our dreams. Maybe we need to practice *failing well*, which means we accept the likelihood of some failure as part of playing the game and we strategize about ways to make sure our unavoidable failures do not sideline us permanently (Linehan 1993a).

The second obstacle to participating is impulsivity. Participating, by definition, is intentional and involves acting from wise mind. Impulsivity, which is driven by the urges of emotion mind, prompts us to take undue risks and overextend ourselves in the heat of the moment. *I can ski that double black-diamond run even though I'm a beginner,* says emotion mind. Or *He seems really nice; maybe I'll go home with him.* Impulsive behavior, like impulse buys, nearly always causes remorse. The more we act on impulse the more we expose ourselves to situations that cause us to distrust ourselves in spontaneous situations. We may find ourselves alternating between impulsivity and avoidance while missing out on participating.

Overcoming Obstacles with Behavioral Activation

Behavioral activation (BA) is a popular treatment that has been shown to reduce depression symptoms (Dimidjian et al. 2006; Dobson et al. 2008). Some aspects of BA look a lot like the skill of participating. For example, activity scheduling, which is part of both DBT and BA, is useful for anyone who has problems with emotion regulation (Linehan 1993a). When we experience painful mood states or intense emotions such as depression, grief, or anxiety, it becomes harder to engage in our usual activities, because energy may be low or it may be tempting to avoid people when feeling dysregulated. The urge when feeling this way is to avoid anything that requires effort or is challenging, even if the activity is potentially rewarding.

BA appears to work at least in part because it focuses on getting people to commit to following through with activities even when they don't want to. These scheduled activities fall into two broad categories: *pleasurable activities* and *mastery activities,* which build confidence and a sense of competency (Dimidjian et al. 2006).

People who avoid, whether due to depression or to intense emotions, sometimes lose touch with the experience of pleasure—a condition known as *anhedonia.* Both BA and the skill of participating help people focus mindfully during pleasurable events and mastery events by having us notice any feelings of pleasure and mastery as they arise in the moment (Linehan 1993a; Addis and Martell 2004). With this practice, anhedonia diminishes, and experiences of pleasure and mastery increase (Dimidjian et al. 2006.) Let's look at how to use participating when engaging with pleasant activities and mastery activities.

Increasing Pleasant Activities

Increasing pleasure in your life when you have intense emotions is easier said than done. People who stop experiencing pleasure from activities usually stop engaging in them. Without the stimuli of ongoing pleasant events, the pleasure centers of the brain shut down, making matters worse (Naranjo, Tremblay, and Busto 2001). Re-engaging with pleasurable activities over time reverses this trend. Mindfully increasing pleasurable and confidence-building activities works to restore enjoyment and decrease depressive symptoms (Dimidjian et al. 2006) and helps people reduce vulnerability to intense emotions (Linehan et al. 2014). Participating in a pleasurable activity means being fully aware in the moment of all the aspects of that activity, savoring all its sights, sounds, smells, tastes, and touches. By throwing ourselves into pleasure wholeheartedly, participating distracts us from thoughts that diminish our pleasure—thoughts such as *This really isn't that enjoyable, It will be over soon, I shouldn't have tried this,* or *I don't deserve this* (Linehan 1993a).

Increasing Mastery Activities

Addis and Martell (2004) note the importance of mastery activities in the treatment of depression. Mastery activities may or may not be pleasurable but they can give us a sense of accomplishment, move us closer to a goal or help to solve a problem. When we are in the grip of intense emotions it can be difficult to do such mastery activities as filling out forms, keeping track of bills, or going to the gym. Scheduling mastery activities works in the same way as with pleasant activities. We make an intention to engage, schedule the time, and then throw ourselves into it fully. Whatever the task, we try to remain present and focused until it is complete. While the activity may not be much fun, when we are finished we are likely to feel better than if we had spent the time ruminating over our problems and dwelling in painful emotions. In fact, research shows that when we can do this on a more consistent basis we are likely to experience increased confidence and improved mood (Dimidjian et al. 2006).

One way we can get ourselves to participate in mastery activities is to practice "self-management." Self-management is the practice of delaying gratification until a goal is achieved and then rewarding oneself for completing the project. An example of self-management is promising ourselves that if we wash, dry, and fold our huge pile of laundry on Saturday morning we can go to the movies on Saturday afternoon. Thus if we do the laundry, we go to the movies. If we don't, we stay home. When we can manage ourselves by building in rewards contingent on our own "good behavior," we gain mastery over procrastination and our mood is likely to improve (Addis and Martell 2004).

Another type of mastery is succeeding in getting ourselves to do things that are in line with our goals but that fall just outside our comfort zone. We have to coax ourselves to go to a mixer to make new friends or attend the pottery class we've paid for but feel like skipping. After we complete an activity we've previously avoided due to our mood, we feel a sense of mastery, which con-tributes to our feelings of self-confidence and hope (Hope, Heimberg, and Turk 2006). We add in a reward for the hard work of facing fear, and self-management is achieved. When we do all these activities by remaining focused in the moment, we are practicing participating.

Participating requires that we get active and engage with our lives. We cannot participate while lying in bed with the covers pulled over our heads. We have to get up and get involved with life. When we choose to participate we immediately find our-selves face-to-face with what needs doing, and our mastery tasks are ready for our attention. In choosing to participate we tap into wise mind and follow the DBT dictum to avoid avoiding (Linehan 1993a).

Exercises for Getting Back in the Game

Have you been socially isolated for a while? Here are ten steps, in increasing order of difficulty, to help you get back in the game. Take them at a pace that feels just a tiny bit uncomfortable to chal-lenge yourself.

1. Go to a neighborhood coffee shop. Chat about the weather with someone in line or behind the counter. Smile and make eye contact. Don't judge yourself or the other person about the interaction. Then sit and drink your beverage in the company of others. Pay attention in the moment to the moment.

2. Go to a farmers' market or a flower market. Walk around and speak to the vendors about what they are selling. Ask what a particular flower or vegetable is called, how hard it is to grow, and so on. Be open to however the interaction unfolds. Stay for forty-five minutes, focusing on remaining present for the experience.

3. *Make a list of all the people whose birthdays you would like to acknowledge and then take steps to do so. Send a card or postcard, write an e-mail, or make a phone call on or near their birthdays.*

4. *Call up an elderly relative or neighbor you have been avoiding and have a nice chat or, better yet, a visit. Bring food, flowers, or pictures to show. Stay at least thirty minutes and fully engage.*

5. *Ask a friend or family member to go with you to a free concert or lecture. After the event, have coffee together to discuss what you heard. Practice being in the present moment and not focusing on whether or not you like or agree with anything.*

6. *Volunteer to work at a community event that is in accordance with your values, such as handing out water at a fun run or selling raffle tickets for a school project. Look for something you'd like to do more than once. Don't be concerned with how successful you are or whether you have fun.*

7. *Offer to help a neighbor, coworker, or friend with a task such as raking leaves, shoveling snow, figuring out something on the computer, or resolving a problem with paperwork. Throw yourself into helping. Don't worry about whether they seem appreciative enough or whether you feel you really helped. Don't think about how you need someone to call you up and offer to help. Be that person for someone else and see what happens.*

8. *Take a beginning class in drawing, painting, or calligraphy and do the best you can. Do not judge your efforts. Frame one of your art works and hang it where you will see it, to remind yourself of your effort.*

9. *Take an introductory lesson to learn a percussion instrument such as marimba or drums. Throw yourself into learning. See if you can have fun.*

10. *Go to a dance where you don't have to have a partner (such as a Sufi or African dance) and join in the circle. Try not to judge yourself or anyone else for how well they go through the movements. Plan to go at least twice.*

This concludes our discussion of the what skills of observing, describing, and participating. If you have not already done so, you may want to review these skills and exercises and find ways to practice them. In the next three chapters we will focus on the how skills—nonjudgmentally, one-mindfully in the moment, and effectively—additional tools we can use to help us reach wise mind.

Chapter 7

NONJUDGMENT DAY

IS COMING

When I was much younger I was emotionally unstable. I drank too much and slept around. After a suicide attempt in my twenties, I was diagnosed with bipolar disorder. Before my diagnosis, I described myself as a "bad person." After my diagnosis I described myself as a "bad, crazy person." Even in my early thirties when I'd been sober for years, kept a job, and had some friends, I was still "no good" in my own mind. I thought anyone who wanted to get close to me was either a fool or a loser. All of this started to change when I stopped judging myself all the time. —Willa, 38

The Problem: Judgments
Intensify Emotions

For many of us, judging others and ourselves feels right, especially when we are emotional. We learn this kind of judgment in childhood, mainly by being judged ourselves. We judge ourselves when we are disappointed, angry, or afraid. We judge others when they don't measure up to our standards for behavior, appearance, or beliefs. Seeing things in black and white, right and wrong, can be emotionally validating because it agrees with the way our emotion mind sees things. Unfortunately, judgments increase emotions and decrease clarity. Judgments destroy perspective and narrow the mind. The more we judge, the more we distort and the more our emotions take control.

A certain amount of judgment comes naturally. As hunters and gatherers, we had to distinguish between wholesome and poisonous plants, learn which animals were worth expending the energy required to hunt them, and know which people were friendly and which were potential threats to us or to our tribe. Thus we learned the good and bad plants, the right and wrong animals, and the good and bad people. This shorthand, passed down through generations, communicated information important to our survival (Diamond 2012).

In families, schools, churches, and communities, children are taught the shorthand of "good" and "bad." "Good" is whatever is preferred by our culture, such as being clean, obeying the rules, and not causing trouble. "Bad" is whatever our society dislikes, such as being dirty, flouting the rules, and being demanding. These lessons are important for a child's survival, especially in the social sphere (Diamond 2012). Over time, however, the rules change, from group to group and region to region. For example, it was once quite acceptable to smoke cigarettes. Smoking was considered "good," even fashionable and sophisticated. Now smoking is considered "bad"—a smelly, unhealthy habit practiced by people who should know better.

The shorthand of judgment persists because it communicates efficiently. As children we have limited skills to understand why one behavior is preferred over another. We are told that hitting is bad and picking up our toys is good. These messages transmit the parents' wishes with the force and power of emotion and get their point across quite well. "I don't like it when you hit me" or "I would appreciate it if you picked up your toys" don't have the same rhetorical punch.

Though efficient, the shorthand of judgment limits information. Let's take the shorthand statement, "Pete is a weird old man." Instead of learning that Pete is an avid birder who rides a bicycle and volunteers at the library, the shorthand calls to mind a negative stereotype. The same is true for "hot babe," "soccer mom," or "nightmare boss." When I describe someone with a stereotype, I limit my possibilities of perceiving that person as an individual.

An extreme example of how good/bad shorthand distorts reality is prejudice. If we believe that people who belong to specific cultural or racial groups, who espouse particular religious or political viewpoints, or who live in certain neighborhoods or regions are "bad," then we are likely to disregard any information that might suggest another possibility. We may even deny well-established facts because facts could complicate our wish to believe what we want to believe about people we judge as bad. Prejudice allows us to disregard the facts and remain in emotion mind while also feeling fully justified in hating others (Czopp, Monteith, and Mark 2006).

The most damaging judgments, however, are those we level at ourselves. Intense self-judging behavior is learned in an invalidating environment of childhood (Linehan 1993). When we are persistently told as children that we are bad, lazy, stupid, overly sensitive, or a disappointment, we internalize these judgments as facts about who we are. Every time we make a mistake, we interpret it as evidence that we are defective. We also overlook valuable evidence that counters these judgments. If, as children, we were constantly confronted with our failures, we may ignore or downplay our accomplishments when they do occur, no matter how significant they might be (Linehan 1993).

Judging one's own needs and emotions as bad is common among people who struggle with a punishing inner judge. The inner judge, taking a page from the playbook of the invalidating environment, insists that it is bad to have certain emotions or to have needs that make demands on the environment. *If you weren't so _____, you wouldn't have needs and emotions that inconvenience others or cause them to criticize you!* says the inner judge. We fill in the blank with our favorite judgment and enter the hell of self-loathing, condemned for the sins of having basic needs and emotions.

The Solution: Nonjudgment

The solution to the problems associated with the good/bad dichotomy is the skill of nonjudgment, the first how skill (Linehan, 1993a). How skills delineate how to practice the what skills. Thus nonjudgment is a crucial part of the skills we have already learned; observing, describing, and participating all include the element of nonjudgment.

When we observe nonjudgmentally, we notice specific characteristics without shifting into judging them. If we are looking at a spider, for example, we notice the shape of its body, the length of its legs, whether it is attached to a web, and what the web looks like. As we observe, we resist indulging in thoughts of how bad and ugly the spider is, judgments that are likely to increase fear and disgust. Instead we can examine it to see whether it resembles any spiders we know to be poisonous, such as a black widow or a brown recluse.

Next we describe the spider. Rather than saying how evil looking it is, we verbalize the facts only—its size, species, behavior, and so on. We can even do research to learn more about the spider so we can describe it more accurately, including its habits and habitats.

Finally, when we participate with the spider, we act from wise mind. We don't necessarily have to kill it just because we despise spiders and find them scary and horrible. We surf our emotional urges, such as whether we wish to smash the spider or save it. We consider the possibility of being bitten by the spider. We consider what would happen if we left it alone. If wise mind tells us to kill the spider, then we do. If wise mind suggests we can safely put it outside or leave it alone, we do that.

We all have emotional reactions to spiders, such as fear and disgust, interest and curiosity. Emotional reactions are not in and of themselves judgments, but they can lead to judgments. Whenever our emotions are strong, practicing nonjudgment can help us re-regulate and avoid falling into emotion mind.

The problems associated with judging spiders may not be significant (other than contributing to unnecessary spider deaths), but when you consider how you might judge your in-laws, your neighbors, your boss, or yourself, it is easy to see the problems with judging. The skill of nonjudgment also can be effectively applied to your own being, including your body, life, character, and worthiness.

Judgments engage with our emotions and stimulate them. Nonjudgment helps us to reduce the emotional thoughts and words and become less emotionally involved. "Downregulation" is a medical term defined as the process of reducing or suppressing a response to a stimulus (Merriam-Webster 2014). Psychologists have borrowed the term to refer to any process that causes a person to be less reactive to emotions. Nonjudgment thus helps us step back from emotional thinking and enter wise mind's waiting room. To become adept at assuming a nonjudgmental position, we have to practice frequently and accept that we will never be perfect. With diligent practice, nonjudgment becomes second nature.

Let's break the concept of nonjudgment into steps and examine each step.

Assume a Nonjudgmental Position

What does it mean to assume a nonjudgmental position? First we have to be willing—to want to try. Sometimes we are emotionally attached to our judgments and to the act of judging, especially regarding ourselves. For example, we might not want to give up the idea of ourselves as being a failure. Perhaps we have thought that for so long and with such intensity that it seems more like the truth handed down from on high. Letting go of that judgment might cause us to feel at risk, as if it is somehow protective to believe this about ourselves. Letting go of judging in general might feel like traveling through a country with no landmarks. How will we know what is good or bad, right or wrong?

To assume a nonjudgmental position, we only have to try it out and see how it feels. We can always go back to judging if we feel we must. In fact, judging is so automatic for most of us that it is nearly impossible to give it up completely, except intentionally and in the moment. The first step is being willing to try.

Observe and Describe the Judgments

The next step is to slow down and notice your judgments (Linehan 1993a). Judgments can come so fast and furiously that we might not even notice them as judgments. We can start by observing a bad feeling and then describing that feeling to ourselves. Let's say that we feel a friend has been monopolizing the conversation. If we say, *I notice I am feeling judgmental toward Dylan*, this moment of recognition builds in a brief pause.

Once we've noticed what we are feeling, we next describe the facts of the situation. The facts are just the facts. We don't have to pretty them up or reframe them as "good" instead of "bad."

We don't have to make them reflect more positively on Dylan, as in, *Dylan is well educated, so of course he talks a lot.* Nor do we have to invalidate ourselves, as in, *If I weren't such a wimp I'd break into the conversation.* And, of course, we don't want to give in to the urge and yell, "Dylan, you are such a know-it-all!" Rather, we need to describe to ourselves the facts and feelings that are affecting us. *I am reacting to how much he is talking. I am feeling afraid to break into the conversation.* This is not judging but stating the facts and how they make us feel. If the facts change, our opinions will change. We don't need to form an opinion of Dylan, the situation, or ourselves beyond these simple facts. Nonjudgment does not make a problematic situation go away. But it can keep us in touch with the facts and help us better regulate our emotions.

Focus on the Consequences

Another step in reaching a nonjudgmental position is to consider the consequences of the behavior we are judging (Linehan 1993a). Certain behaviors have predictable, well-established consequences. For example, it is well known that smoking cigarettes contributes to health problems. So rather than saying, *Smoking is a bad, stupid thing to do,* we can simply state, *Smoking causes heart and lung problems.* And rather than saying, *People who smoke are idiots who don't care about themselves,* which assumes we understand people's motivations, we can say, *People who smoke put their health at risk.* In both instances these reframes are factual statements of the consequences of smoking.

If we don't have enough facts to determine the consequences, all we have is our hunches, intuitions, and opinions. Expressing our opinions as opinions establishes the fact that our opinions can only be taken so far. So, for example, if we think someone is less than truthful but don't have the facts to back up our hunch, we don't rush to judgment that this person is a liar. Instead, if we need to say anything at all, we could say, *I have a hunch that he is not telling me the truth, but I have no evidence to back up my hunch.* Making such mindful distinctions keeps us from rushing to a conclusion based on little or no evidence. Gaining distance from suspicions not grounded in facts brings us closer to wise mind.

Don't Judge the Judging!

People can become alarmed when they notice how many judgments go through their minds in a short while. This realization can evoke a lot of self-judgment (Linehan 1993a). When we first start practicing nonjudgment we can feel like we are the most judgmental person in the world and that becoming less judgmental is hopeless. We might even feel like a hypocrite for trying.

Many years ago, I noticed that I was particularly judgmental in airports. Airports are crowded, stressful places, and I noticed that my reaction to my own and others' stress was to respond with judgmental thoughts. *That man is an ass,* I would say to myself about someone pushing forward in line and bumping me with his suitcase. Then I would feel guilty and judge myself. *What is wrong with me? I am so judgmental!* The end result was that I felt alternately angry and guilty even as I continued to judge others and myself.

When I started traveling a lot to teach DBT, I decided to make airports my place for intensive practice of nonjudgment toward others, and also toward myself. When a judgment arises, rather than either dwelling on it or blaming myself for having it, I simply let it go, using Teflon mind. I have found that, while nonjudgment is hard to do, it pays off. I am more focused in the moment, more relaxed, and less reactive when I practice, which in turn makes flying, though rarely enjoyable, at least tolerable. I have noticed my judgments overall have decreased a lot, both in frequency and in intensity.

•   Maya's Story

Maya, a twenty-nine-year-old woman, was a writer whose first novel won a prestigious prize. With her second novel, she was in the throes of writer's block. When I first met her, she had passed her deadline by over a year. Maya had intense shame and self-loathing associated with what she interpreted as "my utter and complete failure as a writer."

Maya reported that her problems started when she began her first big revision. At the time, Maya would sit at her computer, write a sentence or even a paragraph, then read it aloud and start in on the criticisms. *This is garbage*, she'd say to herself. *I am losing it.* Then she would delete what she'd written and start over, the sense of dread and self-hatred growing the more she wrote and deleted. Finally, overcome with emotion, she simply sat at the computer and cried in frustration and self-loathing. After months of attempting the revision, Maya started spending entire days pacing the floor of her apartment, unable to write a single word. She had begun noticing that during these days her internal monologue was particularly brutal. *You fooled them the first time*, she would say to herself, *but this time they'll see you for the one-hit wonder you are. You don't have the talent for another round. You are a bad writer.* She was intensely anxious and miserable and pressure was mounting.

Maya was used to high expectations. "When I was growing up, Mom was like a Marine drill sergeant. She was never satisfied. Her favorite thing to say when she thought I was slacking was, 'Being smart is not good enough. You can be smart and a worthless failure.' I guess I never believed I was a failure before. The problem is, now I do."

Maya agreed to try for a full week to compose only, without revising. As she wrote she pushed aside any evaluations of what she was writing. *I am writing now;*

that is all, she said to herself like a mantra. Maya agreed not to even read over what she had written and to be vigilant about judgmental self-talk and negative predictions about future outcomes. She was anxious as she began, but gradually she relaxed into the process and wrote as many as ten pages each day. "I hope I don't find out this is all garb—er, not usable," she said. But she kept on writing without revising.

Once Maya was able to write freely without becoming paralyzed by her judgments, we considered how she could return to revising. "I am amazed at how anxious this makes me," she said. "I notice how brutal and constant my judgments are. I would never talk to anyone the way I talk to myself!" Over the next few weeks, Maya revised and practiced commenting on her work without resorting to judgmental language. "It really isn't all that helpful to condemn something as 'garbage' anyway," she said. "That doesn't tell you how to fix it." Instead of blanket condemnations, Maya would say, "This section needs more clarity," or "I think this descriptive passage goes on a little too long and might lose the reader." With this kind of criticism, Maya was free to revise without fear of failure overtaking her. She came to accept that her process with this book was more challenging than with the first book. "The first book just rolled right out of me," she said. "This one is much more challenging. I have to encourage myself through this and refuse to attack myself or my work." By focusing more on her experience of writing and revising and less on producing a perfect product, Maya relaxed into her task. After three months, she sent a section to her editor and got feedback that the book was shaping up nicely. The relief she felt was almost overwhelming.

"I am starting to forget about whether this book is as good as the first one," Maya said. "It's just a different kind of book. If the critics like it, great; if not, I'll figure out how to deal with that too. But I know one thing for sure, I couldn't have completed it without learning to assume a nonjudgmental position and just write." Maya's second novel did not win awards like her first one, but it did get widely and mostly positively reviewed. When I saw her last, she was happily at work on a third novel and having no problems with writer's block. "I remembered that I love to write," she said. "I am not thinking about whether it is going to win awards. I just want it to feel right to me. And so far, it does. "

The Obstacle: Distinguishing Judgments from Preferences, Values, and Discernment

Preferences, values, and discernment are not judgments, but they sometimes get confused with judgments. Preferences are opinions that we hold strongly: *I don't like sodium vapor lights because I prefer the dark.* This statement is not a judgment. However, if I say, *Sodium vapor lights obscure the stars, and the people who install them are stupid,* I have paired a fact (*obscure the stars*) with an opinion (*the people who install them are stupid*). Judgments state opinions as if they are facts. Stating opinions as facts creates confusion and increases emotion. We may suppress facts that don't support our opinions or contort reality to reflect our emotions.

Values are preferences or beliefs that we hold strongly. Expressing our values does not constitute making a judgment. For example, if I say, *I do not like the taste of pork,* that is a preference. If I say, *I do not eat pork for religious reasons,* that is a values statement: my religion prescribes certain dietary rules and I value following those rules. If, on the other hand, I say, *Anyone who eats pork is a no-good fool,* I have just made a judgment (while also insulting bacon lovers everywhere). Stating a value as a value allows us to recognize that it is not a fact, but an opinion. We may strongly hold that value, but stating it as a fact will only inflame our passions, put relationships with anyone who disagrees at risk, and make us highly vulnerable to emotion mind. An easy place to start using nonjudgment is to express a value as a value and a preference as a preference.

Discernment is the kind of judgment we refer to when we describe behavior as "showing good judgment." Discernment allows us to see or understand differences and is a necessary skill that we use every day. We are discerning when we derive an opinion based on facts. This can be the basis for deciding who deserves our vote, which car we want to buy, which dog is the best representative of its breed, or even whether a piece of fruit is ready to eat. We see this kind of judging in a court of law, when deciding whether or not the accused broke a law. Do we have adequate information upon which to base our decision? Which information is relevant and trustworthy, and why? When there are not enough facts upon which to base a conclusive opinion, we step back from making a judgment. Should new facts arise, the judgment may change. These are ways to know that we are exercising discernment rather than judgment.

Below are exercises to help you strengthen your practice of nonjudgment.

Exercises to Reduce Judgments of Others

1. *Count your judgments of others.* This exercise is particularly useful in helping you practice observing judgments of others and stepping back from them (Linehan 1993a). It operates like Teflon mind, in that no effort is made to reframe the judgments. The object is to notice judgments occurring and then let them go.

Get a little counter-clicker that golfers use to count their strokes. Carry it with you when you go to the airport, the gym, your doctor's office, a class, a family dinner, or anywhere you find yourself making a lot of judgments about other people. Simply keep tally. Don't try to reframe; simply note and count the judgments. Later, if you are so inclined, you can graph them as to location and frequency over time.

2. *Reframe on the fly.* Here, rather than counting the judgments as in the exercise above, your effort is to restate them using nonjudgment. As soon as you notice yourself judging someone or something, step back and reframe the situation as it pertains only to the facts. Don't put a spin on it; don't restate it to the positive. Simply look to the facts and restate your judgment as fact. In reframing, the statement *That woman is an idiot!* becomes *That woman pulled out in front of me and endangered us both.*

Exercise to Restructure Idealizing and Demonizing Judgments of Others

The object of this exercise is to bring our attention to important people in our lives that we either idealize or demonize. The feelings we have about the people we choose for this exercise are not likely to change in their nature—that is, we are not likely to stop esteeming one person and disliking another. The negative emotions we feel regarding the person we dislike may decrease in intensity, at least in the moment and perhaps over time, however, while the positive emotions we feel for the person we esteem are unlikely to decrease. At first this practice may feel overwhelming, especially if we have been avoiding contact with the negative emotions regarding the person we dislike. The more we practice, however, the more access we will have to the down-regulating properties of nonjudgment. Noticing our tendency to idealize or demonize people will help us step back from this emotion mind behavior that is rooted in judgment and can blind us to the reality that all people have both strengths and shortcomings.

1. Select two people: one whom you greatly esteem, admire, or respect; the other someone you dislike intensely or hate. These people can be living or dead, and can be known to you personally or even be public or historical figures.

2. On one sheet of paper write the name of the esteemed person, followed by ten one-word judgments about him or her, such as *brilliant, wise, kind,* or *loving.* These may not feel like judgments, but write them down anyway. On a second sheet, do the same for the disliked person, using more judgments, such as *arrogant, greedy,* or *callous.*

3. Beginning with the esteemed person, unpack each of the words that are shorthand expressions of your respect into statements of factual evidence. For example, suppose your esteemed person is your grandmother. If you have the word *brilliant,* you might describe her as *learned to speak English after coming from her home country when she was sixty.* For *wise,* you might say, *fed her family well from traditional recipes on very little money.* And so forth.

4. Turning to the disliked person, unpack each judgmental word with facts. If this person is your supervisor at work, for *arrogant,* you might say, *walks into my office, interrupts my phone conversations, and tells me what to do.* For *greedy,* you might say, *talks frequently to me about how much money he makes.* For *callous,* you might say, *doesn't seem to be concerned about giving me a raise.*

5. If you have judgmental words you cannot unpack, simply circle them and come back to them later. With a cooler head you may be able to find ways to reframe them. If you cannot find a factual basis for them, you can just put a line through them.

Exercise to Reduce Judgments Toward Yourself

The object of this exercise is to observe and describe and then restructure how we talk to ourselves about ourselves. These activities work with both positive and negative judgments of the self.

1. List your judgments. Write down as many judgments as you can about yourself. Stick with the judgments you are most likely to hear in your internal monologue. Don't worry about judgments you have heard from others unless you also subscribe to them. Include judgments about your body, face, clothes, hair, intelligence, values, personality, life history, degree of success, and talents or lack thereof.

2. See if you can reframe each judgment as a statement of fact, using the what skill of describing. If you judge yourself as *weak*, you might reframe this as *cannot yet resist overeating on most days*. If you judge yourself as *a loser*, reframe it as *don't have as many friends as I would like*. Work with a focus on consequences: *As a result of my alcoholism, I lost several jobs and am now underemployed*. If the judgment has no basis in fact, put a line through it and acknowledge it as nonfactual.

3. If you have a judgment that is also a statement of fact, state it without the tone of judgment. For example, if you judge yourself as *fat*, state it as *I have a body mass index of 29.5*. If you judge yourself as *bankrupt*, state it as *I filed for bankruptcy last year*.

4. Don't neglect the judgments you have about yourself that are positive. For example, perhaps you often say about yourself that you are smart, kind, or caring. Write down as many positive judgments as you can and reframe those also. For example, instead of *kind*, you could make a list of behaviors or activities you do that you consider kind, such as *volunteer at the animal shelter*. Look for statements of fact that illustrate the shorthand descriptors.

Nonjudgment is one of the most difficult of all the mindfulness skills, and a great deal of practice is needed to get the hang of it. The payoff is that reducing judgments also reduces our emotion dysregulation, improves our relationships, and increases self-compassion.

• *Jared's Story*

Jared, a forty-one-year-old man, entered DBT at the recommendation of his psychiatrist. He had stopped using heroin and was taking Suboxone for his opiate addiction. Jared had used heroin off and on for about five years. Prior to that he had abused prescription opiates. His income from a trust provided his financial support, so he did not have the kind of pressures from his environment that many people with addictions have.

After six months in DBT class, Jared had not improved in his skills use as much as he wanted. He remained very depressed and hopeless. He refused to let go of the option of killing himself, though he would make commitments to stay alive for a month at a time. Jared's attendance in skills group had been spotty, and his use of skills was limited. Other than suicidal behavior and the possibility he would return to drugs, the main problem Jared faced was his intense judgment of himself and others.

One day, Jared discontinued Suboxone without telling anyone and a week later he attempted to overdose on drugs. The event that prompted Jared's suicide attempt was an argument with Tom, his partner of four years, over their joint operation of a small inn. Tom managed the kitchen, supervised the employees, and kept the books, working sometimes sixty hours a week, in contrast to Jared's average of about twenty hours a week. After the overdose, Tom broke up with Jared. He moved out of Jared's house and started applying for other positions. Jared was deeply hurt and angry with Tom and with himself.

"Who can blame the poor guy?" Jared said. "I've been a bastard to him. But I'm better off without him, the prick." His face contorted with pain.

Jared's persistent self-invalidation, judgments, and pessimism were impenetrable. He adopted more and more extreme statements on behalf of his own worthlessness and the vanity, greed, and cruelty of others. I pointed out that a commitment to staying alive was required to remain in therapy. "Okay," he said, "but I don't deserve help. I'm not really worth it."

Jared made a commitment to practice restructuring each judgment and self-invalidation he uttered aloud in session. Each time he had to unpack a judgment, we learned more about his fears, shame, disappointments, and even hopes. He became less emotionally vulnerable because he wasn't always inflaming his emotions with extreme statements. By reducing his judgments, Jared also reduced his unrealistic expectations of himself and others. He began to accept himself enough to have hope for his life.

"I used to live in a constant barrage of self-hatred," Jared said one day. "I don't think I could even hear what anybody else was saying to me. I still catch myself judging all the time. But at least I recognize it! Too bad I couldn't have learned this before Tom left."

Nonjudgment is a skill that helps us see reality as it actually is, rather than through the scrim of emotion mind. When we begin practicing seriously, we immediately experience some emotional down-regulation and increased clarity of mind. At the core of nonjudgment is a willingness to eschew judgment of the self. Even when we are deeply disappointed in ourselves, have

THE MINDFULNESS SOLUTION FOR INTENSE EMOTIONS

fallen short of our expectations, or have indulged in an orgy of judgment of others, we turn away from self-judgment. As soon as we do, our compassion for ourselves increases.

Practice Loving-Kindness

Metta, or loving-kindness, is an ancient Buddhist practice. Its essential focus is wishing someone to be free from suffering and to find peace. There are no judgments involved and no reframing. To engage in this practice (for which audio is available at http://www.newharbinger.com/33001), you must be willing to let go of thoughts of hatred or vengeance. I learned this particular way of practicing metta from my friend and colleague Randy Wolbert. It is helpful in showing us what we need to do to practice peace, the ultimate goal of nonjudgment. Recently metta has been effective as part of a treatment for PTSD (Thompson and Waltz 2008; Hinton et al. 2013).

1. Tear a sheet of paper into six pieces.

2. On the first piece of paper, write the name of someone about whom you have little or no opinion, either positive or negative. This person could be a neighbor, a work acquaintance, or someone you encounter while shopping, such as a clerk, waiter, or proprietor.

3. On the second piece of paper, write down the name of someone who is annoying to you and whom you sometimes judge. This could be a work colleague, relative, friend, or acquaintance. This is not someone who has really hurt you, but simply someone toward whom you frequently feel judgmental.

4. On the third piece of paper, write the name of someone you profoundly judge and dislike intensely, or even hate. This person can be someone you know or a public figure, living

or dead. You could use the same person as in the "Idealizing and Demonizing" exercise earlier in this chapter.

5. On the fourth piece of paper write the name of someone you greatly esteem, admire, and respect. Again, this person can be someone known to you or a public figure and can be living or dead, and it could be the person used in the "Idealizing and Demonizing" exercise.

6. On the last sheet of paper write your own name.

7. Turn over the first piece of paper and regard the name you have written. Say to yourself, *May _____ (say the name) be free from suffering and find peace.* Notice how you feel.

8. Turn over the second piece of paper and regard the name you have written. Say to yourself, *May _____ be free from suffering and find peace.* Notice any emotions or bodily sensations. Notice thoughts arising, but do not follow them. Continue with your practice.

9. Go through each piece of paper. For each name say, *May _____ be free from suffering and find peace.* Notice the thoughts, emotions, bodily sensations, and action urges that arise. Do not push anything away. Do not cling to anything. Finally, when you arrive at your own name, repeat the phrase. Notice how it feels. Allow yourself to feel whatever you feel. When you are finished, do not evaluate or judge your practice. Simply put it aside. You may wish to save the papers to do further practice.

10. Practice as frequently as you like. Increase the time you practice from five to fifteen minutes.

Nonjudging helps us to downregulate emotions that intensify when we judge things as good or bad, right or wrong. When we practice this skill we no longer need to state our opinions as facts, unless they are. We can label our preferences and values for what they are, without judgment of ourselves for having them or of others for having different ones. We can see the consequences of certain behaviors, harmful or helpful, and describe them as such without judging. The diligent practice of nonjudgment leads to increased clarity about reality and increased acceptance of others and ourselves.

Chapter 8

THE POWER OF FOCUS: ONE-MINDFULLY IN THE MOMENT

When I'm going through a rough time or feeling really emotional for some reason, the hardest thing for me to do is focus. My mind is so caught up in whatever I'm stressing about that I just can't concentrate. At home I start one chore, like cleaning the litter box, then drop that and go to another, like doing my laundry. The end result is that the cat litter gets emptied but not refilled and the laundry gets washed but not dried and it mildews. At the restaurant where I work, I go into the kitchen for a customer request, get caught up in an argument with the cook, then forget what I was after, go back to my tables, and get yelled at. Even when I'm not freaked out I'm always doing two or more things at once, like driving and putting on my makeup or talking with my mother and surfing the web. It's especially bad when I have PMS. Everybody tells me I really need to focus, but I just don't know how. —Adrianne, 33

Multitasking is often defined as doing two or more things at once. However, it is impossible for our brains to focus on more than one thing at a time. Thus when we multitask we are actually toggling back and forth between two foci of attention. Some tasks require only an easy, low-risk toggle, such as folding clothes while watching television or having a conversation while eating dinner. Tasks that require rapid toggling, however, can cause significant stress, put us at risk for mistakes, and make us more vulnerable to emotions (Rubenstein, Meyer, and Evans 2001). For example, a driver talking on a cell phone is as impaired as a driver who is over the legal blood-alcohol level (Strayer, Drews, and Crouch 2006). We are more likely to multitask when we are distressed, and multitasking itself causes distress (Rubenstein, Meyer, and Evans 2001).

The Problem: Multitasking Makes Us More Vulnerable

We may think multitasking helps us get things done more efficiently, but in fact, multitasking is highly inefficient. Each movement between tasks constitutes an interruption, switches our focus, wastes time, and contributes to mistakes (Rubenstein, Meyer, and Evans 2001). A study of work interruptions conducted at the University of California, Irvine, found that, on average, it took nearly half an hour for workers interrupted at their desks by coworkers to return to the tasks they were doing, resulting in a significant increase in mistakes after the interruptions (Mark, Gonzalez, and Harris 2005).

Multitasking also makes us less aware of real threats in our environment. A lifeguard engaged in conversation doesn't notice a child drowning (The Daily Mail Reporter, United Kingdom, April 19, 2013). A woman listening to an audiobook while walking on a train track doesn't hear the train and is run down (*The Minneapolis Star Tribune*, May 2, 2013). A zookeeper talking on a cell phone while cleaning a cage doesn't notice the stealthy lion before it swats and kills her (Associated Press, March 8, 2013). We read about these kinds of accidents every day.

Nonetheless, because of the overwhelming demands of our lives, at times we are forced to multitask. Some jobs, such as mother, air traffic controller, soldier, or emergency medical technician, require frequent multitasking. When we are in such demanding environments, we must constantly assess the priorities and toggle from one demand to another based on each decision, increasing the likelihood that we will experience emotional distress. For example, a mother who is bathing her toddler when her infant awakens and begins to cry must decide how to attend to both as quickly and safely as possible. These kinds of situations arise for her dozens of times a day. No wonder she feels exhausted at bedtime!

Multitasking is especially stressful when the demands competing for attention are of equal intensity and importance, such as when two airplanes need the same runway or when a pressing meeting at work conflicts with an important personal occasion such as an anniversary celebration (Rubenstein, Meyer, and Evans 2001). Stress hormones interfere with short-term memory and contribute to stomachaches, headaches, and back pain as well as suppressed immune functioning (Schneiderman, Ironson, and Siegel 2005). The National Institute for Occupational Safety and Health reports that exposure to unremitting stress on the job can contribute to depression and heart disease (NIOSH 1999). Chronic multitasking can make it more difficult to relax and focus on one thing at a time, even when the opportunity to do so appears (Mark, Gonzalez, and Harris 2005). Thus multitasking makes us more vulnerable to errors, risks, and stress, thereby increasing any problems we already have with emotion regulation.

The Solution: One-Mindfully in the Moment

The solution to the stress and vulnerability of multitasking is to take time to focus. Practicing one-mindfully in the moment (OMM), the second how skill, can help us develop this focus (Linehan 1993a). To practice OMM, we need to (1) stop multitasking, (2) bring attention into the present, (3) select one activity to do, and (4) continue to focus on that activity without judgment (Linehan 1993a). We can practice OMM while working or playing, alone or with others, while moving through activities slowly, quickly, or at a normal speed. It can be practiced for a few minutes, an hour, or longer. As with all the how skills, OMM can be combined easily with any of the what skills (observing, describing, and participating) to good effect and is also compatible with the other how skills (nonjudgmentally and effectively).

OMM is deceptively simple yet effective for calming emotions and increasing access to wise mind (Linehan, 1993a). While resolutely doing one thing at a time, we begin to notice thoughts and emotions coming and going. When we feel the urge to multitask, we surf the urge as if it were a wave until it naturally dissipates, like a wave on a beach. Thus while paying bills online we resist the urge to check e-mail; while cleaning we resist the urge to return phone calls; and while driving we resist the urge to read the text that just arrived. These wise choices reduce stress, risk, and errors, and actually save time. We become less distracted and harried and more in touch with wise mind.

Practicing OMM can contribute to a calmer, less intense emotional experience even if we are not chronic multitaskers. We can reduce stress by choosing to eliminate even seemingly benign multitasking habits such as reading while eating, listening to a book on tape while driving, or moving from one uncompleted task to another simply out of boredom or habit. Instead we can practice OMM and deliberately complete one task before starting the next while keeping our attention in the present moment. When judgments or worry thoughts arise, we can let them slip out of our awareness. When we find ourselves day-dreaming, we bring our focus back to the now. Mundane activities such as filing, cooking, dressing, or putting away toys can become meditative activities; driving to work can be a time of awareness and acceptance; and getting ready for bed can transform into a time of making a quiet connection to the breath.

Must we always do things so deliberately and one-mindfully? Of course not. Most of us would not be able to keep up with busy schedules without combining some simple, familiar tasks. However, the more we practice OMM, the more likely we are to notice its benefits. With fewer distractions, we notice more, remember better, and feel calmer and more centered. Plus, doing one thing at a time mindfully engages our short-term memory: we are more likely to keep track of time and remember important details, which contributes to a further reduction in stress (Zeidan et al. 2011).

Because of its calming effects, OMM is a good skill for getting through a crisis (Linehan 1993a). When we are beset by intense emotions, the urges to act become quite compelling. The skill of OMM gives the mind something other than those urges to focus on, allowing us to tolerate the emotion without acting on the urges and possibly making the situation worse. OMM quiets the ruminations and distortions of emotion mind. Anchored in the moment and focused on the task before us, the mind can settle into the breath while the body carries out whatever activity is before it.

Simple physical tasks are especially helpful for the practice of OMM. We can weed the garden, empty the wastebaskets, brush the dog, mop the floor, make the bed—each task one at a time, while breathing, focusing in the moment, and allowing our minds and bodies to settle. Such work may not make us feel better *right away*, but it is unlikely to make us feel worse if we are focused by OMM. In the meantime our emotional sensations and urges slowly subside. Instead of engaging in problematic behavior or staying in a state of emotional paralysis, we have accomplished some simple tasks. When the mind is engaged in physical work, we can get through a crisis—and also have a cleaner house!

The power of simple work to calm the mind is well known. The Shakers, a religious sect that flourished in the nineteenth century, practiced work as prayer as they grew their gardens and made beautiful, functional furniture. Their saying was "Hands to work, hearts to God" (Burns and Stechler 1984). Physical work performed one-mindfully in the moment as prayer or service is part of many present-day spiritual communities and retreats. Working one-mindfully in the moment can put us in touch with wise mind, allow us to accept reality as it is, and appreciate work as a simple gift.

The Obstacle: Problems with Executive Functioning

If you find it hard to focus on one thing in the moment even when you are not distressed, you may have problems with executive functioning of the brain. Research has shown that people who prefer to multitask often score low on tests of executive functioning, which is the organizing and prioritizing role of the prefrontal cortex, described in chapter 2 (Sanbonmatsu et al. 2013). The box that follows lists the abilities associated with effective executive functioning of the brain.

One aspect of executive functioning is the ability to use something called *working memory*. Working memory can best be described as a set of processes that allow us to use the information present in both short- and long-term memory to solve problems or complete tasks. A good example of the use of working memory is the process we use when adding up a column of figures. Working memory helps us remember the subtotal of each column as we add the next column toward the goal of the final sum. While short-term memory allows us to retain information important in the short term, this information degrades quickly when not used (Cowan 2008). For many people, the act of multitasking creates obstacles to both short-term memory formation and the functioning of working memory (Ophir, Nass, and Wagner 2009). When working and short-term memory don't function well, we forget important details, leading to increased errors and associated stress.

Do you experience strong urges that distract you from a task when you really need to complete it? Research has shown that people who frequently multitask have a much harder time blocking out distractions when they work than those who multitask infrequently. Frequent multitaskers have problems with starting tasks, dealing with details, and managing time (Sanbonmatsu et al. 2013), problems that are associated with impaired executive functioning of the brain (Barkley 2012).

Executive functioning of the brain may be affected by attention deficit disorder, traumatic brain injury, dementia, certain learning disabilities, and depression (Barkley 2012). Chronic emotion dysregulation also interferes with executive functioning. Anyone in grief or an emotional crisis may experience a temporary breakdown of their ability to plan activities, organize themselves, and transition smoothly from one activity to another. The practice of OMM, while somewhat more difficult under these circumstances, may lead to improvement in executive functioning (Zeidan et al. 2010). OMM may also help us stay more focused on what behavior is expected in a given context and make us better able to read social cues.

Abilities Associated with Effective Executive Functioning

1. Initiating and completing tasks and obligations. Prioritizing tasks in a way that contributes to completion.

2. Planning events that are important to you—such as a move, a work project, a trip, or a family occasion.

3. Organizing space and materials so that personal possessions, important papers, tools, and other necessary items are accessible and in order.

4. Modulating emotions with reason. Regulating emotions based on facts.

5. Having an awareness of how one's behavior affects oneself and others. Noticing when your behavior is making others uncomfortable.

6. Inhibiting inappropriate behavior and resisting urges to behave in ways that are inconsistent with social norms.

7. Transitioning from one activity to another without undue distress.

8. Using short-term and working memory to complete a task or fulfill an obligation.

Source: Barkley 2012

Overcoming the Obstacle: Acting in Awareness

Research on mindfulness has looked at whether people with attention problems can benefit from mindfulness practices that teach *acting in awareness*, another name for "one-mindfully in the moment" (Sanbonmatsu et al. 2013). Studies indicate that adolescents and adults with attention problems—including depression, ADHD, traumatic brain injury, and even mild dementia—show benefit from such mindfulness practices (Greeson 2009; Grossman et al. 2004; McMillan et al. 2002; Bedard 2003; Paller et al. 2014). One-mindfully in the moment is easy to learn and can reduce anxiety and improve focus even when executive functioning is impaired. Here are some exercises that can strengthen your focus muscles and increase your ability to be one-mindfully in the moment.

Practicing One-Mindfully in the Moment

1. *Schedule a daily practice.* Select one routine activity and engage in it one-mindfully every day. Drink your morning coffee, drive or walk to and from work, cook, or complete sleep hygiene tasks, doing each task one-mindfully. Make these activities a daily form of meditation. Notice how you feel while doing them and immediately after. Do not evaluate the exercises or your ability to do them; simply do them, staying present as much as you can.

2. *Reduce overall multitasking.* Whenever you feel stressed, notice whether you are multitasking. Consider which task is your priority and focus only on that task for a while. Or see if you can find a way to do the tasks sequentially and one-mindfully rather than multitasking. Can you wait until you get

183

to the office to make that phone call? Can you sit at the table and eat your breakfast rather than trying to eat in the car?

3. *Step away from the media.* Turn off the radio or television; put aside your tablet or computer; turn off the ringer on your phone; and focus on the most important task at hand.

4. *Eat mindfully.* Do not read, watch television, or talk on the phone while eating. When you eat alone, eat mindfully. Chew each mouthful before taking another bite. Put down your fork between bites. Don't take seconds until you have finished what you have on your plate. Pause to check in with your stomach. Are you still hungry? When you eat with others, attend to the social nature of the meal but don't lose track of eating. Listen to and participate in the conversation, but pause and breathe before you take another bite or serve yourself more food. Make eating the primary activity and conversation secondary. Put down your fork and swallow before you begin speaking.

5. *Be present in conversation.* While on the phone, do not surf the web, read e-mail, fold clothes, or wash dishes. Sit down if you can. Focus all your attention on being present with the person with whom you are speaking. In meetings, simply breathe, listen, and speak as prompted by wise mind. Don't write notes, daydream, or scroll through your phone. Try not to doodle unless there is no other way you can focus. When conversing with a friend or family member, bring all your attention to the conversation. Listen without thinking about how you want to reply. Don't interrupt. Stay present in the moment to the conversation.

6. *Give and receive touch one-mindfully.* Whether you are having sex, giving or receiving a massage, petting your cat or dog, changing a diaper, or giving a child a bath, bring your whole attention to the practice. Feel the touch. Be the touch. Don't let your mind wander or stray. Experience the tactile interac-

tion fully, without distraction. Do not judge your experience or become distracted from what you feel. Try to remain fully present until the touch experience is complete.

7. *See your work as service.* Choose one aspect of your job and conduct it as if you were performing service to God, the Universe, or your higher self. Give considerable thought to which part of your work you want to use for practice. The simpler the task, the better. Once you have selected that piece, commit to practicing one-mindfully. For example, if you work as a health care professional, choose one patient to approach using OMM and seeing your work as service. Tend to that person's health care with your full attention, as if you were caring for someone you love dearly, such as a family member or close friend. Gradually extend the practice to all of your patients. If you work in a call center and have to deal with irate customers, focus your attention between calls and commit to bringing your higher self fully into the next encounter with a customer, without judgment. Do your best, but do not evaluate or become attached to whether you "succeed" at pleasing the person or solving a particular problem. One-mindfully attempt to stay as present as possible no matter what happens, using other skills as needed. Notice how it feels to do this. Then choose another aspect of your job to focus on as service.

8. *Appreciate nature.* Walk in a forest or desert, on the beach, or in a park or garden, noticing and appreciating all that you see. Do not allow your mind to wander to discursive thoughts. Focus on observing while walking, and notice what you experience outside yourself. Do not follow distractions. Allow yourself to fully feel any appreciation or wonder that may arise in your experience.

9. *Walk a labyrinth.* Labyrinths for walking meditation are available in many places. If there is one near you, plan a visit. Take your time making your way through the twists and turns,

noticing your thoughts coming and going. Notice urges to step over the boundaries, to be finished, or to walk away. Notice especially any emotions that arise. Continue until the end, simply walking and letting go of everything else.

10. *Appreciate other humans.* Sit where you can observe other people. One-mindfully appreciate how each person is unique, each has a unique set of fingerprints. Notice everything you can about that person and no other. Bring to mind how each person was a zygote, embryo, fetus, newborn, baby, toddler, child, teenager, and so forth. Each had parents who either loved them or didn't. Visualize each person as having her own dreams and desires, likes and dislikes, hopes and fears. Don't try to figure out what her dreams are. Simply appreciate that each person, like you, has her unique human qualities. When your mind wanders, bring it back to one-mindfully appreciating other human beings.

• *Lindsey's Story*

Lindsey, a thirty-four-year-old single mother, was a talented graphic artist who was attractive, bright, and lovable. In part due to her inability to focus, Lindsey constantly lived on the edge. As Lindsey would say, both truthfully and judgmentally, "My car is marginal, my house is a wreck, my job history is sketchy, and my finances are a disaster." The only part of her life that was somewhat organized was her care for her ten-year-old daughter, Ella.

Lindsey recognized that she needed to learn skills to help her focus. *Maybe if I could get off to a good start in the morning*, she said to herself. Her efforts to learn OMM began with one simple task: to make her bed each morning one-mindfully. She told herself that she could

186

not do anything else while making her bed, and that she couldn't just throw the comforter over the rumpled sheets and pillows. She also had to resist hyper-focus, such as making the bed with hospital corners. The assignment was to make the bed well, while breathing and focusing in the moment, a task that should take perhaps three minutes. Still, because of her habit of staying up past midnight and sleeping until the last moment, it took more than a month to get this new behavior established.

"I still don't like the morning, but I don't hate it anymore," Lindsey said. "Making the bed has become like my meditation. When I get right up and make my bed one-mindfully, it starts my day better."

For a second task, Lindsey decided on getting up before Ella, making Ella's lunch, and getting her to school on time. Ella expressed how much she liked having her mother make her lunch, which reinforced Lindsey's efforts. Practicing OMM while making her bed was a warm-up exercise for that goal.

After the routines of making the bed and getting through breakfast were established, Lindsey started making Ella's lunch one-mindfully. This task was more difficult because Ella would be talking to her, the phone might ring, and other distractions would increase as the morning progressed. But eventually, Lindsey's practice paid off. Ella went to school with a good breakfast and a homemade lunch. Unfortunately, they often departed too late for an on-time arrival at school. Achieving on-time arrival at school regularly took months of effort. Eventually, Lindsey succeeded, and as a result, she also improved her record of on-time arrival at work.

"On the days I get to work on time it is easier for me to settle into what I need to do," Lindsey acknowledged. "I'm getting to be a regular ace at OMM and I've noticed how much better I feel as a result. I'm not always screwing up!"

Once the morning routine was established, Lindsey was ready to try an evening ritual. After putting Ella to bed at nine o'clock and turning off the lights in the rest of her apartment, Lindsey began a set of activities that were easy to do one-mindfully and contributed to better sleep hygiene. She turned down the thermostat or opened the window to cool the room, turned on the reading lamp by her bed, and turned off her computer. She set her alarm on her phone and plugged it in to charge, then took a shower, brushed her teeth and hair, put on moisturizer, and slipped into bed. Each of these activities was done one at a time, slowly, deliberately, and one-mindfully no matter whether she felt calm or upset.

Once in bed, Lindsey could read or listen to music, but not get on her computer or phone. It was a struggle to establish these new habits, but Lindsey had noticed that when she used media late at night it was much harder to get to sleep before midnight. She was gradually able to turn off the electronics by nine thirty and unwind, and eventually she shifted her bedtime from one or two in the morning to eleven o'clock at night. At first, it took her longer to actually fall asleep, but eventually her circadian rhythms adjusted and she awoke earlier and more refreshed. Better sleep paid big dividends for Lindsey in the form of improved emotion regulation.

The practice of OMM increased Lindsey's awareness of her own mind and the urges she experienced around spending. "I've learned that I need to shop one-mindfully," she said. "If I go on autopilot, I end up with a lot of stuff I don't need. Last week I was ruminating about work when I went shopping. I spent an extra thirty dollars on things like artisanal cheese and out-of-season fruit." Lindsey committed to using a phone app to track her spending. Tracking slowed her down and made her more mindful of her impulses to buy, which helped her to pay for the things she really needed. Having the cash reduced the chronic shame Lindsey felt about always being short on funds.

The practice of OMM also helped Lindsey in her relationships with peers and family. Family members, friends, and boyfriends were constantly asking Lindsey to do things—such as to go out partying or lend them money—that she knew in her wise mind she either could not or should not do. These requests, especially from family, were the hardest for Lindsey to resist, and giving in to them contributed to being constantly in crisis.

We arrived at a plan for how to handle these requests. Whenever she was going on a date, out with friends, or visiting a family member, Lindsey would set a meditation timer on her phone to ring every fifteen minutes to remind her to focus. When the bells rang, Lindsey would take a deep breath, focus on herself in the moment, and remind herself of what she was doing and why.

"Last weekend I was at Mom and Joe's. Their dog had puppies and they are overwhelmed with finding homes for them all. They were even talking about taking them to the shelter. They were giving me the sales pitch and all of a sudden my meditation bell went off. I can't imagine what they thought, but that bell got me to say no to taking a puppy! The puppies were cute and all, but that is the last thing I need right now! In the past I am sure I would have gone home with at least one."

The second practice we implemented was to get Lindsey to notice whenever someone was making a request of her and to be prepared to answer thoughtfully. She could choose from two different replies: "I would like to say yes, but I need to think it over. Can I get back to you?" or "No, I really can't do that." Mastering this skill gave her a sense of empowerment. Lindsey's friends even appreciated her clarity, because now when she said she would do something she was less likely to call back later with regrets and excuses.

One day, late in our work together, Lindsey told me a story: "My boss came to me last week while I was finishing the spreadsheet for the end of the quarter. I have always been late with these reports in the past, plus they've been full of errors. My boss always criticized me for this. But this quarter I am right on schedule. I even had time to double-check my work. Anyway, she came up to my desk just as I was printing the final copy. She started to grill me, thinking I was going to be late. I went to the printer, got the document, and put it in her hand. She looked so surprised! She walked away without a word. Later she came back to my desk and apologized. She even complimented my accuracy. Then she asked me if I wanted to take on more spreadsheets, and I said, 'I would like to say yes, but let me get back to you.' Later I was able to come back and say, 'What I want to do is the graphics for the marketing campaigns, not the spreadsheets.' She agreed to let me!" Lindsey's sense of pride and self-efficacy had her beaming.

Mastering the skill of OMM was a turning point for Lindsey. She had a tool that allowed her to focus, accomplish tasks, and resist distractions. As a result, her intense emotions felt more under her control. Lindsey will probably always have to manage her attention issues and emotions, but OMM has become her go-to skill and she is rightfully proud of her results.

In summary, the more we know about multitasking, the more we realize how problematic it can be—causing us to be inefficient, error prone, and forgetful. Multitasking puts us at risk for accidents and increased emotional and physical stress. The opposite of multitasking is focusing on one thing at a time, the skill of one-mindfully in the moment.

Practicing OMM introduces a small oasis of calm into our days and increases our ability to appreciate each activity. As with all the other mindfulness skills, OMM has the effect of waking us up to ourselves in the moment. In becoming more awake and aware while engaging in tasks, we also become calmer and more efficient. Even if we have significant obstacles to OMM, such as ADHD or traumatic brain injury, we can become better with practice, increasing the likelihood that we will reach our goals. Engaging in effective behavior toward goals is what our next skill, *effectiveness*, is all about.

Chapter 9

GET YOUR GOAL: ACTING EFFECTIVELY

Last April, my stepsister Jessica asked me to be a bridesmaid in her wedding. I was really happy. We weren't close but I had always wanted us to be. The wedding was going to be a lot of fun—just what I needed.

Jessica is two years older than me. In school she hung with the jocks and was super popular. I had no real friends other than a girl named Taylor. In tenth grade, Taylor started to play volleyball and lost interest in me. She made friends with all the jocks, including Jessica. I felt left out and hated Taylor for dropping me.

When I heard Jessica had asked Taylor to be her maid of honor I didn't know what to do. How could Jessica do this to me? She knew I hadn't spoken to Taylor in years. In tears, I told Jessica I couldn't be in her wedding if Taylor was going to be and tried to explain why. She didn't understand, of course, and was really pissed at me. Of course I wasn't in the wedding. I didn't even go. —Madison, 23

Did Madison want to be in Jessica's wedding or did she want to control who Jessica chose to be in the wedding? Had Madison been clear about her goal, she would have considered the rule that the bride gets to choose her maid of honor. Applying that rule would have helped Madison realize it wasn't Jessica's responsibility to make Madison feel comfortable with Taylor; rather it was incumbent upon Madison to figure out how to get along with Taylor, at least well enough to be in the same wedding party. But because Madison was unclear about her goal and had few other skills at her disposal, she used her anger to try to get what she wanted from Jessica. Anger and tantrums had worked for Madison sometimes in the past, but these behaviors were ineffective in this situation.

Emotions demand that we act on urges regardless of the consequences. *Forget about your long-term goals and values*, emotion mind tells us. *Forget about how others feel. Don't think about how you'll feel tomorrow.* When in emotion mind, you are tempted to toss aside your goals for the sake of an urge or use any means, including unskillful ones, to get what you want. Almost by definition, such behavior is ineffective, especially in the long run.

The Problem: Emotions Distract You from Your Wise Mind Goal

Intense emotions not only interfere with problem solving, they also can cause long-term damage to our relationships. If we were raised in an invalidating environment, we may have been ignored when we behaved well or made requests in a reasonable tone, and we may have learned that if we screamed and cried or acted in extreme ways long enough, someone might occasionally give in to us and give us what we want. Unfortunately, this kind of learning makes it more likely that tantrums will become part of our

194

repertoire (Linehan 1993). The people who give in to us in the short term often resent us in the long term for our behavior.

Emotionally demanding behavior, even when it is unintentional, gets labeled as manipulative. Madison wasn't intentionally manipulating Jessica when she became tearful and angry about Taylor being maid of honor. She was simply acting on her emotional urges. But Jessica felt manipulated and became angry with Madison. Their relationship was damaged, impeding Madison's long-term goal.

Many skills are involved in the process of going after a goal. The good news is that all of them can be learned. We need mindfulness skills to recognize what we want. We need interpersonal skills to ask others for what we need and to say no to what we don't want. We need skills to tolerate the distress of not getting what we want right away or at all and skills to resist urges to act in ways that might make things worse. We have to set aside "by any means necessary" and embrace "use skillful means." We need effectiveness to organize all of our skills and help us attain our goals (Linehan 1993a).

The Solution: Effectiveness

Effectiveness, the third how skill, tells us how to use skillful means to achieve a goal (Linehan 1993a). Effectiveness is both a mindfulness skill—in that it keeps us focused on what we truly want—and a problem-solving skill, in that it outlines a process. This process can be broken down into five steps.

1. *Know your goal.* To do what works you have to know what goal is most important to you. Your primary goal should be one-pointed. Try to articulate it in one sentence, such as *I want to ask for a raise.* Getting clear about the goal is the starting point on the road to effectiveness.

2. *Check your goal with your wise mind.* If you consult wise mind about your goal, does it agree that this goal is truly what you want? Is the goal in harmony or in conflict with what you know to be true? Asking for a raise by itself is not likely to conflict with wise mind. But suppose your motive is *I want a raise because my coworker got one and I don't think it's fair.* Suddenly the emotional content of *it's not fair* may interfere with your ability to use the skill of effectiveness. By checking your goal with wise mind, you can get more understanding out of step 1. Ask yourself, *What is my true goal—to ask for a raise or to complain about life not being fair?*

3. *Break your goal down into objectives.* The next step is to break the goal down into a series of small objectives—the steps needed to reach the goal. The smaller and more concrete the steps, the better. Small steps keep you focused, help you remain patient with what could be a slow process, and show you exactly what is needed. In asking for a raise, some steps to consider would be to (a) come up with a rationale for why I deserve a raise, (b) prepare what I am going to say, (c) arrange for a time to talk with my employer, and (d) prepare myself for the possibility of having to take no for an answer.

4. *Use skillful means.* Being effective means doing what works to achieve your goal—no more and no less (Linehan 1993a). The skill of effectiveness is similar to choosing the middle path in Buddhism. The middle path refers to charting a course between polarized extremes, such as insisting on your own way or giving in to others. Walking the middle path requires that we balance our objectives in any situation with the demands of the environment in which we find ourselves. We play by the rules and let go of imagining some idealized environment

where everything is fair and no rules stand in our way (Rathus and Miller 2014).

5. *Don't get distracted from your goal.* Emotions can get in the way of staying focused on the goal. Madison's goal was to get closer to Jessica, and she saw being her bridesmaid as a perfect opportunity. Madison was distracted by anger, however, when Jessica invited Taylor to the wedding party. The skill of effectiveness prompts us to remember our goal even when emotions arise and promote their own agendas. When circumstances prevent us from having our goal exactly as we want it, effectiveness helps us focus on walking the middle path. Had Madison been able to use effectiveness, she might have put aside her emotion mind urges about Taylor and enjoyed being part of the wedding.

• *Matt's Story*

Matt works full-time for a small family-owned nursery, caring for plants, assisting customers, and helping out in the office. He likes his job because he loves horticulture and it is an easy bike ride from home. The pay is not good, but the company's policies are flexible. This allows him to take time off to pursue his other passion—working on an associate's degree at the community college, one course at a time. This semester Matt is taking a course on Buddhism. Matt is also in recovery from alcohol abuse and has completed DBT, so he has a lot of skills on board.

Matt likes the people he works with, especially the owner, Fred, a kind man in his mid-sixties. Matt is not so fond of the owner's son, Jason, who comes and goes from the workplace seemingly at will and doesn't pitch in with heavy jobs such as unloading trucks. Matt once saw a pay stub left on his desk by accident, which showed that Jason makes more than he does.

When Matt was hired, he was promised a significant raise after his first employee evaluation. After a series of delays related to the owner being sick, Matt's evaluation is about to happen. He is eager to get a raise; his roommate just moved out and he'd like to forgo getting another. Matt has a clear goal (step 1) of getting a significant raise, from twelve dollars an hour to at least sixteen.

When Matt and Fred finally sit down for his evaluation, Matt can see that Fred is not feeling well. He praises Matt's job performance, describing his work as excellent and saying he relies on him. He mentions Matt's knowledge of horticulture, his skill with customers, and his willingness to work hard. Fred doesn't bring up the topic of money, except to mention that a drought and competition have caused the business to be stagnant, something Matt already knows. Matt starts to feel worried about his raise. What is Fred trying to say? Fred clears his throat and tells Matt he has just been diagnosed with a serious and advanced form of cancer and that while he is undergoing treatment Jason is going to take over as general manager.

Matt feels afraid for Fred, then angry, then confused. Is asking for a raise still his goal? Matt checks his goal against his wise mind values (step 2). Do they still match up? Right now Matt is in emotion mind. He is thrown off his game plan by Fred's announcement of his serious illness. Now he knows why Fred has missed so much work, often leaving him, Evelyn, and Luis alone at the store. He feels worried about Jason being in charge. He is even worried that the business might fail, leaving him jobless. But most of all he feels worried about his raise. Should he ask for it or not? Emotion mind says, *Who cares if the old man is sick? You need your raise!* and, alternately, *Now you can't ask for a raise; that would be cold-hearted.* Emotion mind might also say, *You can't work for Jason; he is a lazy bum,* or *If Jason is going to run this place, I'm out of here.* All this noise in Matt's head may make it impossible to remember his goal.

Matt consults his wise mind: *What is my goal?* Wise mind answers, *To ask for the raise.* Matt knows this is wise mind by the clarity, simplicity, and calmness of the response. Then he asks, *Is my goal still in harmony with my values, given Fred's illness and Jason taking over?* Matt listens for wise mind while Fred finishes talking about how he will be leaving in a week and will be back at work a month after that. Wise mind says, *To ask for your raise is still a goal, but now there is a new context, including many emotions. Proceed with caution.*

"Fred, thank you for your evaluation," Matt says. "I am glad to know how much I am valued as an employee. I am so sorry to hear about your diagnosis. I really hope the treatment goes well and that you can return to work feeling strong." Thanking Fred for his kind words in the evaluation and expressing his concern for Fred's recovery are effective interpersonal behaviors. These behaviors communicate to Fred that Matt heard the most important pieces of his communication and acknowledged the importance of their relationship. But what about acting on his goal? Matt decides to build in a pause. Building in a pause is an effective way to allow wise mind time to arrive on the scene.

Step 3 instructs Matt to break down his goal into objectives and then pursue each objective skillfully. Since Matt is unprepared to proceed, he allows the conversation with Fred to end. He will come back when he has established a revised set of objectives toward his goal. Matt spends some time consulting with his mother and sister, both of whom are good sounding boards. He needs to consider what rules apply in this situation. Matt, with the help of his mother and sister, comes up with two objectives.

First, he decides to put his cards on the table. Matt will tell Fred that he still wants the raise because it was promised to him and he needs the money. Since DBT, Matt has made a habit of asking for what he wants and saying no as needed. Fred has responded well in the past to clear requests and has been straightforward with Matt, so Matt feels that being direct with one another is part of their relationship. Matt's mother and sister agree that this is a wise course.

The answer to his second question—whether to tell Fred his feelings about Jason running the business while Fred is away—is not so clear. Jason's attitude, nonattendance, and lack of collaboration really bother Matt. Jason is also uncommunicative and nonresponsive to Matt's efforts to engage with him. Matt thinks Fred and Jason have a somewhat difficult relationship, but Jason is Fred's only child and will likely inherit the business.

Now it is time to use skillful means (step 4). Matt thinks that being clear with Fred about the raise will be playing by the rules of his values and the workplace. But he isn't sure what rules apply about telling Fred his feelings regarding Jason. Matt decides to seek advice again.

Matt's mother says not to mention his misgivings about Jason to his father. Doing so will only upset Fred, who is not likely to put anyone else in charge. "Keep your feelings to yourself and start looking for another job," she advises. She further predicts Matt won't get the raise and the business will fail. Matt recognizes his mother's fear is a distraction and lets it go (step 5).

Matt's sister says he should tell Fred his concerns about Jason. Fred deserves to know how unreliable Jason is because it is nearly the spring season and there will be a lot of extra work. "Maybe you can convince Fred to make you manager instead of Jason. Then you'd get your raise," his sister says. Matt cannot decide which is the right course, but he recognizes that thinking about becoming manager himself is also a distraction (step 5).

After further inquiry into wise mind, Matt decides that bringing up his misgivings about Jason to Fred wouldn't be effective. Fred is aware of Jason's shortcomings. Pointing them out will not serve the purpose of getting Matt a raise, nor will it make his job more tolerable while Fred is on sick leave, and it could cause harm.

Now that he has figured out the plan thus far, Matt has a third consideration. What should he do if his request for a raise is denied? Should he threaten to quit? After all, he was promised a raise, and if Fred denies him he would be breaking that promise. Matt imagines how hard it will be to tolerate Jason as a boss while feeling he is being treated unfairly. After much consideration, he decides not to quit while Fred is in the hospital. He feels it would not only be unkind to Fred but also go against one of Matt's other values, which is to leave jobs with relationships intact and the possibility for a good recommendation. Therefore, no matter what Fred says about the raise, Matt decides to play by the rules and continue to do his job. He will try to interact with Jason in ways that are skillful, at least until Fred comes back from his surgery. By then, Matt's semester will be over and it will be easier to change jobs if the raise doesn't come through. In the meantime, Matt will probably have to find another roommate, which will be the hardest part. He will have to work to accept this reality so it doesn't distract him from his goals.

Having thought through his objective, Matt feels much calmer and more detached. All he can do is ask. The answer is not up to him. Once he has his answer he also has a game plan. The plan prepares him to proceed. Matt is walking the middle path he learned about in his Buddhism class.

Matt has only one objective at this point, which is to have the raise conversation with Fred before he goes on sick leave. He plans his strategy using skillful means, even writing out exactly what he wants to say. He will find Fred when he is not preoccupied and is feeling well enough and when no one else is around. Matt decides to approach Fred first thing in the morning, before anyone else comes in. On the day in question, Fred is in his office with a cup of coffee, scrolling through his e-mails and apparently in a good mood. Matt has memorized what to say to avoid distractions. "Fred, do you have a minute?" Matt asks at the door. Fred looks up, nods, and offers him a seat.

"Last week we had my performance evaluation. At the time, I was hoping we could discuss my pay, but we didn't get to it. I know you are going to be out for a month and you have a lot on your mind, but I still feel it is important for us to talk about a raise for me now, as was promised when I was hired. Can you tell me if I can get that increase? I think knowing will help me get through the next weeks with you gone. We have a lot of spring jobs to do and I will be working my hardest."

Matt has just used his best assertiveness skills and played by all the rules. He chose a good time to ask, asked the right person, and behaved in a way consistent with his values (Linehan 1993a). He asked clearly and directly for what he wanted, acknowledged that it was a difficult time to ask, and told Fred how it would benefit him to give Matt a raise (Linehan 1993a). Matt avoided bringing his discomfort with Jason into the conversation, thereby remaining focused on his goal without the distraction of his emotions. Matt has done all he can, and it is now out of his hands.

Fred can say yes or no. He can ask Matt to wait. He can hem and haw, saying first no then yes, or first yes then no. If Fred says no, Matt can ask, "What do you think we should do about my raise?" (Linehan 1993a). Matt keeps his eyes on the goal and on his game plan. He wants the raise he was promised. But he is focused on using skillful means no matter what. He may or may not get his raise, but he will hold onto his relationship with Fred, who has been his employer for a year, and retain his self-respect by behaving in accordance with his values. Matt accepts the real situation he is in, be it fair or unfair, and moves forward without clinging to getting the outcome he wants. He reminds himself that his life will not be ruined if he doesn't get the raise. Matt has chosen to practice nonattachment to the outcome. At the same time, the course he has plotted gives him the best chance, from the perspective of his wise mind, of getting the raise he wants.

As it turned out, Matt did not get his raise and he had to take another roommate. When Fred returned from sick leave, Matt took a job working in the university greenhouses, which had better benefits and room for advancement. On his last day, Fred came to his truck to say goodbye. "Sorry to see you go, Matt," he said, handing Matt an envelope with a thank you note and a cash gift. "You can get a good reference from me anytime." Matt's self-respect was strengthened by his effectiveness, even though he didn't get his goal.

Even when we behave in ways that are effective, sometimes we won't achieve our goal. Circumstances may make it impossible. People may want to obstruct us. Even if people want to give us what we want, they may be prevented from doing so for other reasons, such as promises made to other people, or economic, political, or other factors (Linehan 1993a). This is reality—it isn't what we think it should be. It isn't right. It isn't fair. It just is.

What is the effective way to cope when we lose a negotiation and don't get something we really want or need? The skill of effectiveness recommends looking at the big picture. No, you didn't get your goal, but perhaps you learned some things that will help you achieve goals in the future. And chances are, because you were focused on being effective, your relationships weren't damaged. Most important, you have increased your self-confidence and self-respect by using skillful means, no matter what the outcome. You can be proud of yourself.

The Obstacles: Ten Ineffective Habits of Emotion Mind

The story of Matt illustrates highly effective behavior. Unfortunately, all of us have experienced obstacles to being effective, some of which can be habitual. To master the skill of acting effectively, we have to become skillful at recognizing and overcoming some habits of emotion mind that make us prone to ineffective behavior patterns.

1. *I'd rather be right than effective!* When you find yourself saying, "It's the principle of the thing," chances are you are more interested in being right than being effective. Getting into pitched battles to prove you are right is a luxury most of us can't afford if we want good relationships. The insistence on being right can make other people feel annoyed or even bullied. What is your goal?

Do you care more about being right just now or about being effective?

2. *It's not fair!* When we focus on something not being fair, it is as if we refuse to accept this unfortunate reality: life isn't fair. We want the rules to suit us, and until they do we are likely to remain disgruntled, especially when the unfairness directly affects us or someone we love. In fact, the value of fairness is considered to be one of our core human values—one that appears to be well established in us as social animals. Research has shown that babies as young as six months old can recognize and will prefer fairness to unfairness (Schmidt and Sommerville 2011).

   However, once we are out of middle school, the complaint "it's not fair" is unlikely to address the problem. If we really want things to be more fair, chances are we have to use skillful means to advocate for justice and cultivate patience.

3. *Revenge!* When someone hurts us or blocks our goals it is natural to feel angry (Linehan 1993a). Acting on anger, however—especially holding grudges and seeking vengeance—is frequently ineffective (Linehan 1993a). When we fuel anger with ruminations and fantasies of settling the score, we become filled with revenge. Acting from revenge has negative effects on mood (Price 2009). There is an old saying that revenge, like acid, causes more damage to the vessel in which it is stored (you) than to the person it is eventually poured upon. It is impossible to move on with our lives after conflict while clinging to hatred and fantasies of revenge.

4. *"Cutting off your nose to spite your face."* Becoming so angry about not getting your way that you act against your own interests is another ineffective behavior (Linehan 1993a). This form of vengeance victimizes you

and carries a tinge of martyrdom. An example of such behavior is refusing to ask your friend for help getting to the doctor because you think she should see what you need and freely offer. But the friend who "should have known" is not a mind reader. As a result of not asking, you don't get to your appointment and you run out of medication. You may express your resentment or suffer in silence, but in either case you are the one who is hurt. It's your job to ask for what you need.

5. *Blame, blame, blame.* Whether we are blaming ourselves or someone else, blaming is a setup for being ineffective. Blaming ourselves for everything makes us more vulnerable emotionally and distracts us from taking responsibility for the parts that actually are ours. If we feel we are responsible for everything going wrong, we don't have to look at the few things we could improve. Instead we set about crucifying ourselves. As they say in AA, "Get off the cross; we need the wood."

    Blaming others also distracts us from taking responsibility. If it is "all Richard's fault," then we believe there is nothing we could have done to create a different outcome. There are situations in which nothing we could have done would have changed the outcome—situations such as being sexually abused as a child, robbed at gunpoint, or hit by a drunk driver. In many other situations, however, had we been more skillful we might have had a different outcome, or at least feel more accepting of the outcome. It is easy to blame your spouse when she starts yelling and overlook your own contribution to the conflict. What was it you said that made her so angry? Could you have said it another way? Refusing to look at your behavior and blaming her for everything will keep the two of you stuck and hopeless. Walking a middle path with blame increases effectiveness.

6. *Giving up.* Giving up is quitting when there is still a chance you can achieve your goal. Giving up (not showing up, or quitting, or stomping off) is the result of giving in to emotion mind, which says you don't deserve your goal or your goal isn't worth all the hard work. A special form of giving up is being so passive when action is needed that your goal simply slips through your fingers. Examples of this behavior are waiting until the end of the semester to begin a research paper and then finding you cannot do it, or not applying for a job for which you are qualified until it is too late.

   Giving up is not the same as letting go. Letting go is making a wise mind choice not to cling to a particular outcome that is out of your hands. Letting go is practicing nonattachment. You can let go of an outcome but continue to strive toward your goal. Giving up is declaring "game over" for your goal before the clock has run out.

7. *Self-invalidation.* When we self-invalidate, we judge ourselves as defective, attributing our emotions, thoughts, and actions to weakness, dysfunction, or failure, without considering whether this is true. Self-invalidation is often learned in the invalidating environment growing up. According to Linehan, the more we self-invalidate the more emotionally dysregulated we become (1993). Thus self-invalidation puts us into the clutches of emotion mind and interferes with acting effectively.

8. *Clinging to past hurts.* Ruminating about past hurts is an emotion mind behavior and is inconsistent with a life worth living. Staying stuck in complaining and focusing on feeling victimized, treated unfairly, judged, and misunderstood are all incompatible with a stable, healthy mood. If your goal is to feel better, the habit of negative thinking is ineffective. Dwelling on past hurts can be

associated with depression and PTSD, for which effective treatments are available.

9. *Perfectionism.* There is a saying: "The perfect is the enemy of the good." Perfectionism can be so pervasive that we feel paralyzed to do anything for fear the results won't be good enough. By definition, then, we can't achieve our goal if we never even try. Perfectionism, like self-invalidation, has its origins in the invalidating environment where, under the pressure of constant criticism, we simply gave up trying. Perfectionism is a highly ineffective habit of emotion mind.

10. *Avoidance.* Procrastination, denial, and passivity are examples of avoidance behaviors that get in the way of being effective. *Ah,* we say to ourselves subliminally, *I don't want to deal with that now. I'll deal with it later, when I feel more like doing it.* Relief floods in, rewarding our decision, and making it more likely we will decide to procrastinate some more. It feels so good (for a moment)! Meanwhile the problem, and our avoidance of it, grows. *That's not really a problem,* we say to ourselves, often with a bit of relief. *I don't need to focus on it.* Passivity is avoiding learning how to problem solve, take responsibility, and make changes in our behavior. An example of passivity is not having a spare tire or a jack in your car while your tires go bald. You become a helpless situation waiting to happen.

Practices to Reduce the Ten Ineffective Habits

1. *Walk the middle path.* In an argument, look for the truth in the opposite perspective. Agree to disagree. Notice when your passion about being right is alienating others and step back.

2. *Work for fairness.* Make a habit of considering fairness as an ongoing project in your life. Ask yourself, *What can I do to make this situation more fair? What will work?* Work to increase fairness in environments that are important to you, using effectiveness.

3. *Reject revenge.* Reduce urges for revenge by distracting from revenge fantasies and eliminating judgmental ruminations and self-talk. When you encounter someone toward whom you feel vengeful, either in your thoughts or in person, try to avoid him politely or be as courteous as you can sincerely be.

4. *Give up being a martyr.* Ask for what you need. You may not get it, but at least you have given yourself a chance. If you don't get what you want or need in spite of your effort, try again in another way, using effectiveness. Similarly, practice saying "no" effectively when you are asked to do something you believe is not beneficial.

5. *Eat the blame.* Rather than blaming others, take responsibility for your part in not achieving your goal. Say to yourself, *What have I learned from this? What can I do now that will work?*

6. *Stay in the game.* Hang in there with your goals. Persist with determination. Encourage yourself; cheerlead yourself. Be willing to fail but keep playing.

7. *Turn off self-hate radio.* Use Teflon mind when you hear yourself using words of self-invalidation. Don't argue; just let the words slip out of your mind.

8. *Count your blessings.* Keep a gratitude journal, and write a few lines every day on what brings you joy and makes you feel grateful. Research shows that a gratitude journal can be as effective for your mood as medications and have fewer side effects (Emmons and McCullough 2003).

9. *Practice self-acceptance.* Celebrate all that is "good enough" in you, all that you love in yourself. Enumerate and embrace your faults and failings and practice "loving" them. Be resolute in your unwillingness to be critical of any efforts you make toward your goals, no matter how minimal or whether they are successful. Write a poem or a song about your strengths. Write some humorous haiku about your weaknesses.

10. *Avoid avoiding* (Linehan 1993a). Cultivate a habit of listening closely to your wise mind whenever you feel the urge to avoid, such as not going to a party, not completing a task, or not paying a bill when you have the money. Notice the tiny bit of relief that accompanies the decision to avoid. Label that little relief as your enemy and instead approach the thing you want to avoid. Then notice the big relief you feel when you complete an avoided task. That big relief is your friend.

Overcoming Obstacles by Playing by the Rules

The ten ineffective habits of emotion mind all refuse to recognize basic social rules. Madison did not acknowledge that the bride gets to choose her maid of honor; Matt did realize that his employer would feel loyal to his only son. Acknowledging these rules can help us be more effective in the face of obstacles.

Accept Reality as It Is

The obstacles of emotion mind all have one thing in common—they don't accept reality. A simple example comes from the reality of personal finances. Let's say I really want a new car. My old car is unreliable, a gas-guzzler that stinks when I turn on the heater, but I own it free and clear. I wish I had enough income to afford payments on a car, but I don't. If I don't accept this limitation, I may spend a lot of time looking for a car to buy instead of considering what I can do to make the car I own more reliable until I can afford another. Searching for a new car does not solve my transportation problem and leaves me feeling frustrated.

When the Rules Are Unclear, Check Your Values

Rules can be straightforward or obscure. The rules for passing through the security line at the airport, playing gin rummy, or driving in the fast lane on the interstate are usually clearly defined, as are the consequences of not complying with the rules. Some rules are less clear. What rules should we follow when interacting with relatives who criticize us, friends who hurt our feelings, or authority figures who have deceived or harmed us? We may get conflicting advice from books or people we consult and may spend hours trying to decide which advice to follow. Ultimately, when the rules are unclear, we have to check the rules against our values and rely on wise mind to help us figure out how to proceed.

Refer to Rule #1, Even When You Don't Want To, or Accept the Consequences

Sometimes we really don't want to follow the rules. Rules may inconvenience us or get in the way of something we want. Let's start with an inconvenient rule, such as a rule of reciprocity. For example, you and your friend attended the same community college and you graduated a year ahead of her. She came to your graduation, which meant a lot to you at the time. Now it is your turn to attend hers but you don't want to go. You find graduations long and boring. You consider lying to her about a more pressing commitment, such as a family member being sick. If you lie, you will lose self-respect and she might find out that you lied. If you tell her the truth, that you don't want to go, it will hurt her feelings. Still, you do not want to spend an entire Sunday sitting in the bleachers watching the academic parade, feeling bored. This is an inconvenient rule! No matter what you do there are consequences you don't like. You need to consider your goal: what is more important, keeping the friendship or avoiding the graduation? If keeping the friendship is more important, then you can look for ways to make the graduation less boring and more fun, such as by, finding friends to sit with during the ceremony, mindfully noticing your environment, or if all else fails, listening to an audiobook on your phone during the times you are bored.

A rule also can block a goal that is important to us. Suppose there is a drought and the neighborhood has been told that we can water gardens only once a week. We have just put in three fruit trees and they need a soaking at least three times a week to become established. What should we do? Situations like these present a conflict between our values and our desires. Let's say we believe that the shared resource of water must be respected and we want to comply with the rules, but we also want our trees to survive. Effectiveness prompts us to do some creative problem solving, such as catching water in the shower to save for our thirsty trees.

Some rules so violate our values that we feel we must break them. When Rosa Parks broke the rules of segregation by taking a seat in the front of the bus, her goal was to change the rules, and an objective toward that goal was to get arrested. Ultimately her behavior, along with the behavior of countless others in the civil rights movement, was effective toward the goal because the participants were prepared to accept the consequences for breaking the rules. Eventually, and with enormous sacrifice, they forced society to see how repugnant those rules were.

• *Maggie's Story*

Maggie was a Marine veteran who had served in Afghanistan. At the time, as a female she was not supposed to be in combat, but her role as a driver put her in harm's way on a daily basis. Although there were other women in her unit, Maggie was frequently the only female in her immediate vicinity. She always tried to pull her weight and generally got along well with the guys, which wasn't always easy. She even tolerated a fair amount of teasing about her gender that some would consider harassment. She loved her work and hoped to advance in the ranks and make the Marines her career.

Maggie's job was to drive soldiers and Marines to and from various posts for duty. One day, Maggie was alone in the jeep with a Marine corporal she did not know. She was to drive him to a post about 50 kilometers away along a road that she had driven many times. In the middle of nowhere, the corporal asked Maggie to pull over so he could relieve himself. He got out of the Humvee, walked a few feet away, and began urinating. Maggie got out too and stood with her back to the man and lit a cigarette. In a moment he had his arm around her neck and her right

213

arm pushed high up her back. "Easy way or hard way?" he hissed under his breath. Maggie struggled to get free, trying to burn him with her cigarette. He punched her so hard in the back that she fell to the ground. Then he raped her.

Not long after she returned to base, Maggie reported the rape to her commanding officer. She remembers being examined and filling out paperwork. Two weeks later she was transferred to a different unit in Kabul, out of transport and into vehicle maintenance. She never saw the corporal again, nor did she hear anything further about the rape charges.

At her new post, Maggie didn't know anyone. She received medication for back pain, but didn't take it because it made her nauseous. She found herself newly fearful of the other men around her, none of whom she knew. She tried to tough it out. Three months later Maggie discovered she was pregnant.

Due to military rules, it was difficult for Maggie to terminate the pregnancy. She was told she could obtain an abortion privately if she paid for it herself, but the process might take months and would require travel to Europe. Maggie was torn about what to do. She didn't have a lot of savings and she wasn't sure she could handle an abortion, especially if she had to wait. She decided to do nothing, realizing it would mean the end of her career. When she was five months pregnant, she was discharged from the Marines and sent home. Maggie felt disgraced and talked to no one about the rape. Her family did not know how she had become pregnant, but they accepted her home. Back pain continued to plague her. Around the time of her baby's birth she began having symptoms of post-traumatic stress from the assault, including nightmares and flashbacks.

When Maggie first went to the VA to try to get benefits for herself and her daughter, she was told there was an eight-month wait for an evaluation. When the evaluation came around, she was told that she had degenerative disk disease but that it was not connected to her service, so she would not receive benefits. Maggie found out that she could ask for a second evaluation, so she did. At that evaluation four months later, the board established a 20 percent "service connection" to her back injury. As a result, Maggie was to receive a small stipend and access to medical care. She was prescribed oxycodone for her pain, but decided not to take it, fearful of becoming addicted. She was put on another waiting list to be evaluated for her PTSD. In the meantime, she found out that the man who raped her was serving time in a military prison for another rape but had never been charged for raping her.

Maggie first showed up for therapy when her daughter was fifteen months old. A small, wiry woman with a buzz cut and large, dark eyes, Maggie was accompanied by her mother and her daughter, Tabitha, a big, happy baby who toddled around the waiting room. Maggie lived with Tabitha in a mobile home on her family's small farm. Her parents, who were semiretired, took care of her daughter whenever Maggie was able to work. Back pain prevented her from doing the kind of work she loved, auto mechanics. She had gotten a temporary job working for the state, but when that ran out she didn't know what she would do.

After I had completed my assessment of Maggie's PTSD and heard her story of the sexual assault, I asked Maggie about her goals. "I don't really have any now," she said, looking at the floor. "When I was a kid I wanted to be a Marine. I wanted to work on tanks." She looked out the window. "We can see how that turned out."

"What do you want now?"

"I never think about what I want. I used to want to get as far away from home as possible. I never thought I'd be living at my parents' with a baby. I never even wanted children. Now here I am. I can't even afford to go to school. I can't do much because of my back injury. I guess I just want to see Tabby grow up."

Maggie described her childhood as "pretty happy." She was an A student and the starting third baseman on her championship high school softball team. Prior to enlisting she had attended two years of technical college, gaining a certificate in auto mechanics. The hardest thing for her to talk about was that her mother's brother had molested her. He had said that if she told anyone, terrible harm would come to her and her family. She never spoke of it.

Maggie had nightmares and flashbacks from Afghanistan and her back pain was chronic and sometimes severe. The only joy in her life was her daughter. Somehow the facts of Tabby's conception didn't interfere with Maggie's relationship with her. "She's just a baby," she said. "She didn't do anything wrong." I was impressed with how effectively Maggie kept her trauma and her love for her daughter separate.

Maggie focused on survival day to day. Her favorite skill was effectiveness. "Every day I have to figure out how to take care of Tabby, take care of myself, and not go crazy. I figure out what works and that is what I do. I think that's pretty effective."

"But what about your future?"

"I don't feel I have a future at this point."

After learning DBT skills, Maggie focused on her PTSD. Gradually, Maggie's flashbacks and nightmares decreased. She was able to think of the rape and not panic, dissociate, or go numb. She also took a course in pain management that included mindfulness meditation. She began to practice ten to fifteen minutes per day, which helped her to manage her pain better. Her mood slowly improved.

As she started feeling better, Maggie began to think of her life beyond mere survival. She began to dream about moving to the city and enrolling at the university. One day at the end of a session Maggie suddenly said, "I think I know what I want to do, finally. I want to study mechanical engineering." She looked as if saying this surprised her.

To go after this goal, Maggie would need enough money to rent an apartment and put Tabitha in a good daycare, both of which seemed impossible. Still, now that she had a goal—step 1 in acting effectively—she felt more energized.

One month later, Maggie got a letter from the VA. "They've scheduled the hearing for my PTSD claim," she said anxiously. "It's in a month." Maggie had dreaded the VA hearing, which would determine whether she would be compensated for the rape. She had filed her claim nearly two years ago and then had put it out of her mind. Now it loomed before her.

Maggie feared that the disability board would disbelieve her, blame her for the rape, and even humiliate her. Even though she knew it was not entirely rational, Maggie also feared that Tabby would somehow be harmed in retaliation for her seeking a service-connected disability. Maggie wondered if her fears had something to do with the molestation by her uncle.

"I don't even know for sure how this could hurt Tabby. But it scares me so much I just don't know if I can face it."

Maggie had never told her family about how Tabitha was conceived, and they had never asked. Maggie was afraid that if she admitted Tabitha was conceived by rape her family would turn against her child. In her wise mind

Maggie did not believe this would really be the outcome, but nonetheless the possibility tormented her.

The stakes for the claim hearing were high. Maggie would have to answer a lot of questions and she might feel triggered by them. If her claim were allowed, however, she would receive some compensation for all she had experienced since the day she was raped. She would be able to afford to go to school and have daycare for Tabby. She would not have to worry about working jobs that were damaging to her health just to survive. She could make up for the loss of her military career with another career that would help her make a new life. The rewards for having the VA acknowledge what had happened to Maggie would be substantial, not only materially but also psychologically. Maggie would triumph over the adversity that had held her down for so long.

"The man who raped me is in prison for raping someone else. And Tabby is living proof it was him! It should be a slam-dunk. I should get disability for myself and also for her. It is only fair! But I am so scared. I feel like I am back out on that deserted road where it all went down. I didn't deserve what happened to me, but it happened. I do deserve to get compensated, but maybe I won't. I just don't know what to do."

After a lot of struggle, Maggie decided to face what she feared. "I don't think it would be effective for me not to face this fight," she said, wiping away tears. "This is the chance for me to tell my story. I don't think I can live with myself if I don't go in there and stand up for myself. And my family will finally know the truth about what happened to me, for better or worse." Maggie had checked her goal against her wise mind values, step 2 in acting effectively. These values required her to go forward, even to face her fear that speaking up would somehow hurt her daughter.

Once Maggie had committed to presenting her case she went into action. She found out everything she could about the rules of the disability world and did her best to comply with each one. She pulled together all of her discharge documents and made a timeline of her tour of duty, including the dates of the rape, her discharge, and Tabitha's birth. She included a folder of pictures of her daughter, now almost four years old. Maggie practiced imagining the disability hearing in great detail so she could prepare herself for the emotions that might arise. These actions employed step 3 (break your goal down into objectives) and step 4 (use skillful means).

To deal with her worst fear, Maggie decided to discuss Tabitha's conception with her brother, who was also a veteran and very supportive. "Hey, Maggie," Anthony said, hugging her after she told him. "I've known all along. Don't be afraid. We all love Tabby no matter what, and you, too." Maggie was relieved after this conversation but still worried, especially about what her father would say.

Maggie told me later there was one moment during the hearing when she lost some of the control she had so carefully cultivated. The hearing was conducted before three men and one woman, who sat slightly above Maggie at a long table on a dais. The main administrator, an older man, asked her why she did not inquire into charges being brought against the Marine who raped her. "Didn't you realize that you needed to make sure you pressed charges?"

"No, sir," Maggie said, quietly, "I was told the chain of command would take care of that."

"And you didn't follow up on that?" he persisted.

"No, sir, I had a lot of other things on my mind."

"Really? Like what?"

"Like pain from a back injury and also getting transferred to a new unit."

Maggie said she felt like calling him a few names at this point. "I wanted so badly to tell him off! But I remembered the skill of effectiveness. Much as I wanted to attack him, I didn't think that would help me achieve my goal. I just focused on the goal." Maggie followed through with step 5, not being distracted from her goal.

When it was over she was exhausted but proud of herself. There would be more facts to assemble, such as paternity test results, additional medical and psychiatric records, and other details. But this part, the part she dreaded most, was over, and Maggie had handled herself "like a champ," according to her brother.

The decision wouldn't come for another several months. "I am not going to go crazy while I wait," she told me, grinning. "It wouldn't be effective."

Maggie never told her mother and father directly about the rape and her pregnancy. It was now out in the open but still no one spoke of it. It was just the way her family handled such things. On the day of the hearing and in the weeks afterward, however, her family conveyed in many ways their love for her and their unconditional acceptance of Tabby. Maggie no longer believed her family would reject her daughter. "I feel like I've taken off a hundred-pound pack I've been carrying since the rape," she said. "I think I've finally come home from the war."

Five months later, Maggie received a letter informing her that she was given 100 percent service-connected disability for her back and the rape. The pay and benefits she received allowed her to move and enroll at the university. Tabby would attend the university daycare program. I lost touch with Maggie after her move, but last May I got an announcement of her graduation—she received a B.S. in engineering. Enclosed in the invitation was a picture of Tabby in her baseball uniform. "Thanks,"

Maggie had written on the back of the picture. "Very Effectively, Maggie."

The hurdles Maggie faced seemed insurmountable to her when she first entered treatment. She was suffering from PTSD and chronic pain; she was a single mother, underemployed, and living in an isolated rural area. Even with a supportive family, Maggie had to face her fears. She tried to play by the rules, but the system failed her. To rebuild her life she had to find goals and navigate by her wise mind. Whenever hopelessness about her situation or anger at the injustice she experienced prompted her to give up or escape, she refocused. Even in the last months, before she heard the decision about her award, Maggie practiced encouraging herself. "I'm a Marine," she said. "Grunts can do anything."

Practices to Strengthen Effectiveness

The skill of effectiveness is actually a process, the key components of which are skills in themselves. These skills include clarifying your values, prioritizing, setting goals, and being assertive. The following exercises will strengthen these key component skills.

1. *Clarify your values.* Undertake a process to learn more about what you value and why. Values include ethics, moral principles, and what you believe makes life worth living, even fulfilling. Perhaps you received instruction in values in religious education or from your family of origin. Now is the time to make sure the values you inherited are really your own. Get as clear as possible about what you believe, want, and are willing to work toward achieving. Are there conflicts in your values that cause you to feel confused, such as valuing being debt free but wanting a lot of luxuries you can't afford? Enlist the help of a wise friend, clergy person, or therapist to have

an in-depth conversation about your most deeply held values. Seek out books, videos, and lectures on values and test what you learn against how you feel. Translate your beliefs and desires into goals. For example, you may value community but find yourself socially isolated. What steps would be effective toward increasing community in your life?

2. *Prioritize.* What are the most important things and who are the most important people in your life? Are you giving them the priority they deserve? Are you putting the things and people you value most—such as your children, your health, or your stability—first? If not, why not? What is getting in the way? Take time to reflect on what is needed for your priorities to be reflected in your choices. Do you need to give something up or change some habits to have time for your priorities? Are you willing to do this? If so, make a commitment to yourself and get help to follow through. Prioritizing will help you be more effective in setting goals.

3. *Set short-term goals.* Sit down once each week and spend some time thinking about your short-term goals. What would you like to achieve in the next week? Your goals can be as simple as *take a ten-minute walk three times this week* or as ambitious as *complete the big project at work*. Make sure the goals you set require the right amount of effort—not too much or too little—and that they are achievable in the time frame you have in mind. Plan ahead how you will reward yourself after accomplishing your goal, such as by going to a movie, sleeping late on Sunday, or taking comp time at work. The practice of providing reinforcement for yourself after you accomplish objectives is called self-management (Linehan 1993). Self-management skills increase your ability to be effective.

4. *Set long-term goals.* Spend at least thirty minutes each month reflecting and writing or talking about your long-term goals.

Allow yourself to dream a little about what you would like to see in one year or up to five years. Start to plan toward long-term goals. Write in a journal or on a calendar about your plans for the next year or discuss your plans with a trusted friend or advisor. For example, do you plan to change jobs, move to better housing, save money, take a trip, or go back to school? Set some goals for yourself and start to follow through. Break down each goal into objectives and take the first step. Knowing your long-term goals can help you stay on track with short-term goals as well. Keeping your long-term goals in mind will increase your effectiveness in keeping your behavior in line with your goals.

5. *Assert yourself.* Learn, practice, and master skills for assertiveness, such as the DBT Interpersonal Effectiveness skills, covered in Linehan's skills training manual (Linehan et al. 2014). These skills outline in detail how to ask for what you need and how to say no in such a way that you are most likely to achieve your objective in the situation, keep your relationships healthy, and maintain your self-respect.

Acting Effectively Pulls It All Together

One way to look at the skill of effectiveness is that it operationalizes wise mind. Effectiveness pulls from all the skills in your repertoire to help you figure out what you want, solve problems, keep relationships, and achieve your goal. While there are many obstacles and barriers to acting effectively, the five steps outlined in this chapter will help you master this important skill.

Now we have completed our discussion of the seven mindfulness skills: first wise mind, then observing, describing, and participating (the what skills), and acting nonjudgmentally, one-mindfully in the moment, and effectively (the how skills). Let's turn our attention to some powerful acceptance skills, which will help us use the skills we've already learned to best effect, even in times of intense distress. These skills are radical acceptance, turning the mind, and willingness.

Chapter 10

LETTING GO OF SUFFERING THROUGH ACCEPTANCE

I will probably never fully recover from Simon's death. But now, ten years after burying my son, I can finally wake up and face the day without dread. Sorrow and grief remain my daily companions, but I no longer have the excruciating suffering of those first years. I no longer expect him to come running in the back door any minute with a turtle or a beetle to show me. Even though he is still in my heart, I have accepted that he is gone from this world forever.

About six years ago, I was trying to help an acquaintance who had just lost her daughter at the hands of a drunk driver. I noticed she was refusing to accept her daughter's death. "It shouldn't have happened," she kept insisting, sobbing. "They should enforce the law!" I remembered feeling exactly that way when Simon died. For many years I would say to myself, "He shouldn't have gotten sick. He was so healthy and so strong!" Listening to her made me realize that I had stopped questioning and refusing to accept reality. I had begun to accept. I had acquired a tiny foothold in the peace that acceptance brings.

I am not sure what it takes to let go of suffering and accept reality, but I know it is more than time alone. It is time plus a willingness to let go of wanting things to be other than they are. And when reality acceptance happens, a seed of peace can grow right alongside the pain. —Rena, 55

Legend has it that when Siddhartha Gautama was growing up as a prince in northern India in the sixth century BCE, he was protected by his father, the king, from any contact with illness, old age, suffering, or death (Nhat Hanh 1998). It would seem that the king had a big problem with reality acceptance to think he could protect his son from these painful facts. Of course, his effort was doomed to fail.

When Siddhartha was in his twenties, he decided to explore outside the palace grounds. On the first day, accompanied by a servant, he ventured forth and encountered an old man. "What is wrong with that man?" he asked his servant. "Sire, he is old," answered the servant. "Will that happen to me?" the young prince asked. The servant answered, "Yes, it will." Siddhartha returned home, and that night he felt restless. The next morning he again wanted to go out of the palace grounds. That day he encountered a diseased person. Again he asked if he might ever become diseased, and again his servant told him the truth. On the third day, the young prince saw a corpse being cremated. "What is wrong with that man?" he asked. "Sire, he is dead and his body is being turned to ashes." But this time Siddhartha realized that what happened to other men would likely also happen to him. He realized that he too was subject to the painful conditions that everyone faced, and he felt troubled. On the fourth and last day, Siddhartha met a *sadhu*, a holy man, who encouraged him to relieve his suffering by renouncing the world and going off in search of enlightenment. Convinced, Siddhartha left his comfortable palace and his family, including the young wife and son he loved, and set out on a journey to find the truth.

Siddhartha spent many years living the austere life of a wandering hermit without attaining the knowledge he sought. Nearly in despair, he sat down under a tree, determined to meditate until he reached enlightenment. Finally, Siddhartha experienced a profound and lasting realization. He then began the teaching career that made him famous as the Buddha, or the Enlightened One.

The Problem: Life Is Painful

In his first talk to his disciples, the Buddha outlined his under-standing of the human condition. He also presented his teach-ings on how to become free from suffering. The Buddha didn't consider himself a spiritual teacher but rather a healer (Batchelor 1998). His insights are known as the Four Noble Truths. The most important part of these truths is that even though life is painful, we don't have to *suffer*. Suffering is optional and arises from a refusal to accept reality (Nhat Hanh 1998).

The Four Noble Truths

1. *To be alive is to experience pain.* No matter how privileged or lucky we are, eventually all of us will experience death—in most cases preceded by old age or physical illness. We cannot avoid loss, sadness, disappointment, fear, and frustration. Human nature is imperfect and so is the world in which we live. No matter how we strive, all things—including all pleasures, accomplishments, and everything and everyone we love—will eventually dimin-ish and be lost. We and everyone we love will die.

2. *In the face of so much pain, suffering arises.* We suffer because we refuse to accept the reality described in the first noble truth. We want external things, experiences, and relation-ships to be perfect, permanent, and fully satisfying. We live in the illusion that it is possible to have constant plea-sure and to avoid anything we find unpleasant, painful, or aversive. Throughout our lives, we continue to grasp at this false dream of fulfillment, causing us to experience one bitter disappointment after another. And because we cling, we suffer. The more we suffer, the more we cling. The origin of suffering is the clinging, the attachment to our illusions and to reality being other than it is.

3. *It is possible to bring our suffering to an end.* To achieve freedom from suffering, we have to give up clinging to the idea of always getting exactly what we want, and also to accept painful things that happen to us beyond our control. It is not that we have to give up wanting to have pleasure and avoid pain in the first place. Everyone wants that! We simply have to stop *clinging* to having things our way. This, of course, is easier said than done. Clinging to having what we want and recoiling in agony when faced with what we don't want is the definition of suffering, but it is also human nature. (Think of a two-year-old having a tantrum.) We actually have to learn how to accept reality when it is painful and even when it is mildly dissatisfying. We even have to let go of clinging to our own pain.

4. *Ordinary people can attain freedom from suffering.* Ordinary people—this means us! In the Buddha's day it was believed that ordinary people had no hope of ever transforming their suffering. Only people who renounced the world and lived as monks could find such peace. But according to the Buddha (and many teachers today), a person does not need to renounce the world. Instead, he or she needs to live in the world with acceptance of reality and according to some basic principles, which the Buddha called the Eightfold Path, a topic covered later in this chapter. Acceptance of reality and mindful practice of the Eightfold Path can lead anyone to inner peace and freedom from suffering (Nhat Hanh 1998).

Deliverance: A Story

Here's a story that illustrates how the Four Noble Truths and reality acceptance skills work together. Imagine that you just built a beautiful cabin on a river at the end of a quiet country lane. The house has lovely views out every window. At night you can fall asleep under the dark sky to the sound of crickets and the river flowing by. There isn't a neighbor in sight. You believe you have finally attained your goal of permanent pleasure.

One day you come home and notice a new driveway cut into the lane across from yours. You hear the sound of a big truck, which now comes into view, pulling a long trailer on which sits a beat-up, turquoise double-wide mobile home. By nightfall, the house is installed in such a way that you can see it through the trees, right out your living-room window. As you go to bed that night you hear bluegrass music. You hate bluegrass music. Enter the First Noble Truth: life means pain.

How can this have happened? You were told that land would never be sold! You believed you would one day buy it! Your illusion of bucolic paradise is ruined! The Second Noble Truth, that suffering is caused not by the pain itself but by clinging to things being different, is now in play. Soon enough you see that your new neighbor has a dog and a passel of children who come to your house and bother you. You don't know what to do to get your elusive paradise back. You are in torment.

Along comes the Third Noble Truth: if you stop clinging to reality being different from how it is, you may find peace. For months you struggle to accept the changes to your world. If you accept reality, you will have to give up your dream of how things should be. Reluctantly, you decide to try.

A friend advises you to meet your neighbors and try to develop some kind of relationship. You decide it can't hurt to be neighborly. Thus arises the Fourth Noble Truth: there is a path to letting go of clinging.

You knock on their door. You have brought a vegan casserole and a recording of a string quartet to welcome them to the neighborhood. They answer the door and invite you in, offer you some barbeque, and turn up the bluegrass. After sharing a meal, they invite you to church and ask you to join them in a word of prayer. You are an atheist but you bow your head. They give thanks for having you as a neighbor.

After a few weeks you start to radically accept their dog, even though he barks a lot. (*Radical acceptance* is described in the next section.) He is a big, happy, yellow mutt who goes for walks with you along the river. You learn to enjoy their children, especially the little girl who likes to read and who borrows your books. She made you a macramé bracelet and brought you an empty hummingbird nest she found. You begin to look forward to her visits and finally accept her invitation to come again for dinner (even though you bring your own food). You eventually enjoy the company of the entire family and sometimes sit on their porch in the evening, laughing and talking. There are subjects you avoid bringing up, but all in all you feel radical acceptance of them and from them. Your efforts to get to know them have reduced your suffering so much that on the occasional night when you are sitting on your back porch with their dog at your feet and you hear bluegrass music above the river and the crickets, you feel a sense of peace and acceptance with things exactly as they are. You have not reached enlightenment, perhaps, but you are certainly closer.

The Solution: Willingness, Turning the Mind, and Radical Acceptance

Even if we want to accept, when we are in pain it takes time, skill, and effort. *Willingness, turning the mind,* and *radical acceptance* are tools to help us, especially in the face of egregious hurts, such as having an incurable illness, irrevocably losing a loved one, having endured abuse in childhood, or other painful realities we cannot change. These tools are also useful in situations we cannot change easily or quickly, such as having a grinding, low-paying job or inadequate housing, or being obese, or feeling isolated and lonely. Willingness, turning the mind, and radical acceptance even help with smaller setbacks and disappointments by allowing us to accept pain moment by moment instead of turning to harmful behaviors to avoid our pain. The more we accept, the more our suffering decreases and the more our lives can assume a peaceful and balanced course.

Willingness

The first reality acceptance skill is willingness. Willingness is an attitude we can adopt when faced with a problem. We take a stance that is flexible and can-do, even in the face of fear. We will not avoid, hunker down, turn negative, or give up. We will go toward the problem or the pain with courage and without clinging desperately to the outcome we want but may not be able to achieve.

When our wise mind says that we must endure, willingness helps us be ready. Willingness will keep us flexible but grounded, mentally and emotionally prepared, and in touch with all the skills in our repertoire. Being willing is bringing our best to a grueling task, a crisis, or just everyday life. It is the opposite of a "bad attitude."

An example of willingness is volunteering to be the designated driver at the bachelor party to keep everyone safe and to keep your commitment to yourself to stay sober, rather than either getting smashed like the others or skipping the party completely (unless you are very early in sobriety and skipping the party is the only way that will work). Here are some exercises to help you increase willingness and proceed toward whatever you are avoiding facing.

Exercises to "Get the Feeling" of Willingness

1. *Letting go.* Find a warm pool or hot springs and practice floating. Lie on your back and let go of tension in your body. (You

may wish to have someone spot you while you undertake this exercise.) Allow yourself to rise and fall with your breath. Notice how it feels to let go of clinging to your position in the water. When you are completely relaxed you should be able to keep your face above water easily even as your body rises and falls with your breath. Experience being willing to be supported by the water.

2. *Willing body*. Practice deepening your breath and relaxing first your face and hands. Let your arms hang loose at your sides, unclench your fists, and turn your hands gently to palms up. As you practice willing body, continue to pay special attention to relaxing parts where you chronically hold tension, such as your buttocks or shoulders. Encourage yourself by saying, *I may not like this but I can accept it.*

3. *Assume a half smile*. Half smile is a skill that uses the hardwired connection between facial muscles and the brain to change the way you feel (Linehan 1993a). Soften your eyes and brow and completely relax your face. Ever so gently turn up the corners of your mouth until you can feel a little tickle in your brain. That tickle is your brain responding to your serene facial expression. It need not rise to the level of a full smile to be effective, and it should not become a mask or a grin. According to Linehan (1993a), a half smile is different from masking because you are choosing this facial expression of peace and acceptance just for yourself, not for anyone else.

4. *Encourage yourself*. Gently coax yourself to accept a situation by repeating phrases such as *I can get through this, This will be over soon*, or *I am being strong right now*. Say to yourself, *I am proud of myself for being so brave* or *I am handling this pretty well*, when indicated. Allow yourself to cry as needed and provide comfort for yourself. Don't indulge in self-pity (*Everything bad always happens to me*) or self-judgment (*I am such a failure*). Instead, validate your difficulty and your efforts with

kind, encouraging self-talk, as in, *Of course this is hard, but I am coping with it.* Self-encouragement and self-validation will increase your willingness.

Turning the Mind

The second skill for accepting reality is turning the mind. Our minds operate independent of our will. Left to their own devices, our minds tend to go on autopilot and find their way to painful places of worry, loss, judgment and nonacceptance. This tendency is more pronounced during times of depression and anxiety and when we are in the aftermath of loss or trauma. Turning the mind is bringing our attention back, again and again, to acceptance of what is, even when we are beset by urges to ruminate or avoid or when we are in the presence of intense emotions, flashbacks, or dissociative behavior.

Turning the mind marks the choice between tolerating distress and acting on our emotions, triggers, addictions, compulsions, or other strong patterns. Emotion mind would have us believe that we are helpless in the face of these strong drives and that we have no choice but to follow the tendencies of the mind into problematic behavior. We feel that we can't help ruminating when we are depressed, drinking when we are lonely, or dissociating when we are triggered. But even in the presence of triggers, or when addictions, obsessions, and compulsions are strong, even when auditory hallucinations or mania are on board, we still have choices. We can turn our minds away from avoiding, giving up, or giving in, and return to acceptance. If we acknowledge, *I am experiencing pain*, we can figure out how to deal with the pain, including getting help to avoid relapsing into problematic behavior.

Turning the mind is like standing at a crossroads and then taking steps on the path to wise mind (Linehan 1993a). Each

233

time we turn the mind we strengthen the power of awareness and increase the likelihood that we will choose the wise mind path when we again find ourselves at a crossroads. The more we choose this option, the more confidence we gain in our ability to turn the mind and the easier it becomes.

We can see this clearly when we meditate for long periods of time, such as at a retreat. Whenever we try to be still we see the tendency of the mind to wander constantly. If we just let our minds wander, we begin to feel bored, restless, and even miserable. When we practice turning the mind, we choose again and again to bring attention back to our inner awareness, in the moment. Thoughts and bodily sensations will still come and go, but we will not follow them. By turning the mind we settle into what Tibetan meditation teacher Sakyong Mipham (2004) calls "peaceful abiding." We can stay there for longer and longer periods of time, enjoying the peace and quiet as fruits of our practice.

Turning the mind can be as quick as turning a car or as slow as turning an aircraft carrier. After a big loss, we may have to work hard for a long time to turn the mind toward acceptance. When my first marriage came to an end, I remember awakening before dawn to the sudden realization that my husband was gone. I had been blissfully unaware while I was asleep. Now, newly awake, I felt all over again the sadness and fear of this new reality. I would lie in my bed dreading the day to come, shedding tears, and feeling hopeless. Gradually, I would drag myself out of bed, make coffee, and sit for a few minutes with my cup, working up the courage to face the day.

During that time I would be encouraged by telling myself that all I had to do was get through that day. I didn't have to worry about next month's bills or the years of loneliness my mind was imagining. I turned my mind away from regretting mistakes I'd made or being angry with my husband for things he'd done. I turned my mind away from wishing it could be different or

234

fantasizing about a magical reconciliation. I tried as hard as I could to accept reality as it was, nothing more or less. Then I got up, made breakfast, and packed lunches, turning my mind again and again. By the time I woke my children up, I had glued myself together enough to focus on their needs. It got a tiny bit easier each day, but it took a lot of effort for a long time.

Early in the process, my therapist told me that eventually I would be happy again, accepting that all of this had happened. I did not believe what she said and I was more than a little annoyed with her for saying it. However, she was right. Eventually I was happy again. Eventually, I so fully accepted what had happened that I could say I was happily divorced. By then I was living a new life that could only exist because the old life had come to an end. My new life was born out of countless times of turning my mind toward acceptance. Below are some practices that will help you turn your mind.

Practices to Strengthen Turning the Mind

1. *Notice the content of your thoughts.* Are you dwelling on suffering? If so, turn the mind. Whenever you notice yourself dwelling on your pain, say to yourself, *I'll go home now,* and return to the path of acceptance by observing your breath. (Downloadable audio for this practice can be found at http://www.newharbinger.com/33001.)

2. *Notice the content of your speech.* Are you complaining, whining, blaming, or judging? Turn your mind toward acceptance. Say aloud, "I have been focusing on the negative. I think I'll give that a rest."

3. *Notice your body posture.* Are you tense and constricted? Frowning and hunched up? Turn your mind and relax your body. Begin with three deep cleansing breaths and then relax

your face, jaw, shoulders, and neck. Stretch your arms and legs. Release the tension you are holding in your body, tension that could be a result of nonacceptance.

4. *Ask for help.* Be receptive to universal wisdom. Welcome any indication that grace and harmony exist. Light a candle to represent your intention to accept. Place your hand on your heart and say, with your full attention, *May I find peace in my heart.* When you feel lost or even abandoned by all that you believe in, don't give up. Never give up hope that you will have the strength to accept. Remember, you only have to accept in the moment, for the moment.

Radical Acceptance

The third skill of reality acceptance is radical acceptance. This skill is "radical"—from the Latin *radix*, meaning *root*—because it requires acceptance at the very root of reality. We recognize what we are feeling in the moment and regard that experience with compassion (Brach 2003). This means accepting completely and letting go of deriving any outcome whatsoever from our effort to accept. We do not cling to the magical thought that somehow our acceptance will create the changes we wish would happen. In fact, we let go of even the expectation that we will feel better after having accepted. Radical acceptance may not make us feel better, but it is likely to help us tolerate our pain better—no small consolation.

As Linehan (1993a) points out, accepting does not mean that we see the situation as good or something that "should have been." Let's say we were abandoned by our parents at a young age and grew up in foster care. We spent many years praying for our parents to return and claim us, but they never did. Now that we are grown we are trying to come to terms with the sadness and loss we feel about our parents' abandonment. Radical acceptance means simply accepting the facts—we were given up by our parents, period. Radical acceptance helps us step aside from *this shouldn't have happened to me*. It does not include rationalizing or making up stories to try to feel better, such as that our parents tried hard to keep us but couldn't or that growing up in foster care was better than living with our parents, unless we know those things to be true.

The skill of radical acceptance doesn't require us to put a brave face or positive spin on reality. We are free to use these coping strategies if we choose, but we should be careful that they don't keep us from fully accepting reality, especially how much it hurts. To say *this was God's will* may help some of us accept a painful experience. On the other hand, believing something heinous that happened to us was "God's will" may prevent us from allowing ourselves to acknowledge how random and cruel the event still feels to us, thereby getting in the way of total acceptance and the healing it brings.

Radical acceptance is not about the future. We are not in radical acceptance when we say, *I will never recover from this*. We can only accept the facts, not any extrapolation or prediction from the facts. Acceptance of reality takes no stance on whether reality is good, bad, or indifferent. It simply says, *This is real and I accept it as real*.

The key to radical acceptance is that we can only accept reality in the moment and for the moment. You can only accept for right now that You have pain and numbness in my feet that will not go away and that doctors cannot seem to diagnose. You cannot accept this painful reality for all time because to accept for the future is impossible. Perhaps You will be cured one day— who can say? You can only accept reality for this moment. Similarly, I can only accept for right now that my dog is dead and I miss her terribly. Tomorrow I will have to accept again. The acceptance of today will help but will not accomplish acceptance of loss forever.

When my son was five years old, he was playing in the front yard with his trucks when he found a dry, flattened frog in the driveway. "Momma," he said, "this frog is very dead."

"Yes, it is," I remarked, looking at the little desiccated frog.

"Will it come back to life?" he asked, looking up at me anxiously.

"No, honey, it won't. Would you like to bury it?"

"Yes," he said solemnly, and we dug a hole near the steps and buried the little frog with ceremony. Later that morning, he came into the kitchen and asked me, "Momma, does everything die?" My heart sank. I had anticipated this might happen, but suddenly I felt completely unprepared to lead my son out of the Garden of Eden.

"Yes, son," I said. "Everything that is alive dies."

"Will you die?"

"One day. Probably a long, long time from now, when you are all grown up."

He was quiet for a few moments. "Will Papa die?"

I nodded. "Yes, but probably when he is very old, older than Granddaddy."

Again, he was quiet for a few moments, as if considering whether to ask the next question. I squatted down beside him and waited.

"Momma, will I die?" he finally asked in a voice just above a whisper.

All of us come to the realization of mortality at some point in childhood. For many it is one of the first harsh realizations about our nature. Other realizations will follow—so many that life can seem like one painful awakening after another. Without a doubt, the distribution of suffering is not an even one. Some people, beginning in early childhood, experience more loss, pain, and injustice than others. Children who grow up in a struggle for survival, whether because of poverty, war, abuse, or neglect, or because they have not felt loved and been kept secure, can feel haunted for life by their experiences. Catastrophic loss in adult-hood, such as the death of a child, contracting a terrible disease, or losing all your possessions and your livelihood, can transform a happy life into one of suffering. Refusing to accept terrible pain does not make it go away. Radical acceptance doesn't either. But it does help us bear the painful reality.

In the case of my son, his confrontation with death was for-gotten for the rest of that day, but at bedtime, when I was tucking him in, it came up again. "I'm worried about my animals," he said. "I don't want them to die." He took several stuffed animals from his toy box and tucked each one in beside him, assuring them they would be safe all night. Then he took his favorite, a soft, floppy bunny that had belonged to his father, and clasped it to his chest. "You are old, so I will hold you," he said. "Momma, you can read my story now; we're ready." He was asleep before his story was over. For the moment and to the degree that he could, my little boy had accepted that everyone and everything dies.

To strengthen your grasp of reality acceptance, practice this contemplation exercise.

Exercise: Contemplate the Impermanence of All Things

Find a photograph of the earth from space. Consider that the earth was created about 4.5 billion years ago and will likely be absorbed into the expanding, dying sun in 7.6 billion years, thereby being completely destroyed. Gaze at the photograph and contemplate how every human being and every animal and every bit of life ever known by us dwells or has dwelt on this planet, and everything on earth is impermanent. Contemplate what this means to you. When your mind wanders, bring it back to the photograph of the earth and the awareness of impermanence. Try to hold the image in your awareness.

The Obstacles: Willfulness and Clinging

Willfulness is the opposite of willingness. Willfulness is stubbornness, rigidity, attachment, and clinging. Willfulness often arises out of fear or perceived threat. We may be willful because we are afraid of our pain or are afraid we don't have what it takes to resist the urges of emotion mind. We might believe we will lose something essential if we let go of clinging to our attachments. We might fear being forced to do something we don't want to do or to give up something we can't have but still desperately want. Sometimes we become willful when a desire is so strong we don't even want to resist it, even though we know giving in to the desire won't be good for us.

One way that we cling to pain is to keep asking ourselves why a particular thing happened to us or to someone close to us. Any pain that we interpret as random seems especially hard to bear. *Why did I get laid off? Why did my mother get cancer? Why was my child killed?* Asking *why?* can indicate nonacceptance of the fact that everything is caused. When we look at events leading to either a natural or a human-made disaster, we see that they are chains of cause and effect. So, too, are many choices people make that seem impossible to understand or accept, such as becoming addicted to drugs or committing a crime. It may be painful at first to contemplate the facts. It is also painful to accept that we don't know or will never know all the facts. But in the long run it is easier to accept when we stop asking, *Why did this have to happen to me?* and start accepting that it did.

We may not be able to change a particular situation, but we can choose to take steps to prevent a similar situation from happening to us or someone else. This is why parents who lose children to gun violence get involved in gun safety and those who have experienced cancer themselves or in their families often become dedicated to trying to prevent it in others or to work toward finding a cure.

240

Below are practices that can help reduce willfulness and clinging in order to begin accepting things just as they are.

Practices to Reduce Willfulness and Clinging

1. *Letting go of why.* Whatever you are struggling to accept, try letting go of asking *why?* Instead try to track, as best as you can, the chain of events leading to whatever has occurred. For example, *I got laid off because my local company was sold to a multinational conglomerate that moved our jobs to Bangladesh to reduce labor costs* or *My mother got cancer because she was exposed to radon gas in her home for thirty years unbeknownst to her.* Or recognize that you may not ever know the cause. When you find yourself asking *why?* step back and take a deep breath. Replace *why?* with the phrase, *It happened. I don't know why and I may never know. I don't like it, but I accept it.*

2. *The yes meditation* (adapted with permission from Brantley 2007). Allow about ten minutes for this practice. Sit comfortably in a quiet place where you won't be disturbed. Settle your mind and body with slow abdominal breathing for about a minute. Then allow your awareness to be open to anything that arises. It may be discomfort, such as physical sensations, thoughts, or emotions, or it may be pleasant or neutral stimuli. Allow whatever arises to be present and identify it in your mind. It could be pain in your jaw, or feeling tired, peaceful, or comfortable. It could also be *sadness arising at conflict in my relationship, worry about my daughter's performance in school, the clock ticking, a lot to do today,* or *going on vacation.* Allow the thought or sensation to be present as you breathe in. On the out-breath say *yes* to whatever arises. The meditation then becomes *pain in my jaw, yes; very tired, yes;*

241

sadness about Bob, yes; worry about Lisa, yes; clock ticking, yes; a lot to do, yes; excited about going on vacation, yes; and so on. When your mind wanders too far into the thought or sensation, bring it back to *yes* on the out-breath. If your mind becomes still, you can keep practicing this exercise with *this moment* on the in-breath and *yes* on the out-breath.

• Liza's Story

Liza, fifty-two, was recently widowed and had a sixteen-year-old daughter, Morgan. Liza's husband, Mitchell, had died of an aneurysm six months before. "He kissed me goodbye in the morning and by noon he was dead," she said.

Mitchell had been a successful art dealer and gallery owner. Since the gallery provided most of their income, after Mitchell's death Liza decided to close her small family law practice and try to keep the gallery open. In the chaos that accompanied taking over Mitchell's business, Liza came across information that led her to believe he misrepresented some of the art he sold in the year before his death. She also found letters and cards that made her think he was sexually involved with several of his clients. "We had been happy," she said. "At least I thought we were happy. I was so completely stunned that for weeks I couldn't even feel angry. Now I can't even cry anymore. I am furious at him."

Not long after these discoveries, Liza started having severe anxiety. "I walk around all day with a lump in my throat like I swallowed a marble. I feel like I am going to cry from aggravation any minute. My stomach churns and my head aches. I don't sleep longer than three hours at a stretch, and I'm up before five o'clock in the morning, wide-awake. The medications they gave me do nothing for any of it."

Liza's daughter was faring better. "It was very hard for Morgan at first. It was so sudden. But she is adjusting— doing much better than I am, in fact. She doesn't know any of this stuff about him. Sometimes I'd like to tell her. Of course I won't, but I can hardly stand it when she goes on and on about what a great father he was. Sure, a great father who was lying to his family and cheating his customers." Liza sobbed. "I hate him now."

"I haven't talked with anyone about this," Liza said. "I would rather die than have it get out. First of all, I don't know what the repercussions will be about some of the lies he told. I could get sued and lose everything, or the gallery's reputation could be destroyed. If people found out about the affairs I would be so ashamed I just couldn't stand it. I can't even bring myself to talk to an attorney, and I *am* an attorney!"

Liza found it impossible to accept all that was happening to her. Not only had she lost her husband, but her identity as a happily married woman was called into question, making it harder to be a widow, too. Liza was experiencing complicated bereavement, a type of grieving that can intensify and prolong painful emotions (American Psychiatric Association 2013).

At first Liza had tried to wall off everything but anger. She wouldn't allow herself to feel sadness for longer than a few moments. Meanwhile, anxiety had flooded her, filling in all the spaces where grief was suppressed. She feared that acknowledging her sadness would incapacitate her, but anxiety was taking a toll. And she was procrastinating about dealing with problems at the gallery. "Honestly, I just tend to willfully ignore things I don't want to see."

Eventually, Liza did meet with an attorney friend about Mitchell's misrepresentation. The attorney advised her to disclose the misrepresentations to the customers affected and be prepared to buy back the art involved. She could use a small contingency fund Mitchell had established for buy-backs.

"I feel hugely relieved now about the gallery. I'm trying to accept that there were things about Mitchell's business dealings I had always wondered about. I know now that he was less than honest. I think I had seen the signs of it in the past but refused to look at them. I won't do it like he did. I may not make as much money, but I want to be able to sleep at night."

Liza was still struggling to accept the fact of Mitchell's infidelity. "I feel like a fool for believing in him all those years. I want to take down all his pictures in the house. I feel like it was all a lie—every bit of it. I just have to put the past aside, I guess, and not look back. But sometimes Morgan wants to talk about her father, and I just don't know what to do!"

Liza knew that her nonacceptance was getting in the way of parenting her daughter, but she was still too angry to practice willingness. To grieve Mitchell's death fully, Liza needed to accept that he had been unfaithful. She acknowledged that he had always been flirtatious with other women and she had tried not to notice. She admitted knowing that he had a casual attitude toward the truth long before she discovered evidence of his most hurtful lies. She struggled to accept that she could never completely forgive him for what he had done and perhaps never resolve her complicated emotions.

"I have been trying for so long to make it all harmonize. It's as if I want a happy ending after all this pain. But the reality is, there is no happy ending. When

I look at my life I can no longer separate the pain from the joy."

Finally, Liza was ready to face her grief over Mitchell's death. She allowed herself to feel the pain of missing his body and the warmth of him in bed, feelings she had tried to banish when she first uncovered the infidelity. She cried when telling me about how much she had enjoyed their conversation, how they loved to cook together, and how he and Morgan were so close. She recalled their last anniversary together, when they had climbed above the tree line in the mountains and made love in a little meadow far off the trail.

"I went to the wedding of some old friends over the weekend. It is a second marriage for both of them. The man performing the wedding had two carafes of wine, one red and one white. He said the red one symbolized pain and the white one symbolized joy. After he pronounced them husband and wife, he poured the two carafes together into a third carafe and they both drank from the mixed wine. At first I thought it was a little corny, then I had this realization that this is exactly what my life is. I can't drink from just one carafe, either joy or pain. It's all mixed up together."

Liza's intense and complicated emotions had gotten in the way of practicing reality acceptance after her husband died. Her reaction to discovering his deceptions was willfulness. She shut down all of her emotions except anger and allowed her mind to wander over anger-fueled thoughts and fantasies. Perhaps because she avoided sadness she was plagued with anxiety instead. Only by willingly facing and accepting all of the convoluted, complex pain could she deal with the realities of widowhood and eventually heal.

Increasingly, Liza turned her mind away from rumination about how things shouldn't be as they were.

Instead, she bravely embraced what was true. Liza radically accepted that her marriage had been a deeply flawed one, but one she nonetheless cherished, and one that she would honor for her daughter's sake. Accepting these painful realities set Liza free to go on with her life.

Pain, as we know, is unavoidable. However, we can learn and practice skills that help us create the possibility of a life without suffering. Let's turn to ways we can synthesize these skills and live more mindfully.

Creating a Synthesis: Mindfulness Skills and the Eightfold Path

For those of us who have suffered a great deal and struggled to heal, the desire to transcend suffering burns bright. We know it is impossible to escape pain, but we want to free ourselves from suffering. Is it possible for everyday people to find *more than temporary* relief?

When Siddhartha became the Enlightened One, over 2500 years ago, he answered this question. He said that a path to freedom from suffering existed. He called it the Noble Eightfold path (figure 12). The Buddha defined the Path as a way to attain enlightenment, meaning the cessation of suffering and the experience of equanimity. A great deal has been written on the Eightfold Path from a strictly Buddhist perspective. I do not want to suggest that DBT skills are equivalent to the Eightfold Path, or that using DBT skills makes one a Buddhist practitioner. Nevertheless, the mindfulness skills we have been discussing, when practiced assiduously over time, can lead from a "life worth living" to a life lived in clarity and equanimity, similar to Buddha's prescription for ending suffering. Let's take a look at the Path and DBT mindfulness skills together.

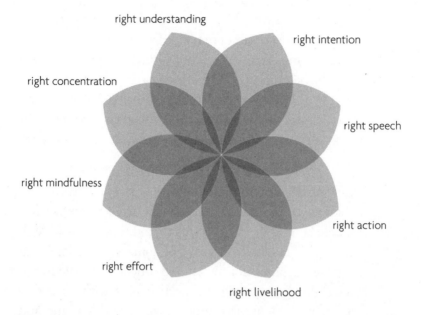

right understanding
right intention
right concentration
right speech
right mindfulness
right action
right effort
right livelihood

Figure 12

1. *Right understanding* traditionally means embracing the Four Noble Truths and understanding that the origin of suffering is the embrace of ignorance, greed, and hatred. When we cling to our desires (getting what we want and avoiding what we don't want) our greed, hatred, and ignorance increase and our understanding decreases. We see ourselves as separate from others and cling to our separateness. In a contemporary skills context such as that of this book, in order to approach right understanding we begin with letting go of clinging to our judgments, our negative preoccupations, and the distortions of emotion mind. A step on the path to right understanding is accessing wise mind.

2. *Right intention* traditionally means paying attention to your intentions because they shape your thoughts, which in turn shape your words and your actions and, finally,

shape your destiny. Intentions set the stage for all that follows. In the contemporary skills context, right intention is paying attention to your ultimate wise mind goals from the beginning of your efforts to the end, to enhance your own well-being and that of others. When we use effectiveness, we are beginning the path toward right intention because we are shaping our destiny with conscious purpose.

3. *Right speech* traditionally means speaking truth and avoiding gossip and malicious or divisive speech. Is what we are about to say true? Is this a good time to say it? Will saying this result in more wholesome connections and increase happiness for myself and others? In a contemporary skills context, right speech begins with accessing wise mind by making use of the skills of describing and nonjudgment.

4. *Right action* traditionally means acting in accordance with certain universal precepts, such as avoiding killing or harming others, stealing, or engaging in sexual impropriety. In a contemporary skills context, we approach right action when we pursue our wise mind goals using effectiveness. By doing what works, playing by the rules, and adhering to wise mind values we can approach right action.

5. *Right livelihood* traditionally means making your living in a way that is not abusive to people or animals. In a contemporary skills context, we approach right livelihood when we do our best to find work that is neither harmful to others nor detrimental to ourselves. The path to right livelihood challenges us to go beyond *it's just a job* or *I am just following orders* and leads us toward work that allows us to act from wise mind, and fully participate in our livelihood.

6. *Right effort* is what is traditionally brought to the practice of mindfulness and meditation, where emphasis is placed on having a clear and stable mind. Right effort means being aware of how negative thoughts arise and distract us from our foundation of inner knowing, whether we are in seated meditation or going about our daily lives. Not everyone will establish a dedicated practice of meditation. Still, the regular practice of turning the mind is a first step on the path of right effort. Whenever we turn our minds away from negative thoughts and urges and become willing to be present to the moment, our minds become clearer and more stable. Turning the mind and willingness are the beginnings of right effort.

7. *Right mindfulness* is also traditionally associated with the practice of meditation. Right mindfulness is the practice of being constantly attentive to the present moment. In a contemporary context, right mindfulness keeps us from wandering into confusion by remaining anchored in the present. When we practice observing and one-mindfully in the moment, we take small but significant steps on the path to right mindfulness.

8. *Right concentration* traditionally refers to the ability to maintain one-pointed focus in order to develop a very clear awareness that allows us see through ignorance. Deep concentration alone does not lead to enlightenment, though it might put us in the vicinity of enlightenment. But now, based on neuroscience, we know that concentrating for long periods of time changes our brains so that we experience more equanimity (Lazar, Kerr, and Wasserman 2005; Siegel 2007). Using all of the mindfulness and acceptance skills described in this book can lead to right concentration, where suffering is eliminated and enlightenment, or peace, is possible.

Chapter 11

THE JOURNEY CONTINUES

In this book I have been discussing mindfulness and reality acceptance skills mainly as ways to manage intense emotions. Most of us know, however, that mindfulness and reality acceptance can offer us much more than a way to calm down. For those of you who would like to strengthen mindfulness in your life by creating a daily mindfulness practice, this chapter discusses some next steps you can take.

Recognizing Your Thirst

Every human being has the capacity for inner fulfillment. You may feel that you have little or no control over your outer circumstances, but everyone has the power to enter into the present moment and accept things just as they are. By choosing to be mindful, you choose to be aware of your inner wisdom. Such awareness, by its very nature, leads to further awareness, including appreciation, contentment, peace, and freedom. Every day you can awaken to an expanded sense of yourself and your world.

You can also fall back to sleep. You can lose touch with yourself, including your sense of joy and freedom. The old habits of nonacceptance, suffering, and acting on emotional urges can return, sometimes with a vengeance. Unfortunately, it isn't difficult to lose a lot of the insight and skill you've gained.

One way to decrease the likelihood that you will fall back to sleep is to establish and maintain a daily mindfulness practice. Making time for a daily practice is one of the most important commitments to yourself you can make. The first step to establishing a practice is to recognize your need for peace.

My teacher Prem Rawat has said that we are all thirsty for peace, even though we may not recognize it. Sometimes we may confuse our need for inner fulfillment with our desires for financial security, an intimate relationship, or a comfortable, harmonious home. While these things are much to be desired, our need for inner peace is more fundamental. We can easily overlook this need as we try to satisfy more material desires. This basic need will endure, however, like a thirst that needs quenching. It will motivate us to find that which will satisfy us in a lasting way.

An Indian story attributed to Sri Ramakrishna describes a musk deer's intense search for the source of an elusive fragrance that is driving him wild with desire. The scent, it turns out, emanates from his own body. Like that scent, both the thirst and the water that quenches that thirst are inside of us. Recognizing this is one of the most important realizations we can have. We see that our attention can go from searching outside of ourselves for satisfaction to looking inside, where peace, fulfillment, and awakening can be found. But how, exactly, should we look inside of ourselves? What path should we take?

Finding Your Path and Teacher

Mindfulness and meditation practices are simple activities or a series of activities that allows us to abide in the present moment, intentionally and nonjudgmentally. There are many different practices, most with ancient origins.

The Path

The teachings that surround mindfulness and meditation practice are called the path. A path could be as simple as doing your daily practice by yourself. Most paths, however, offer a community of other practitioners and may include events, retreats, group meditations, inspirational talks, and service activities. Some paths have a lot of structure, ritual, and beliefs, while others have little structure, few rules, and no outright beliefs. Most paths, both structured and unstructured, also have teachers.

The Teacher

Teachers guide, support, and inspire your practice. A good teacher will inspire you with her personal example and will keep you encouraged by advising you about how and when to practice and by taking a genuine interest in your progress. Your relationship with the teacher may be the main thing that keeps you practicing, especially at the beginning. The teacher's caring, good humor, wisdom, and expertise will keep you practicing when it feels like nothing is happening. For many, interactions with the teacher result in powerful awakening experiences.

How can you determine if a teacher is for you? The best way to recognize a prospective teacher is to sample her teachings. If the teacher has published books, recorded talks, or posted writings or videos on a website, check them out. Attend a retreat, event, or talk by the teacher. Do you resonate with what is said and with the person speaking? Is she teaching from experiential knowledge of the subject—that is, does she talk about her own experience of mindfulness practice, awareness, and joy—or does she read or lecture from scriptures? Does her message inspire you to learn more? If you are inspired, continue to listen as long as you want without making a commitment. Let wise mind guide you as you consider whether you would want to be this teacher's student. When you feel ready, ask to become a student. If the teacher accepts you, try to be the most dedicated student you can be. If the teacher rejects you, try not to take it personally. She has probably done you a favor.

It is important that a teacher have credentials to teach, called a *lineage*. A lineage is a succession of teachers who, upon retirement or death, pass the baton to one or several of their students. Having a lineage indicates that a teacher has studied with someone who was a respected teacher and that this teacher believed this student was worthy of being a teacher. No one can call himself an attorney, psychologist, physician, accountant, or certified Honda mechanic unless he has attended a recognized training program, passed the required exams, and perhaps been licensed by the state. Similarly, priests, rabbis, roshis, certain ministers, swamis, imams, yogis, and gurus have received training, ordination, or permission to teach in their religion or practice. Having permission to teach from authorities in the lineage does not guarantee that the person is truly qualified, ethical, or effective, but it provides some transparency about a teacher's credentials, background, and approach.

Don't expect teachers to be tame and domesticated. Even when they appear to be tame they usually are not. A teacher can be outrageous, intense, intimidating, aloof, boring, loving, quiet, confusing, hilarious, or all of the above, and still be ethical and effective. Finding a teacher involves risk, which is one reason why many people are afraid to look. You will need to use your wise mind to discriminate between a safe teacher and a dangerous one. If a teacher makes inappropriate requests of you—such as for sex, money, or improper influence—or behaves in other ways that are clearly unethical, listen closely to the discernment of your wise mind. You can express your concerns directly to the teacher, or just walk away if you must.

While money is necessary for organizations to run retreats and events, rent facilities, pay airfare, and even provide livelihood for the teacher, costs are usually covered by attendance fees and fundraising, not by selling the teaching itself. If the fees to participate in the activities seem exorbitant to you, consider how this will affect your participation. If you encounter problems with a path regarding money or perceived ethical problems, seek a path you can accept without having to overlook things that seem like improprieties.

Teachers have different requirements regarding whether it is acceptable for their students to study with them and another teacher simultaneously. If a teacher requires that you study only with her, recognize that you will be committing to and developing in that one practice. This can be useful, especially for the first years of practice. Other teachers will not ask for exclusivity or even for a commitment from you. They may make no commitment to you either, beyond the specific event you attend with them.

What about having no teacher at all? The main advantage of this choice is that it avoids all the risks I raised above about the teacher. The main disadvantage is that practice without a teacher is hard to maintain and can suffer from a lack of inspiration or clarity. Imagine other activities you would never consider undertaking without a teacher, such as learning to fly a helicopter or having a natural childbirth. Establishing a daily practice of mindfulness or meditation requires a great deal of discipline, nourishment, and guidance, and you can easily get off track or become confused. Without a teacher you are at risk of giving up when the going gets rough.

If you choose to practice without a teacher, I recommend that you gather together with other practitioners and sit with them for at least forty-five minutes a week, share readings, and discuss books on mindfulness. Perhaps you will find this enough structure and inspiration to keep your daily practice going. It may encourage you to look for a teacher when you feel ready.

The Community

Whether your participation is as limited as attending an occasional talk or as comprehensive as joining a monastery, it is likely you will encounter other seekers at least occasionally as you walk your path. The company of fellow students is one of the features of a formal path. Your fellow students can provide encouragement, support, and inspiration, and sometimes their modeling will bolster your efforts to stay focused. Fellow students and other seekers can also be a great distraction. Their behavior as you work together, sit together, and listen to one another and to your teacher may provoke judgments or the fear of being judged. The challenges presented by your fellow students can confuse you enough to cause you to abandon your practice. The same challenges can contribute to your growth in discernment, however, if you remain in touch with your wise mind when interacting with fellow travelers on the path.

What About My Religion?

People sometimes wonder if having a mindfulness practice will interfere with their religion. Since mindfulness practice is not about beliefs, rites, rituals, scriptures, or the afterlife, it should not conflict with any religion. You might want to inquire first into any mindfulness practices that are part of your religious heritage. As mentioned in the introduction, many religions have a mindfulness tradition, such as centering prayer in Christianity, Sufism in Islam, and the Kabbalah in Judaism. You may have been raised in (or still practice) a religion in one tradition and be drawn to a different kind of mindfulness tradition, as did Pat Hawk, a Zen Master (roshi) who was also an ordained Catholic priest.

Next Steps: Effort and Grace

Sometimes our awakening arises from enlightenment experiences that happen all at once and are mysterious in nature, sometimes from day-to-day revelations that we can understand as part of the limitless unfolding of reality. In my experience, the process of awakening is enhanced by my effort and something I call grace.

My effort is to sit down and practice daily, when I feel like it and even when I don't. My effort is to listen to my teacher and to my wise mind every day. My effort is to be willing to feel and notice and appreciate as much as I can.

Then there is grace, defined by some as "the unmerited favor of God" (Stein 1973), and which can also be seen as a quality freely available in the universe. To me, grace is freely available if I ask for and accept it. Because it is abundant, natural, and powerful, I don't feel the need to lock it onto a personal God. I see grace in nature, in the people I love, in the courage of my clients, and in my own thirst, which motivates my effort. But I cannot rule out that it comes from God!

I believe that the need for peace is a powerful force that carries us forward even when the going is hard. I also believe that when we make an effort, something equally powerful—grace— meets us and draws us closer to ultimate reality. I encourage you, in your effortful quest to awaken, to be open to the possibility that such grace is available to you and to turn toward it like a sunflower turns toward the sun.

Before I end this book, I want to offer a story that I hope will inspire you to throw yourself wholeheartedly into practicing these skills. A few years ago I was beginning koan study with Pat Hawk, a small, taciturn Zen master with a dry sense of humor. A koan is a Zen riddle that cannot be solved with logic or thought. The student, puzzling over it, is supposed to be provoked into enlightenment. Pat gave me the koan "Count the number of stars in the heavens" (MacInnes 2007).

It was winter and quite cold outside. Each night I would go out and look up at the dark New Mexico sky with the white clotted stars of the Milky Way and begin to count the stars. Immediately I felt frustrated and fidgety and wondered why I was even bothering with this silly task. At my next meeting with Pat

THE MINDFULNESS SOLUTION FOR INTENSE EMOTIONS

I asked, "Am I really supposed to count the stars?" "Just count," Pat said and ended our interview.

For several weeks I did what I was told, counting stars, following my breath. Each night I would wonder which of the stars I counted were actually galaxies consisting of trillions of stars. There were more stars than I could fathom. The numbers fell away, and wordless awe took their place. Looking at the stars I experienced a profound oneness.

I couldn't wait to tell Pat. "Yes," he said, when I finished telling about my experience, "it is all there, isn't it? Even when you can't see it. Every night and all day too." I knew he wasn't talking about stars. He was talking about a larger reality, an astounding and vast one that we sometimes ignore. As you study and practice the skills in this book, encountering obstacles and overcoming them, don't forget the stars!

ACKNOWLEDGMENTS

Many people were instrumental in this book coming into being. Foremost is Dr. Marsha Linehan, the developer of DBT mindfulness skills, who originally suggested I write on this topic. I would also like to acknowledge my early readers, Linda Hube, Amelia Fern Hube, and Ann Koons, and advisors, Ruth Hernan Dunn, Carol Butler, and Ora Munter—all of whom provided critical feedback, wise counsel, and support for which I am most appreciative. Debra Kaufman, friend, poet, and professional editor, who helped me refine my prose with her tactful and parsimonious edits. I also want to thank Felice Marohn, a Buddhist practitioner and scholar, who helped me refine how I linked DBT to Buddhist teachings. Her insights and clarity were invaluable, especially to chapter 10.

My editors at New Harbinger, including Catharine Meyers, Jess Beebe, Nicola Skidmore, Angela Autry Gorden, Vicraj Gill, and freelancer Susan LaCroix, at times understood my meaning more fully than I did, and I feel lucky to have worked with them. I am thankful for the excellent illustrations provided by Miriam Hill, Amy Shoup, and Heather Garnos.

The following people deserve acknowledgment for their support and encouragement: my children, Woodwyn Koons, Rowan Koons, Aaron Scheps, and Dillon Scheps; and my team at Santa Fe DBT, LLC: Bette Betts, Jill Tiedemann, Lisa Woodridge, Felice Marohn, and Alisa Montano, as well as former teammates Beth O'Rourke, Barbara Carter, and Nesha Morse. And most of all I would like to thank my husband Edward Scheps, who supported me unstintingly, listened to drafts read aloud, and tolerated long weekends when I had to work instead of play. Finally, I want to express my love and gratitude to Prem Rawat, my teacher for more than forty years, who continues to inspire and encourage me to practice with his example, wisdom, and compassion. Being his student has been one of the greatest gifts of my life.

RESOURCES

As you explore mindfulness practice you may find that books and other media can provide inspiration and encouragement. Here are some of my favorite resources, coming from a variety of different traditions—religious and nonreligious—including scriptures, poetry, essays, autobiography, how-to books, short readings, websites, and more. I hope you will find this list helpful. My very best wishes on your journey!

Books

Aitken, Robert. 1982. *Taking the Path of Zen*. New York: North Point Press. In this book Aitken Roshi offers gentle guidance for those drawn to Zen, especially in America.

———. 1984. *The Mind of Clover*. New York: North Point Press. This book is my favorite of Aitken's writings on mindfulness in the Zen tradition.

Batchelor, Stephen. 1998. *Buddhism Beyond Beliefs*. New York: Riverhead Books. An avowed atheist and former monk, Batchelor writes about the essential elements of Buddhism with impassioned clarity.

Bays, Jan Chozen. 2011. *How to Tame a Wild Elephant: Simple Daily Mindfulness Practices for Living Life More Fully and Joyfully*. Boston: Shambhala Publications. Bays is a Zen roshi and a pediatrician. Her book is fresh, lighthearted, and insightful, and includes some great exercises.

Borchert, Boris. 1994. *Mysticism: Its History and Challenge.* Cape Neddick, ME: Samuel Weiser. Recommended by Marsha Linehan as the best book on the subject.

Chödrön, Pema. 1997. *When Things Fall Apart.* Boston: Shambhala Publications. Pema Chödrön is a Buddhist nun who offers encouragement and inspiration for anyone going through a difficult time. This book is a favorite for many of my clients.

Chögyam Trungpa. 1973. *Cutting Through Spiritual Materialism.* Boston: Shambhala Publications. This classic offers valuable teaching on developing discernment about spiritual practice from a famous Tibetan Buddhist lama.

Cooper, David A. 1999. *A Heart of Stillness: A Complete Guide to Learning the Art of Meditation.* Woodstock, VT: Skylight Paths. Cooper teaches meditation from a Jewish perspective.

Durgananda, Swami. 2002. *The Heart of Meditation: Pathways to a Deeper Experience.* South Fallsburg, NY: SYDA Foundation. Durgananda, also known as Sally Kempton, writes beautifully about the inner world and inspires us to go deeper into our practice.

Emerson, Ralph Waldo, and Henry D. Thoreau. 1991. *Nature Walking.* Boston: Beacon. This collection of favorite essays from two of America's greatest thinkers of the Transcendentalist school provides inspiration for people who find spiritual solace in nature.

Hafiz, 1999. *The Gift.* Translated by Daniel Landinsky. New York: Penguin Books. A treasure of Islam, Hafiz lived in Persia in the fourteenth century. His poetry is outrageous, funny, inspiring, strangely modern, and very easy to appreciate.

Hoff, Benjamin. 1982. *The Tao of Pooh*, New York: Penguin Books. This book is a fun introduction to The Way (the Tao), especially if you enjoy the attitude of a certain honey-loving bear and his friends.

Kabir. 2004. *Ecstatic Poems*. Translated by Robert Bly. Boston: Beacon Press. These poems by Kabir, a fifteenth-century Indian poet, are mystical meditations on the moment and the ecstasy available to those who seek it. Bly's translations serve them up perfectly for the modern palate.

Keating, Thomas. 2009. *Intimacy with God: An Introduction to Centering Prayer.* New York: Crossroad Publishing Company. Father Keating provides instruction on contemplative Christianity and the practice of centering prayer.

Kelly, Thomas R. 1941. *A Testament to Devotion.* New York: Harper Brothers. Kelly, a Quaker mystic, writes from his deep love of Christ in a way that transcends religion.

Kornfield, Jack. 1993. *A Path with Heart: A Guide Through the Perils and Promises of Spiritual Life.* New York: Bantam Books. This is a good travelogue for the skeptical seeker.

Lao Tzu. 1972. *Tao Te Ching.* Translated by Gia-Fu Feng and Jane English. New York: Vintage Books. This is an excellent translation of the ancient text, accompanied by photographs and calligraphy. Explore the foundation of Taoism, Qi Gong, and Tai Chi, which also strongly influenced Zen.

May, Gerald. 1982. *Will and Spirit.* New York: HarperCollins. Dr. May, brother of Rollo May and also a psychiatrist, wrote on willingness, influencing Marsha Linehan, the developer of DBT.

Mello, Anthony de. 1982. *Song of the Bird.* New York: Doubleday. This book by Jesuit priest and mindfulness practitioner de Mello contains short, funny, and inspiring stories from many traditions, with nonreligious commentary. The stories can be used for solo reflection and for discussion in teams and groups.

Mipham, Sakyong. 2004. *Turning the Mind into an Ally*. New York: Riverhead Books. This book contains clear, simple instructions and encouragement for meditators on dealing with the mind, from the son and lineage holder of Chögyam Trungpa.

Nepo, Mark. 2000. *The Book of Awakening: Having the Life You Want by Being Present to the Life You Have*. San Francisco: Conari Press. This is an excellent compendium of short daily readings and exercises to motivate your practice.

Nhat Hanh, T. 1991. *Peace Is Every Step: The Path of Mindfulness in Everyday Life*. New York: Bantam Books. This Vietnamese Buddhist monk and teacher was a prolific writer whose work is easy to read and imbued with kindness, hope, and encouragement.

Oliver, Mary. 1992, 2005. *New and Selected Poems*. 2 vols. Boston: Beacon Press. Oliver's poetry evokes the joy she finds from immersing herself in the natural world. It is imbued with awakened mystical awareness but not at all religious.

Rawat, Prem. 2013. *The Greatest Truth of All: You Are Alive*. Amsterdam: Words of Peace Global. Rawat is a teacher who brings a nonreligious, practical message about experiencing inner peace. This book is transcribed from his talks given to audiences large and small all over the world.

Rilke, Rainer Maria. 1980. *The Selected Poems of Rainer Marie Rilke* (English and German ed.). Translated by Stephen Mitchell. New York: Vintage Books. A little more challenging than some of the poetry in this list, Rilke is worth the effort. The translation highlights the mystical, nonreligious nature of Rilke's work and includes a beautiful introduction by the poet Robert Hass.

Rumi, Jalal Al-Din. 1996. *The Essential Rumi.* Translated by Coleman Barks. New York: HarperCollins. Born in Afghanistan in the thirteenth century, Rumi remains one of the most popular poets today because of his humor, his emotional intensity, and the sheer beauty of his language. Rumi comes from the mystical Sufi tradition of Islam. This is a very accessible translation.

Salzberg, Sharon. 1995. *Loving-Kindness: The Revolutionary Art of Happiness.* Boston: Shambhala Publications. This is a classic work on *metta*, or loving-kindness meditation, a highly useful practice to increase acceptance and compassion.

Watts, Alan. 1966. *The Book: On the Taboo Against Knowing Who You Are.* New York: Random House. This book inspires further curiosity into the question, *Who am I?* Very provocative, it encourages the reader to inquire into regarding one's "true self."

Yogananda, Paramahansa. 1946. *Autobiography of a Yogi.* New York: The Philosophical Library. This is a classic introduction to the spiritual search from an Indian perspective, and a fun read.

Websites

http://www.newharbinger.com/33001. Audio files for various practices in this book are available for download here.

http://www.dharmaseed.org. Western Buddhist teachings from the Vipassana tradition.

http://www.mindful.org. A resource for mindfulness in daily life.

http://www.wopg.org. Streaming videos and podcasts of Prem Rawat's latest talks from all over the world.

http://www.premrawat.com. Short streaming video direct to camera by Prem Rawat.

http://www.soundstrue.com. Audiotapes, podcasts, and more.

http://www.centeringprayer.com. Information on communities and retreats.

http://www.dharmanet.org. More access to Zen teachers and communities in the United States.

http://www.freemindfulness.org. Free guided meditations.

REFERENCES

American Psychiatric Association. 2013. *Diagnostic and Statistical Manual of Mental Disorders*. Arlington, VA: American Psychiatric Publishing.

Addis, M. E., and C. R. Martell. 2004. *Overcoming Depression One Step at a Time*. Oakland, CA: New Harbinger Publications.

Adler, J. M. 2012. "Living into the Story: Agency and Coherence in a Longitudinal Study of Narrative Identity Development and Mental Health over the Course of Psychotherapy." *Journal of Personality and Social Psychology* 102(2): 367–89.

Barkley, R. A. 2012. *Executive Functions*. New York: Guilford Publications.

Batchelor, S. 1998. *Buddhism Without Beliefs*. New York: Riverhead Books.

Batty, D., and M. Weaver. 2009. "Black Box Confirms Hudson Plane Lost Power in Both Engines." *The Guardian*, http://www.guardian.co.uk/world/2009/jan/20/hudson-plane-crash-black-box.

Beck, J. S. 2011. *Cognitive Behavior Therapy: Basics and Beyond*. 2nd ed. New York: Guilford Publications.

Bedard, M. 2003. "Pilot Evaluation of a Mindfulness-Based Intervention to Improve Quality of Life Among Individuals who Sustained Traumatic Brain Injuries." *Disability and Rehabilitation* 25(13): 722–31.

Behar, E., I. D. DiMarco, E. R. Hekler, J. Mohlman, and A. M. Staples. 2009. "Current Theoretical Models of Generalized Anxiety Disorder (GAD)): Conceptual Review and Treatment Implications." *Journal of Anxiety Disorders* 23: 1011–23.

Bermond, B., K. Clayton, A. Liberova, O. Luminet, T. Maruszewski, and P. Ricci Bitti. 2007. "A Cognitive and an Affective Dimension of Alexithymia in Six Languages and Seven Populations." *Cognition and Emotion* 21: 1125–36 doi: 10.1080/02699930601056989.

Biskin, R. S., and J. Paris. 2013. "Comorbidities in Borderline Personality Disorder." *Psychiatric Times* January 9, 2013.

Borchert, B. 1994. *Mysticism: Its History and Challenge.* York Beach, ME: Samuel Weiser.

Bowen, S., K. Witkiewitz, T. Dillworth, and G. Marlatt. 2007. "The Role of Thought Suppression in the Relationship Between Mindfulness Meditation and Alcohol Use." *Addictive Behaviors* 32(10): 2324–28.

Brach, T. 2003. *Radical Acceptance: Embracing Your Life with the Heart of a Buddha.* New York: Bantam.

Brantley, J. 2007. *Calming Your Anxious Mind.* Oakland, CA: New Harbinger Publications.

Buckingham, W., D. Burham, P. King, C. Hill, M. Weeks, and J. Marenbon. 2011. *The Philosophy Book (Big Ideas Simply Explained).* New York: DK Publishing.

Burns, K., and A. Stechler. 1984. *Hands to Work, Hearts to God.* Documentary film.

Caccioppo, J. T., and W. Patrick. 2008. *Loneliness.* New York: W.W. Norton.

Chapman, A. L., K. Gratz, and M. Brown. 2006. "Solving the Puzzle of Deliberate Self-Harm: The Experiential Avoidance Model." *Behaviour Research and Therapy* 44(3): 371–94.

Chess, S., A. Thomas, and H. Birch. 1970. "The Origins of Personality." *Scientific American* 102–9.

Cowan, N. 2008. "What Are the Differences Between Long-Term, Short-Term and Working Memory?" *Progress in Brain Research* 169: 323–38. doi: 10.1016/S0079–6123(07)000209

Csikszentmihalyi, M. 1997. *Finding Flow: The Psychology of Engaging in Everyday Life.* New York: Basic Books.

Czopp, A. M., M. Monteith, and A. Mark. 2006. "Standing Up for a Change: Reducing Bias Through Interpersonal Confrontation." *Journal of Personality and Social Psychology* 90(5): 784–803.

Davidson, R. J., J. Kabat-Zinn, J. Schumacher, M. Rosenkranz, D. Muller, S. Santorelli, F. Urbanowski, A. Harrington, K. Bonus, and J. Sheridan. 2003. "Alterations in Brain and Immune Function Produced by Mindfulness Mediation." *Psychosomatic Medicine* 65: 564–70.

Department of Health and Human Services, Centers for Disease Control and Prevention (NIOSH). 1999. cdc.gov/hiosh/docs /99–101.

Diamond, J. 2012. *The World Until Yesterday: What Can We Learn from Traditional Societies?* New York: Viking Press.

Dimidjian, S., S. Hollon, K. Dobson, R. J. Kohlenberg, R. Gallop, D. K. Markley, and D. C. Atkins. 2006. "Randomized Trial of Behavioral Activation, Cognitive Therapy and Antidepressant Medication in Acute Treatment of Adults with Major Depression." *Journal of Clinical and Consulting Psychology* n.s. 74(4): 658–70.

Dobson, K. S., Hollon, S. D., Dimidjian, S., Schmaling, K. B., Kohlenberg, R. J., Gallop, R. J., Rizvi, S. L., Gollan, J. K., Dunner, D. L., and Jacobson, N. S. 2008. "Randomized Trial of Behavioral Activation, Cognitive Therapy, and Antidepressant Medication in the Prevention of Relapse and

Recurrence in Major Depression." *Journal of Consulting and Clinical Psychology* 76(3): 468–77.

Eaton, N. R., R. F. Krueger, K. M. Keyes, A. E. Skodol, K. E. Markon, B. F. Grant, and D. S. Hasin. 2010. "Borderline Personality Disorder Comorbidity: Relationship to the Internalizing-Externalizing Structures of Common Mental Disorders." *Psychological Medicine* 41(5): 1041–50.

Ekman, P., and W. V. Friesen. 2003. *Unmasking the Face: A Guide to Recognizing Emotions from Facial Expressions*. Cambridge, MA: Major Books.

Emmons, R. A., and M. E. McCullough. 2003. "Counting Blessings Versus Burdens: An Experimental Investigation of Gratitude and Subjective Well-Being in Daily Life." *Journal of Personality and Social Psychology* 84: 377–89.

Evans, G. W. 2003. "The Built Environment and Mental Health." *Journal of Urban Health: Bulletin of the New York Academy of Medicine* 80: 536–55.

Fuster, J. 2008. *The Prefrontal Cortex*. 4th ed. London: Academic Press.

Gallwey, W. T. 1997. *The Inner Game of Tennis*. New York: Random House.

Germer, C. 2004. "What Is Mindfulness?" *Insight Journal* Fall: 24–5.

Godfrin, K., and C. Van Heeringen. 2010. "The Effects of Mindfulness-Based Cognitive Therapy on Recurrence of Depressive Episodes, Mental Health and Quality of Life: A Randomized Controlled Study." *Behaviour Research and Therapy* 8: 738–46.

Goleman, D. 2011. *Social Intelligence: The New Science of Human Relationships*. New York: Bantam Books.

Gonzalez, F. J. 1998. *Dialectic and Dialogue: Plato's Practice of Philosophical Inquiry.* Evanston, IL: Northwestern University Press.

Greeson, J. M. 2009. "Mindfulness Research Update." *Complementary and Alternative Medicine* 14(1): 10–18. doi: 10.1177/1533210108329862.

Greeson, J. M., M. J. Smoski, E. C. Suarez, J. G. Brantley, A. G. Ekblad, T. R. Lynch, and R. Q. Wolever. 2015. "Decreased Symptoms of Depression After Mindfulness-Based Stress Reduction: Potential Moderating Effects of Religiosity, Spirituality, Trait Mindfulness, Sex, and Age." *The Journal of Alternative and Complementary Medicine* 21(3): 166–74.

Grossman, P., L. Niemann, S. Schmidt, and H. Walach. 2004. "Mindfulness-Based Stress Reduction and Health Benefits: A Meta-Analysis." *Journal of Psychosomatic Research* 57(1): 35–43.

Gunderson, J. 2009. "Borderline Personality Disorder: Ontology of a Diagnosis." *American Journal of Psychiatry* 166(5): 530–39.

Harmon, W., Ed. 1990. *The Classic Hundred Poems.* New York: Columbia University Press.

Hatfield, E., J. T. Capaccio, and R. L. Rapson. 1994. *Emotional Contagion.* Cambridge: Cambridge University Press.

Hinton, D. E., V. Pich, A. Nickerson, S. G. Hofmann, and M. W. Otto. 2013. "Mindfulness and Acceptance Techniques as Applied to Refugee and Ethnic Minority Populations: Examples from Culturally Adapted CBT (CA-CBT)." *Cognitive and Behavioral Practice* 20(1): 33–41.

Hope, D. A., R. G. Heimberg, and C. L. Turk. 2006. *Managing Social Anxiety: A Cognitive-Behavioral Treatment Approach.* Oxford University Press: New York.

Jacob, G. A., K. Hellstem, N. Owe, M. Pillman, C. N. Scheel, N. Rusch, and K. Lieb. 2009. "Emotional Reactions to Standardized Stimuli in Women with Borderline Personality Disorder: Stronger Negative Affect But No Differences in Reactivity." *Journal of Nervous and Mental Disease* 197: 808–15.

Jorgensen, C. R. 2006. "Disturbed Sense of Identity in Borderline Personality Disorder." *Journal of Personality Disorders* 20(6): 618–44.

Kabat-Zinn, J. 1990. *Full Catastrophe Living.* New York: Bantam Books.

Kernberg, O. 1967. "Borderline Personality organization." *Journal of the American Psychoanalytic Association* 15: 641–85.

Killingsworth, M. A., and D. T. Gilbert. 2010. "A Wandering Mind Is an Unhappy Mind." *Science* 330(6006): 932. doi:10.1126/science.1192439

Knapp, M. L., and J. A. Daly. 2002. *Handbook of Interpersonal Communication.* 3rd ed. Thousand Oaks, CA: Sage Publications.

Kristeller, J. L. 2010. "Spiritual Engagement as a Mechanism of Change in Mindfulness and Acceptance-Based Therapies." In *Assessing Mindfulness and Acceptance Processes in Clients,* Ruth Baer, Ed. 155–84. Oakland, CA: New Harbinger Publications.

Lazar, S.W., C. Kerr, and R. H. Wasserman. 2005. "Meditation Experience is Associated with Increased Cortical Thickness." *Neuroreport* 16(17): 1893–97.

Lehman, D. 2006. *The Oxford Book of American Poetry.* Oxford: Oxford University Press.

Linehan, M. M., H. E. Armstrong, A. Suarez, D. Allmon, and H. L. Heard. 1991. "Cognitive-Behavioral Treatment of

Chronically Parasuicidal Borderline patients." *Archives of General Psychiatry* 48(12): 1060–64.

Linehan, M. M. 1993. *Cognitive Behavioral Treatment for Borderline Personality Disorder.* New York: Guilford Publications.

———. 1993a. *Skills Training Manual for Borderline Personality Disorder.* New York: Guilford Publications.

———. 2014. *DBT Skills Training Manual.* 2nd ed. New York: Guilford Publications.

Linehan, M. M., L. Dimeff, K. Koerner, and E. M. Miga. 2014. "Research on Dialectical Behavior Therapy: Summary of the Data to Date." Seattle, WA: Linehan Institute, http://www .behavioraltech.org.

Loori, J. D. 2002. *The Art of Just Sitting: Essential Writings on the Zen Practice of Shikantaza.* Somerville, MA: Wisdom Publications.

Lovelock, J. 2000. *Gaia: A New Look at Life on Earth.* 5th ed. Oxford: Oxford University Press.

MacInnes, E. 2007. *The Flowing Bridge.* Somerville, MA: Wisdom Publications.

Mandler, G. 1984. *Mind and Body: Psychology of Emotion and Stress.* New York: W. W. Norton.

Mark, G., V. M. Gonzalez, and J. Harris. 2005. "No Task Left Behind: Examining the Nature of Fragmented Work." *Proceedings of ACM CHI, Association for Computing Machinery* 321–30.

McIntyre, L. M., M. I. Butterfield, K. Nanda, K. Parsey, K. M. Stechuchak, A. W. McChesney, C. R. Koons, and L. A. Bastian. 1999. "Validation of a Trauma Questionnaire in Veteran Women. *Journal of General Internal Medicine* 14: 186–89.

McMillan, T., I. H. Robertson, D. Brock, and L. Chorlton. 2002. "Brief Mindfulness Training for Attentional Problems After Traumatic Brain Injury: A Randomised Control Treatment Trial." *Neuropsychological Rehabilitation: An International Journal* 12(2): 117–25, doi:10.1080/09602010143000202.

The Merriam-Webster Dictionary. 2014. Springfield, MA: Merriam-Webster. http://www.merriam-webster.com.

Mipham, S. 2004. *Turning the Mind into an Ally.* New York: Penguin Books.

———. 2006. *Ruling Your World.* New York: Random House.

Morgan P., and C. Lawton, Eds. 2007. Introd. to *Ethical Issues in Six Religious Traditions.* 2nd ed. Edinburgh: Edinburgh University Press.

Moore, W. J. 1992. *Schrodinger: Life and Thought.* Cambridge: Cambridge University Press.

Morris, A. S., J. S. Silk, L. Steinberg, F. M. Sessa, S. Avenevoli, and M. J. Essex. 2002. "Temperamental Vulnerability and Negative Parenting as Interacting Predictors of Child Adjustment." *Journal of Marriage and Family* 64(2): 461–71.

Naranjo, C. A., L. K. Tremblay, and U. E. Busto. 2001. "The Role of the Brain Reward System in Depression." *Progress in Neuropsychopharmocological and Biological Psychiatry* 25(4): 781–823.

National Institute for Occupational Safety and Health (NIOSH). 1999. "Stress…at Work." Publication 99–101. Department of Health and Human Services. http://www.cdc.gov/niosh/docs /99–101.

Nhat Hanh, T. 1998. *The Heart of the Buddha's Teaching: Transforming Suffering into Peace, Joy and Liberation.* Berkeley, CA: Parallax Press.

———. 2002. *No Death, No Fear.* New York: Riverhead Books.